Three Sisters Ponds

Three Sisters Ponds

My Journey from Street Cop to FBI Special Agent
—from Baltimore to Lockerbie, Pakistan and Beyond

PHILLIP B. J. REID

authorHOUSE®

AuthorHouse™
1663 Liberty Drive
Bloomington, IN 47403
www.authorhouse.com
Phone: 1-800-839-8640

Published by AuthorHouse   05/30/2013

ISBN: 978-1-4817-5460-6 (sc)
ISBN: 978-1-4817-5459-0 (hc)
ISBN: 978-1-4817-5458-3 (e)

Library of Congress Control Number: 2013909333

CONTENTS

Chapter 1 It Takes a Village (Day Village)......................................1

Chapter 2 Growing up in Baltimore 7

Chapter 3 Joining the Baltimore Police Department 21

Chapter 4 Three Sisters Ponds..33

Chapter 5 Recruiting for the BPD...41

Chapter 6 Teaching at the Police Academy...................................49

Chapter 7 Applying for the FBI..53

Chapter 8 Training at the FBI Academy.......................................59

Chapter 9 First Office Agent 67

Chapter 10 The Big Apple...77

Chapter 11 My OP 99

Chapter 12 The Bombing of Pan Am Flight 103 109

Chapter 13 The Office of Professional Responsibility 165

Chapter 14 Hawaii 173

Chapter 15 Alaska...203

Chapter 16 The Vail Fires...231

Chapter 17 Closing Thoughts...245

DEDICATION

▲

I want to dedicate this book first to God. Although I'm not very religious, I cannot ignore his intercessions during critical periods throughout my life—intercessions that in most cases were not obvious or appreciated, except in retrospect.

I dedicate this book to the thousands of federal, state, and local law enforcement officers who put their lives on the line every day to keep this country safe and secure. Their challenges have surely increased since the tragic events of 9/11.

I dedicate this book to my mother. It was only after her death that I realized how much she had influenced my life, for better or worse, and that I became a better and more successful person because of her.

I also dedicate this book to my (poor) wife Bernadette, who put up with my twenty-eight years with the FBI, including all the time I spent away from home and all the transfers to new assignments, which forced her to change jobs and friends each time.

I dedicate this book to my daughter, Maisha, whose conception added meaning and purpose to my life and inspired me to keep pushing. As she has grown up, she has made me immensely proud as a father and grandfather.

I also dedicate this book to my three brothers, Ronald, Donald, and Skip. We have grown to be so different, but fortunately we have not grown apart.

DISCLAIMER

▲

The opinions expressed in this book are that of the author's and not those of the Federal Bureau of Investigation.

ACKNOWLEDGMENTS

▲

I want to thank my best friend, Zander Maurice Gray, who has been a steady and positive source of help, influence, inspiration, friendship, and guidance over the years.

I am indebted to Alex Haley, the late co-author of the *Autobiography of Malcolm X,* for ensuring that the work went to press. A lot of my black brothers and sisters were just as lost as I was when it was published in the '60s. The book saved many of us from ourselves and from our history in this country, and Malcolm X's life, as illustrated, shed light on the challenging future we all would face. More important, this book inspired my inner strength and stimulated my intellectual curiosity—characteristics I would need in order to navigate successfully through life while pursuing my American Dream.

I also want to acknowledge the contribution of the Three Sisters Ponds to my life and career. As this book will make clear, my dreams and goals were identified, framed, and launched from a bench overlooking this majestic site in Baltimore's Druid Hill Park. Thirty-one years later, while sitting on a park bench in Nice, France, overlooking the Mediterranean Sea, I realized just how many of those dreams had been fulfilled.

I must give posthumous thanks to the man who was my sergeant during my assignment to the Baltimore Police Personnel Division, who later became the city's police commissioner. He gave me the opportunity to get my bachelor's degree, but along the way, the example he set as a manager, a person, and a friend helped me develop leadership skills that would benefit me throughout my law enforcement career. He also took on the challenge of trying to teach me how to play basketball—a frustrating effort for him because I had grown up a swimmer. He never stopped trying, although he shook his head every step of the way.

Finally, I want to thank my unit chief while I was assigned to the FBI's Office of Professional Responsibility (internal affairs). I didn't realize how bad my writing skills were until he started bludgeoning my reports with his red pen. The report-writing standard he set for his unit caused most of us to protest, but it also made us improve. He was unrelenting in holding us to his high writing standards and will no doubt be reviewing this book with a critical grammatical eye.

PROLOGUE

▲

After twenty-eight years of service, I'm now retired from the FBI and have settled into the much slower-paced lifestyle and never-ending summer climate of Naples, Florida. Having lived in Honolulu, I consider Naples the Hawaii of the mainland. Since arriving here, I've finally found time to reflect back on my extraordinary thirty-six-year law enforcement career as both a Baltimore City policeman and an FBI agent.

I do recall the particular moment when it really hit me for the first time that I had fulfilled the majority of the dreams and goals that I had set for myself, and how fortunate I was to have chosen a career that had made it all possible.

At the time I had been in law enforcement for thirty-one years. I had just completed my third week of waiting to testify in the murder trial of Lamin Khalifa Fhimah and Abdel Baset Ali al Megrahi, two Libyans we had identified during a three-year, international terrorism investigation as being responsible for the December 21, 1988, bombing of Pan Am Flight 103 over Lockerbie, Scotland, which killed the plane's 259 passengers and crew plus eleven citizens of Lockerbie. The trial was being held on an unused US Air Force base, Kamp Ziest, located in Utrecht, Netherlands.

Waiting around to testify had gotten a little boring, although I was watching the proceedings on a closed-circuit TV near the courtroom. After spending three years of my life working this case (two on the island of Malta as the lead FBI investigator), and then waiting another nine years for it to be brought to trial, I wanted to see the accused bombers in the flesh. So when a couple of other agents waiting to testify suggested that we go into the courtroom and watch the trial in person, I quickly agreed.

It was a very different courtroom scene than we were used to in the United States. Presiding over the trial was a panel of three Scottish judges wearing wigs and robes—they could have come straight from King Arthur's court. The defendants were wearing jalabiyas. They were sitting together and were not in restraints or protected by armored glass. I was shocked by the casualness of their demeanor and by their apparent lack of concern about the proceedings. Though there was significant security in place, I would have preferred to see the accused murderers of 270 innocent people wearing hand and ankle shackles and hot-orange jumpsuits.

As I was just getting comfortable in my seat, Megrahi and Fhimah simultaneously locked gazes with me. Their eyes immediately lit up with panic and distress, and they started talking rapidly to each other. Though we had never met, it was obvious that they recognized me from the intelligence briefings I knew they had received about the FBI and our investigation on Malta. The briefings had probably included photos. They both pointed at me—the black, bald FBI agent who had been pursuing them for years—and they began talking more and more loudly. Their discussion quickly became disruptive to the proceedings, and their attorney complained to the judges about our presence.

All three of us were asked to leave the courtroom immediately and told not to return until we were called to testify. I was embarrassed about being asked to leave, but at the same time I felt good about seeing the defendants in the flesh and finally facing them down. During our three years of investigation, they had returned to Libya, where they couldn't be apprehended. It had taken a lot of hard work, personal sacrifice, and diplomatic pressure by a significant number of investigators from numerous law enforcement and intelligence agencies and governments all over the world to get these two into a courtroom.

Looking Megrahi and Fhimah in the eyes at long last was a bittersweet moment. I was torn between the urge to jump for joy and the urge to jump the railings that separated us so I could physically assault them. Though I had pursued and arrested murderers in the past, nothing in my experience had prepared me for mass civilian casualties. And the defendants' casual demeanor made me suspicious; it seemed to reflect an audacity, an expectation on their part that they were about to receive *more* than a fair trial. *Has a deal already been struck?* I asked myself.

Two days later, on Friday, September 29, 2000, the judges called a three-day recess. I was still smarting from having been evicted from the courtroom, and I was ready for a break. Rather than stay in my Utrecht hotel room for the duration, I decided to complete one of the high-priority items on my bucket list: I bought an airplane ticket to Nice, France.

I arrived in Nice the next morning and checked into a hotel on the Mediterranean Sea, requesting a room facing the water. I went straight to my balcony to catch the incredible view and began calling family and friends back in the States to brag a little. After making my calls, I decided that I needed a closer view of the sea—and I was also hungry. So I stopped at a nearby coffee shop, bought a large cappuccino and a ham sandwich, and then hustled over to the boardwalk.

It was a beautiful autumn afternoon. The world was such a different place then . . . the horrific bombing of Flight 103 had been the world's deadliest recent terrorist attack. Little did we know what lay in store for us just one year later.

On this particular day there was a slight chill in the air, although that didn't seem to bother the crowds strolling along the boardwalk.

A parade of Rolls Royces, Ferraris, Bentleys, Mercedes Benzes, Bugattis, Lamborghinis, and Maseratis slowly worked their way under the palm trees of the Prom des Anglais, which parallels the Mediterranean. Above them, red-tiled roofs, world-class hotels and restaurants, churches, outdoor markets, and parks nestled into the hills rising up from the shoreline of the Côte d'Azur, otherwise known as the French Riviera. The blue-green sea was like glass, and it was dotted with yachts of all sizes and designs sliding in and out of the marinas of neighboring Monte Carlo.

The vista brought to mind the other beautiful bodies of water I'd seen working FBI investigations in far-flung parts of the world: London's Serpentine Lake in Hyde Park; the Nile River in Egypt; Dal Lake in Srinagar (Jammu/Kashmiri), India, at the foot of the Himalayas; the Rhine in Germany; the Seine in Paris; Repulse Bay in Hong Kong; Crescent Bay in Karachi, Pakistan; and the Cook Inlet in Anchorage, Alaska, where white beluga whales roamed. Carefully gripping my hot cappuccino, I found an unoccupied park bench where I could have a comfortable lunch while enviously reviewing the passing flotilla.

As I began to settle in, I was suddenly struck by physical and emotional distress. My body started shaking, each convulsion stealing my breath away. My eyes welled up and then overflowed as I cried uncontrollably. I tried to rest my cup on the bench without spilling it, but to no avail. Putting aside my sandwich, I buried my face in my hands. The combination of the spasms and my loss of emotional control sent me into a panic. *Am I having a stroke? Am I losing my mind?*

I slowly lowered my hands, peering out at the sea through blurred eyes. Then, almost simultaneously, my vision cleared, the shaking subsided, and the realization set in that this moment was about much more than sitting on a bench, eating lunch, and gazing at very expensive boats. I had reached a pivotal milestone in my life, and my startling physical and emotional reaction was God's way of making sure that I couldn't ignore it.

As I said, visiting the French Riviera was the fulfillment of one of my dreams and goals, many of which were launched more than thirty years earlier from a park bench overlooking a different body of water—Three Sisters Ponds, located in a quiet, well-groomed part of Baltimore's Druid Hill Park. In the spring and summer, the ponds were bordered by an array of colorful flowers and tall trees that held nests for a variety of birds. The water was always still as glass and full of vibrant reflections of the surroundings and blue sky.

There is something about being in, on, or near a beautiful body of water that is essential to my existence. Bodies of water have provided the settings for many of my most memorable adventures and challenges, including sailboat racing on the Potomac River and Chesapeake Bay, doing the swimming leg of a triathlon in Lake Michigan, and cruising down the Seine in Paris. When I'm in the water—or even when I can just see it—I feel grounded, connected to all that is good and possible. The water has not only given me solace; it's been the launching pad for my life's dreams and goals.

Over the course of numerous visits to Three Sisters Ponds between 1969 and 1984, I logged countless hours on the bench (or what I called the "throne") reflecting on the past, pondering the present, and wondering what I could do to create a better future. During that period I was very dissatisfied with my circumstances. I was fortunate to be a Baltimore City policeman with a beautiful one-year-old daughter, but my marriage to her mother was failing. I had never done well in school, and facing and then overcoming academic challenges had never been my forte. Although I had improved my education enough to become a policeman, I knew I needed a college degree, because I didn't want to be a street cop for the rest of my life. I wanted to see and experience the world outside of Baltimore. I wanted to travel around the country and the world. I wanted to see Paris, Rome, and the Nile. I wanted to explore East Africa, visit the Taj Mahal in India, and walk the Wall in China. I wanted to have a good job, a great family, a nice home, nice cars—in short, I wanted the American Dream.

So on that fall day thirty-plus years later, as I sat on the bench in Nice and reflected on my life, it came home to me that thanks to all the opportunities and experiences availed to me through my law enforcement service, I had reached the majority of my life goals. The police department and the FBI had offered me a variety of interesting career choices, and with them new experiences, new challenges, and new avenues for personal and professional growth. They allowed me to earn an associate's degree from a community college, which led to a bachelor's degree; they gave me the chance to travel and meet important and interesting people from all over the world, including a US president, and they helped me develop as a leader, ultimately becoming a senior executive with the FBI, leading two FBI field offices as special agent-in-charge.

My dogged determination to succeed was matched by a strong desire to open doors for other blacks to follow in my footsteps. I hope I helped accomplish this in the BPD and the FBI. I'm living proof that no matter who you are, a law enforcement career can take you wherever you want to go.

I would like to share the details of my life's journey in the hope that they might be enlightening, inspirational, motivational, encouraging, and persuasive enough for you to seriously consider a public service career in law enforcement. But even if that career is not for you, I hope the story of my journey will reveal a route to your own dreams and goals.

CHAPTER 1

▲

IT TAKES A VILLAGE (DAY VILLAGE)

I was born on October 27, 1948, in the then-segregated Providence Hospital in Baltimore City, Maryland. It has been said that ambulances would drive by a dozen white hospitals to get blacks to Providence, even when their lives were in jeopardy. At that time, Providence was the only Baltimore-area hospital that would deliver black babies.

I was the second of four sons, and we were typical baby boomers. World War II had ended, and my father had come home from the navy to a peacetime job as a baker at the popular Rice's Bakery in South Baltimore. My mother stayed home to raise her four boys: my older brother Wendell (Skip), born in 1944; my twin younger brothers Ronald and Donald, born in 1950; and me.

We lived in a small, segregated enclave known as Turner Station, located on Bear Creek. Turner Station was tucked away in the far southeast corner of Baltimore County, at the southernmost tip of Dundalk, Maryland. The community began in the late 1880s after the founding of what would eventually become the Bethlehem

Steel Mill and shipyard on Sparrow's Point. When African American men couldn't find homes for their families on Sparrows Point, many went to the Meadows, an area not far away in Turner Station. As this little community grew, it expanded to the water's edge, eventually becoming one of the largest African American communities in Baltimore County.

Turner Station, as I remember it, was a beautiful, peaceful, self-contained town where everyone knew each other and people didn't lock their doors. We lived in the Day Village area, on Peach Orchid Lane; the other areas of Turner Station were Sollers Homes, Turner Homes, and Ernest Lyons. We had all the conveniences of a small town, including gas stations, barber shops, beauty salons, and cabs. We had a seven-hundred-seat, air-conditioned cinema, the Anthony Theater, built in 1946 by our town's first black physician, Dr. Joseph Thomas, who named it after his father. We also had the Village Drugstore, which featured a sit-down soda fountain that gave me a lifetime addiction to Coke floats. At Allmond's grocery, you could run up a tab that you paid when you could. I still remember the store's hand-written notepads containing IOUs.

Due to racial segregation and the town's isolation, most of the businesses in Turner Station were by necessity black-owned and—operated. Our need for self-reliance generated a strong black entrepreneurial spirit.

Turner Station was home to a number of individuals who made lasting contributions to the state and the nation, including Dr. Thomas, who was a businessman and diplomat as well as a physician; Kweisi Mfume, president of the NAACP and a five-term Democratic congressman from Maryland's Seventh District; former NFL star Calvin Hill; and Kevin Clash, the voice actor and puppeteer best known as the voice of Elmo on *Sesame Street* (for which he's also co-executive producer). Another former resident was Robert Curbeam Jr., a graduate of the US Naval Academy who became an astronaut and participated in multiple space flights between 1997 and 2001. His family had lived in Turner Station since 1931.

Most of the houses in Day Village were attached, two-story tract homes. Each home had a coal bin on the street side for winter heating, and many had front entrances that faced Bear Creek. I don't believe anyone owned their homes; they may have been owned by Bethlehem Steel.

If you were a kid growing up in Turner Station, all the adults participated in your upbringing—in other words, if you misbehaved, they would discipline (beat) you as if they were your parents, and then they would report your behavior to your parents, who would discipline (beat) you again. (There were no double jeopardy restrictions in Day Village at that time.)

Bear Creek is a two-mile-wide inlet off the Patapsco River, which ultimately connects to the Chesapeake Bay. When I was growing up there, one side of the creek bordered the black community of Turner Station, and the other side bordered the white community of Dundalk. The white families had boats with boat docks, and their houses were larger and spaced farther apart. I was told never to be caught on that side of Bear Creek—I don't remember what the supposed consequences were, but I do recall being afraid to disobey. I also don't remember seeing many white people in Turner Station; the only ones I can recall were the Catholic priest and the National Guardsmen who came in during our hurricanes.

There were quite a few weeping willow trees hugging our side of Bear Creek, and the neighborhood kids, including me, would spend hours sitting in their thick branches, and hanging and swinging from them as well. Unfortunately, there was a dark side to these trees: they produced the switches my mother would use to beat us. If we disobeyed her, she would order us to go pull them from the trees and hand them to her so she could whip us. Some of these whippings were held in public. You can imagine the scene it caused when my mother would try to pry the switches from our hands so she could use them on us. Today, of course, this would be considered child abuse.

I remember doing a lot of swimming, fishing, and crabbing in Bear Creek. It was like living in a resort, particularly during the summer, when the schools were closed. The only bad thing I recall about the creek was when Hurricanes Diane and Hazel blew through: some of those willows ended up on our roofs and in the creek, which then rose and flooded nearby homes. Bear Creek left an impression on me that lasted a lifetime. It gave me my love of and need for being near the water, as well as a healthy respect for its power. It was also where I first discovered the connection between bodies of water and my aspirations for the future. I regularly perched on one of the strongest limbs of a weeping willow tree at the back of our house, and while gazing out over the creek, I'd daydream for hours about what my life might be like when I grew up.

Our parents raised us with middle-class values. We were Catholic and regularly attended Christ the King Church in town. We didn't own our home, but we took care of it as if we did. We seemed always to have enough food on the table, and because my father worked at a bakery, we had plenty of breads and pastries. If necessary, we would catch and eat the fish from Bear Creek—usually catfish. (We didn't believe in catch and release in those days.) Hot dogs and baked beans were our Saturday dinner staples.

Through third grade I attended Fleming Elementary School, which was built in 1944. I remember my first grade teacher as a particularly encouraging force in my literacy. She was quick to praise and seemed genuinely amazed at my level of reading and writing, regularly showing me off to other teachers and parents. Unfortunately, that was the only glowing educational moment I can remember. It all seemed to go downhill from there.

When I was five or six years old, my parents divorced. They'd never seemed to like each other very much, and one day my father just packed up and left—although I don't remember actually seeing him leave or even saying goodbye. We were never told why he left, and I don't recall being surprised. However, it certainly put a crimp in our cash flow. Mother was suddenly left to raise and feed four hard-headed, hungry boys on her own with child support payments that never seemed quite enough. There weren't many job opportunities for her in Turner Station or in the Dundalk area of Baltimore County. But Mom was too proud to go on welfare.

It became increasing clear that we could no longer afford the rent in Turner Station—my mother would need to find full-time employment, something that, to my knowledge, she had never done before. So my father and some other relatives helped us move to Baltimore City.

CHAPTER 2

▲

GROWING UP IN BALTIMORE

Boundless in its vastness, it engulfs us
We are born in it, made of it, and nourished by it
It fuels our nightmares and placates our dreams
We're challenged to harness it, or be oppressed by its streams

Its veins permissively run throughout our lives
Civilizations have drowned in it, while others have thrived
It has shaped the history and character of the human species
countless wars won and lost for it, some steadied by treaties

I have surrendered to and respect its fickle bearing
It's adapt or die, or spend your life swearing
I've learned to venerate its majesty and relish its splendor
which grounds me and connects me to all the good I
remember

The years of admiring and gazing across its horizons
have given me peace and solace and a few surprises

It's been the launching pad for my many dreams
and my many welcomed challenges found a home in its seams

Sure, I had my fears, maybe too numerous to count
Nothing so enormous that I couldn't surmount
With so much of it dominating the world, with no end
*Finding no better alternative, **I learned to swim***

Phil Reid

We moved to the Walbrook section of Baltimore City in 1956, with the hope of finding a new and better life. Of course, this all depended on Mom finding suitable employment. She complicated things by deciding to pursue a college education while working full-time. She had always wanted to be a public school teacher and was willing to make any sacrifice necessary to achieve her goal.

Walbrook is a neighborhood along West North Avenue in West Baltimore. Coppin State College, where my mother attended school, was located there, and several of Baltimore's major streets—North Avenue, Windsor Mill Road, Bloomingdale Road, and Hilton Street—converged there in an area known as Walbrook Junction, a transportation hub for the Maryland Transit Administration. From Walbrook Junction we would take the electric trolley to the Lexington Market in downtown Baltimore. The market still exists; it's a very popular indoor/open-air venue where you can buy a variety of fresh-cut meats, fish, fruit, vegetables, and sweets.

Walbrook Junction had Fibus Drugstore, where my older brother, Skip, worked as a delivery boy. It also had a Blue Boys sub shop, Acme Food Market, and Schmitz Bakery, where we went every Sunday morning after church to buy fresh blueberry muffins sprinkled with powdered sugar.

We moved into a four-story apartment building that hadn't aged very well. It stood alone on the top of a hill at 3301 Elgin

Avenue and was surrounded by single-family homes—a middle-class neighborhood with mostly black and a few white families. Eugene Allen ("Big Daddy") Lipscomb, the 284-pound, six-foot-six defensive tackle for the Baltimore Colts, lived across the street from us. In those days, football players didn't sign the multi-million-dollar contracts that would have kept a guy like him from having to live in our neighborhood.

Moving to the big city was an eye-opening experience. I was eight years old at the time, and very frightened. I wasn't used to all the traffic and noise, or so many grocery stores and movie theatres. I wasn't used to the crowds and the tall buildings—and, of most concern, the threat of being a crime statistic. I'd never even seen a policeman in Turner Station, but they were everywhere in Baltimore, usually in pairs, and police and ambulance sirens wailed all hours of the day and night. I quickly began to miss Bear Creek. There were no lakes in our new neighborhood. This city life didn't look promising to me at all, but this was my future, like it or not.

Once we'd settled into our new surroundings, my mother enrolled us in St. Cecilia, a Catholic school only a block away from our apartment. It was run by the Sisters of Mercy—but believe me, they showed no mercy to their students, or even to each other; they argued amongst themselves publicly and ferociously.

My three brothers and I became altar boys and participated in many church activities. Because we didn't have much household income, our tuition to attend St. Cecilia School was drastically reduced. Unfortunately, however, we didn't last very long there. When one of my brothers got into a heated verbal exchange with another student (for reasons that are still unclear), the school didn't hesitate to kick us *all* out.

So for the next two years we attended Gwynns Falls Elementary Public School, located on Gwynns Falls Parkway—and I can say that without the Catholic school discipline, I went rogue. I was very disruptive in class and was so bad one day that a teacher justifiably slapped me in the face. It was pretty good slap! I became somewhat of a bully, a status I enjoyed until one of my victims (and apparently a karate student) put me out of the bullying business with a quick kick/punch combination to the ribs.

We missed quite a few meals in those days—a fact that might also have contributed to my poor performance in school. I began stealing food from the Acme Food Market, Penn Fruit Supermarket, and my neighbors' pantries, although I always shared my stolen edibles with my brothers and friends. When a store clerk caught me stealing a pack of Fig Newtons in the Penn Fruit Supermarket, I dropped the package, ran out of the store, and never went back. For years my mother wondered why she could never get me to go there to buy groceries. Even today I can remember that clerk's face.

I was indeed in need of some sort of intervention (possibly an exorcism). Fortunately, my mother found a way to get us back into St. Cecilia School—and it was none too soon. There was a new order of nuns in place, the Oblate Sisters of Providence; they were black instead of white, but otherwise just as mean and strict as the Sisters of (No) Mercy. Somehow I managed to come under their spell and developed a strong reattachment to religion and the Catholic Church. I became an altar boy, and for a time I even considered becoming a Maryknoll missionary priest.

We were very close to the two priests assigned to our parish. Both were very active in the community and respected by everyone. I remember one night when one of them took my brothers and me bowling. I'm not sure whether he was testing racial tolerance at bowling alleys and using us as his guinea pigs, but we stopped at two bowling alleys in Baltimore County, and even though he was wearing his clerical collar we were turned down both times. We were all devastated, and I believe the priest was embarrassed, as well.

My grades didn't improve very much during my two remaining years at St. Cecilia, and I couldn't seem to figure out how to fix the problem. Even getting Cs seemed beyond my reach. I'd hoped to attend Catholic high school, but my grades weren't good enough. I decided to attend Edmonson High School instead, because it had a ninth-grade freshman class. But during my last year at St. Cecilia, we were forced to move very abruptly: my brothers and I came home from school one afternoon to find all our household goods on the sidewalk, with strangers rummaging through them as if they were at a free flea market. Talk about embarrassing! My father and our uncle, a much-respected detective with the Baltimore City Police Department (BPD) paid a moving company to pick up what was left of our belongings and haul them to a new apartment on Druid Hill Avenue, deep into the city. By moving there we were closer to my father's house—although that didn't make his child support payments any bigger, and it didn't make me any closer to him, either.

One ray of hope shined through the sudden move: the Druid Hill Avenue YMCA was located down the street from us. This is where my brother Ronald and I, and many other black kids in Baltimore City, learned not only to swim, but to swim competitively. Once again I was reconnected with the water, which I had sorely missed. This time, however, water wasn't just something to jump into, splash around in, or catch fish in; it was a way for me to develop important, meaningful, character-building attributes that would serve me well through life.

While learning to swim competitively, I saw how diligence, focus, and commitment could lead to improvement. I learned teamwork. As a result of all the hard workouts, my physical appearance began to change, and I found, to my delight, that my female friends noticed and appreciated the change. Competitive swimming taught me what challenges were, and it encouraged me to accept challenges from others and create my own for self-improvement. I learned to be competitive—not just in the pool, but in life.

My mother continued her struggle to finish school, work, pay the rent, and keep food on the table. She still wouldn't consider welfare, although from time to time we received food baskets from St. Cecilia Church.

Because of continuing money problems, we didn't stay on Druid Hill Avenue very long. My mother was struggling to pay the rent, and we were on the verge of having all our household goods put out on the street a second time. My uncle came to our rescue once again.

He brought us into his family's home on Madison Avenue, just a couple of city blocks from Druid Hill Avenue; believe it or not, they moved us into their dining room and kitchen. While it was a major inconvenience for them, they really cared about and welcomed us. This bought us time so my mother could finally graduate from Coppin State and start fulfilling her dream of teaching and earning a steady, middle-class income.

When my mother graduated in 1962, her four sons couldn't have been prouder of her accomplishment. We'd all suffered with her along the way, but it was worth it. Watching her as she pursued and achieved her goal, we learned a great deal about life and what it takes to accomplish something. Mother had a lot working against her. She had to work full-time for pay that was barely enough to feed, clothe, and house us. Through it all she found time to study, go to our PTA meetings, and discipline us as well. She was our hero!

That same year I started the ninth grade at Edmonson High School, as a thirteen-year-old freshman. I continued to struggle academically and began cutting classes. Not until I joined the freshman swim team, which required at least a C average from its members, did I begin to attend classes and make an effort to keep my grades up. My love for swimming and being in the water became my reward for attending classes and getting better grades in school.

I enjoyed being on the swim team and the feeling of camaraderie. Though I did play soccer for a couple of years at Edmondson High, it was swimming that I truly loved. Many of the teams we competed against included black kids who had learned to swim at the Druid Hill Y. I was a pretty good swimmer, but I could have been much better had I not started smoking cigarettes.

Our world seemed to improve significantly once Mother graduated from Coppin State Teachers College and became a public school teacher.

She eventually bought the Madison Avenue home from my uncle, who was retiring from the police department. The house had been in the family since the 1930s, and it was just down the street from Druid Hill Park, where I eventually became a lifeguard at the public pool, working there for four summers. Once again, water played an important role in my life. Because I had become a strong swimmer, I was able to get my first job. Many of the black swimmers who learned to swim at the Druid Hill YMCA became lifeguards at one of the various public pools around Baltimore. We all became very close friends over the years.

One summer in particular, all of us lifeguards were upset about our low pay and dangerous working conditions, and we threatened to go on strike. Mayor Theodore R. McKeldin threatened to fire us all. For some reason I became the spokesperson for the lifeguards; I was interviewed by one of the local TV stations, and I even wrote a letter to the *Baltimore Sun* questioning the mayor's position. I was shocked, surprised, and honored when he responded to my letter to the editor, ultimately agreeing to our requests. We got our raise and increased security at the pools.

In Baltimore you lived or died by each Orioles or Colts game. The Orioles had an overabundance of great players back then: the Robinson brothers, Brooks and Frank; Boog Powell; Davie Johnson; Luis Aparicio; Jim Gentile; Jim Palmer; Dave McNally; Andy Etchabarren; Russ Snyder; Paul Blair; Curt Blefery; Eddie Murray; Rick Dempsy; and many others. The Orioles experienced their greatest success from 1964 to 1983, when they won seven division championships, six pennants, three world championships, and five MVP awards.

The Orioles' first World Series championship team, in 1966, was led by three Hall of Famers: outfielder Frank Robinson, third baseman Brooks Robinson, and pitcher Jim Palmer. Frank Robinson won the 1966 World Series MVP award, as well as the Triple Crown in hitting: he led the American League in batting average, home runs, and runs batted in. The Ripkin boys, Cal and Bill, were young kids then, and we watched them grow up at Memorial Stadium where their father, Cal Sr., was the Orioles' third-base batting coach.

My brother Ronald and I were there during the fourth game of the 1966 World Series, when the Orioles beat the much-favored LA Dodgers four straight games (sweep!) to win the title. It was a pitching duel between the Dodgers' Don Drysdale and the Orioles' Dave McNally. It was a one-run game, with Frank Robinson hitting a solo home run. Ronald and I were on cloud nine after the game—we were so excited that we decided to walk home instead of catching the bus. It was a long walk, but it didn't matter. We still have the ticket stubs from that game.

The Colts had Johnny Unitas, Lenny Moore, Jim Parker, Alan Ameche, Gino Marchetti, Johnny Sample, Alex Hawkins, Dick Syzmanski, Raymond Berry, Jim Mutsheller, Bill Pellington, Steve Myra, Ordell Braase, Art Donovan, and Coach Weeb Ewbank. In the 1958 NFL championship game in New York's Yankee Stadium, the Colts beat the Giants 23-17 in overtime, earning their first-ever championship. The contest would later be known as "The Greatest Game Ever Played."

In those days, Johnny Unitas had his bowling alleys, Gino Marchetti had his fast food franchise, and Jim Parker had his liquor store, all in the Baltimore area. I sure miss the Gino Giant burger—and I still can't get the commercial out of my head. ("Everybody goes to Gino's, 'cause Gino's is the place to go! Yes *everybody goes* to Gino's, 'cause Gino's is the *place* to *go!*") Their special sauce has never been matched.

A memorable experience was seeing Joe Paterno when he came to Edmondson High School to recruit one of our running backs, Charlie Pitman. I believe this was Paterno's first year as Penn State's head football coach. Charlie and I became friends through our high school sweethearts, who were very close. Charlie went on to play four years at Penn State and became an all-American. He was also a great student and a great person in general. He played for two professional football teams, the St. Louis Cardinals and the Baltimore Colts.

⚜

I graduated from Edmondson High in 1966, but it wasn't pretty. I think I held the school record for the most absences in one year. There were about a hundred of us who had flunked one or more classes and were originally told that we couldn't get our diplomas until we attended summer school. But in the end, the principal decided that it wasn't worth the hassle and allowed us to walk across the stage and graduate with everyone else.

Though I wasn't academically worthy of being accepted by Morgan State College, I nevertheless pursued the dream of being a student there, enrolling in the fall of 1966. I'd always wanted to be a part of the school's proud traditions and history. Morgan is an urban college attended by approximately seventy-four hundred undergraduate and post-graduate students—the vast majority of them black, at that time. It was an easy commute from home, the tuition was very reasonable, and most important, many of my friends were going there. Somehow my SAT scores were just high enough for Morgan to let me in; it was the only school that I applied to and the only one that I thought might accept me. Morgan's reputation in the community was that it was easy to get in, but you had to work hard to stay in.

Although I did become a proud Morganite, I didn't change my poor academic ways; after my second semester, I was put on warning. Morgan kicked me out a semester later, but not before I'd had a chance to swim for the school team. Several of the kids who had learned to swim at the Druid Hill YMCA were on the team, too; I had competed against many of them in high school. Over the years they had helped their high schools win meets and even city championships. Now we were all together at Morgan. That school year, 1966-67, we won the CIAA Swimming and Diving Championships under the close mentorship of our coach.

Although I was on the team, I didn't contribute as much as I could have. I was still smoking, and with the combination of too much all-night, early-morning partying and drinking, my performance was certainly affected. When I first arrived at Morgan, the coach asked me to swim a fifty-yard sprint in front of the school's other coaches to show off my talents, and I impressed them with my speed. But it was all downhill from there. I was never able to maintain my speed or get better.

Being kicked out of school meant there were several realities I had to face. I knew that if I wanted a chance at a successful life, I had to get a college education. My problem was that I didn't know how to study, I had no academic discipline, and I couldn't read, write, or articulate well. Frankly, I don't know how I made it through grade school. Now, in the face of this failure, the only hope that I could cling to was the example of my mother's resolve and dedication, and her success against long odds. I knew that as long as I didn't give up on the dream, there was a chance for me, too.

Since I would be out of school for a while, I knew I needed to find a full-time job and make some money. I applied for a job with the Baltimore Gas and Electric Company, for which I had to take a written exam. I flunked it horribly. The HR representative who administered the exam was blunt: he told me that I had failed the exam and that the results indicated that I was not reading or writing above the fourth-grade level. I was embarrassed, devastated, and clueless as to what to do next. I eventually got a job at Bethlehem Steel in Sparrow Point, working as a metallurgical inspector. It paid good money, but there were plans to shut down the plant, and I knew that I didn't want that kind of life anyway. I had talked and listened to other employees there, and I realized there wasn't much of a future at Bethlehem Steel. In anticipation of shutdown, Bethlehem was speeding up production, which gave me plenty of opportunity for overtime. I made a lot of money, which I used to buy my first car and save up tuition money—I was hoping to get back into Morgan someday.

While working at Bethlehem Steel, I met a brother who quickly realized how lost I was and recommended that I read *The Autobiography of Malcolm X*. He was very much a black militant, but we found comfortable ground for communication. At that point in my life, I don't know that I had ever truly read a book from cover to cover.

Once I started reading that book, I couldn't put it down (even though my attention and retention spans were very short, and so I constantly had to reread paragraphs for comprehension). I found myself in that book, and I also began to understand myself much better. As Detroit Red discovered himself, so did I. I realized that my predicament was my own doing and that I had to take control of and responsibility for my own destiny, by any legitimate means necessary. Certainly the black man's history in America isn't pretty, and I easily could have blamed my predicament on the history of racism, but that wouldn't have gotten me any closer to getting my life back on track. If I was to be successful, I had to develop an immediate appetite for learning. Only then could I understand who I was and how and where I fit in this country. Looking back, I realize that meeting that brother when I did was an important and pivotal moment, and it probably saved my life. This was certainly one of those times when I believe God intervened.

I decided that the only viable path for me was to restart my education on my own, and from scratch. So that's what I did—literally. I began with first-grade textbooks—*Alice and Jerry, See Spot Run*—and over time worked my way through twelfth-grade texts. Thank God for the Enoch Pratt Free Library in Baltimore! I began to spend a lot of time in libraries, reading books, magazines, and periodicals. I couldn't read enough about black history, American history, and business, and I tried to keep current on news and issues by reading various local, national, and international newspapers.

I then reapplied to Morgan for the fall semester of 1968. This time I was in a little stronger position to succeed academically. I was pleasantly surprised when they readmitted me (on probation).

That happened to be a tumultuous year at Morgan as well as many other colleges and universities. The assassination of Dr. Martin Luther King Jr. on April 4 had caused an eruption of rioting in Baltimore and around the country; public order had not been restored until April 12.

The riots in Baltimore cost the city an estimated $10 million ($63 million in 2010 dollars). Maryland National Guard troops and nineteen hundred federal troops were ordered into the city. During four days of looting, 288 liquor-related establishments were burned or looted and 190 food stores vandalized. About fifty-seven hundred people were arrested on various charges, mostly for curfew violations. The loss of life totaled six—three by fire, one in an auto accident, and two of gunshot wounds during suspected lootings. Only one person was killed by a policeman. We could see and smell the smoke from our house on Madison Avenue, and some of the rioting and looting took place very close to our house, on Whitelock Street.

That was a time when blacks were finding their political voice and demanding change in college administrations. The Vietnam War had generated a great deal of antigovernment sentiment and especially antimilitary sentiment, which was now spilling onto campuses. After it became the target of several demonstrations and boycotts, Morgan's ROTC program was moved off campus.

I successfully navigated through my classes that school year, while at the same time getting involved in black activism. But by the end of the spring semester I began to realize that I would not be able to return for the 1969-70 school year: my money had run out, as had my mother's. It also began to dawn on me that I was twenty years old and had wasted a lot of my mother's money on education. It was time to leave home and start seriously looking for permanent employment.

That summer of 1969, when I was working as a lifeguard again at Druid Hill Park, a friend of ours stopped by the pool wearing his new Baltimore Police Department uniform. He had just joined the force, and he really looked sharp in uniform. I asked him about his experiences so far: the application process and background investigation, the salary and benefits, and the police training academy. He mentioned that the department encouraged its officers to complete college, paying for tuition and books through a program called Law Enforcement Educational Program (LEEP).

My brother Skip had already joined the BPD, and now I was starting to think about joining, too. My girlfriend at the time was also working summers at the pool, in the girls' locker room. We had been talking about getting married, and so I discussed my idea with her. She thought it was a great plan. I also talked to my brother and my uncle, who by now was retired from the force, and I was encouraged by their comments. I realized that this was the dream job for me. I could provide a community service, which was very important to me; earn a decent salary with health benefits so I could support a family; finish school; and build a retirement income.

I called a police recruiter, who told me that they were looking for men who thrived on challenges, prided themselves on helping others, and were willing to work hard to learn the necessary skills for this challenging but critical job. Police work could be tough, demanding, and unpredictable, he said, but it was also one of the most rewarding jobs you could have. Every day that you wore your uniform and badge, you would be making Baltimore a safer and better place to live for your family, friends, and neighbors. Plus, no matter where in the country you might move, police officers were always needed.

He explained that Baltimore City policemen were assigned to one of nine districts where they were responsible for patrolling and responding to calls. Officers had to have solid analytical skills, because they were in the field the majority of the time and needed to be able to assess situations quickly and correctly for their own safety and the safety of others.

Becoming a police officer was quite simple, he said, but it required a lot of dedication and hard work. You had to be at least twenty years old and a US citizen, with a high school diploma or a GED. Once you'd met those prerequisites, you had to achieve or maintain a high level of physical fitness and use common sense. There would be a background check, and the recruiter reminded me that a career in law enforcement could quickly be short-circuited by "youthful indiscretions." He said that I would have to take the written civil service exam for police officers and pass the physical exam, which included tests of vision, hearing, strength, and agility. I would also take a drug test, and I would be interviewed by a senior officer and/or take a personality test to assess my personal characteristics such as judgment, integrity, and responsibility.

I was sold!

CHAPTER 3

▲

JOINING THE BALTIMORE POLICE DEPARTMENT

Come crying into a world filled with both
promise and despair,
trying to find our way and prosper,
we seek the means to get us there,
but the challenge is knowing what's proper.
Opportunities come and opportunities go
as we seek life's comfort stride.
Some we exploit and some we blow.
Good judgment *will dictate how well we survive.*

Phil Reid

I remember being very excited at the thought of joining the police department. I had always admired my uncle; he personified what a good policeman should be. He was tall, heavy but fit, and tough-looking, with a deep, commanding voice, and he was always chomping on a cigar. One time he challenged me to a footrace that I thought I could easily win, and once we started running, he got up on his tiptoes and sprinted by me with ease. My uncle was also a great family man and very charitable. He certainly took care of us when we needed his help, which included buying our groceries a few times.

I read everything I could about the BPD. I wanted to make sure I knew what I was getting into, and I didn't want any regrets. I understood that it wouldn't be a very popular decision among many of my black friends at that time, but I thought that joining was an opportunity to help change attitudes, because the police would always be part of the black community. I was impressed with the career opportunities it offered me, such as promotions through the ranks and the various jobs within the department—detective, traffic, property, personnel, training. The salary and benefits—including health insurance, retirement benefits, vacation and sick leave, and use of the credit union—were also very attractive.

I applied to the police department in July 1969. I took the test and, believe it or not, I passed. I also passed the background investigation. There was a reservoir in Druid Hill Park that was about two miles in circumference, and I ran around it several times to get myself in running shape for the police academy. Unfortunately, smoking kept me from becoming a great runner.

Because I was not quite twenty-one at the time, I was temporarily placed in the police cadet program; I worked in the records section at police headquarters until I was close enough to twenty-one to join an academy class. I was bored and very anxious to start academy training.

While I was still a cadet, I received my official greetings from Uncle Sam: I had been drafted. This caught me by surprise—now I had to think about whether to get into government service as a military officer or as a police officer. I decided on the latter and appealed the draft notice. I went downtown to the US Custom House, where the draft board was hearing appeals, and I explained that it didn't make a difference to me whether I went into the military or the police force, but that I was already working for the BPD and my preference was to provide my government service as a police officer. I remember the colonel who headed the draft board at the time saying that either service would do the country good, and he tore up my draft orders. *Just like that,* I thought, *this guy changed the direction of my life.*

⁂

I started my police training on September 1, 1969, at the Baltimore Police Academy, located in their Northern District station house.

My class started out with thirty-six trainees and lost a few along the way. It was a fourteen-week program of rigorous academic, physical, defensive, and firearms training. As I recall, the trainees were an odd mix: former bartenders, meat cutters, and security guards; a former news anchor; a former lifeguard (me); and a few college graduates. There were no women in the class.

There were three other black trainees. One of them was very intelligent, with great leadership skills. He led the class most of the way with the highest academic average, and he was the leading candidate for valedictorian until he was beaten out toward the end of the program and lost his opportunity.

The academy put a lot of emphasis on studying the general orders, which contained all the rules, regulations, policies, and procedures covering every conceivable situation. We were told that if we learned and followed the general orders, we would do fine. In addition, we were taught federal, state, and local laws; codes; and various practical law enforcement lessons in the International Association of Chiefs of Police (IACP) training keys—our roadmap for staying out of trouble with the department. The IACP keys were used to keep our training up to date: we read the material and took a quiz at the end. Our police commissioner, Donald Pomerleau, a former IACP executive, introduced the training keys to the department when he became commissioner.

After a few firearm training sessions, they assigned pistols to every trainee except me—I wasn't old enough. I had to wait for two weeks, until I turned twenty-one, before I could get my weapon assignment. It was a long two weeks, and I felt a little left out, but finally I got my own revolver, a six-shot .38 caliber Smith & Wesson.

I found academy training difficult. I had no problem with the physical training, but I had to work extra hard to survive academically, and I'd never fired a weapon before. To get comfortable with it and achieve a passing score, I practiced quick draws and dry firing in my bedroom at home, and I also spent a lot of time at the firing range. I made it through and graduated on December 12, 1969.

During the last week of training we were given our district assignments. I was assigned to the Northern District, based in the same building as the academy. This district covered a section of the city very close to where I grew up. It also encompassed Druid Hill Park.

I was now officially a rookie cop. I had to get used to wearing a uniform every day and an extra belt loaded with a gun, ammunition, handcuffs, a handy talkie radio, a nightstick, a flashlight, and mace. (Later we would also wear hot, heavy bullet-resistant vests under our uniforms.) We had to remember to bring all these things to work every day, because we always started roll call with an equipment inspection while standing at attention.

I was assigned to work with some senior officers for a while before I eventually soloed. I expected that the experienced officers would be testing me.

There continued to be a lot of antigovernment, anti-law-enforcement sentiment in the country as the result of the Vietnam War and the civil rights struggle. We were all "pigs" at that time, and of course, if you were a black cop, you were also an "Uncle Tom" or even an "Uncle Tom pig." There were unprovoked attacks on police in Baltimore and elsewhere around the country, some resulting in their death or serious injury. These were not easy times to be a law enforcement officer, and that was particularly true in Baltimore City.

Fortunately, I loved the job. It was a very comfortable fit for me because I liked the uniform, liked being a black police officer, and wanted to be the model of a great policeman. I lived in the city and enjoyed being a policeman there.

Now that I had a job, the next step was to plan my wedding. Two months after I graduated, I married my Druid Hill Park co-worker in a Catholic church on Valentine's Day—February 14, 1970. It snowed heavily that day. Looking back, I wonder if that was a bad omen for our marriage.

In 1970 there were approximately thirty-five hundred policemen in the Baltimore Police Department, whose jurisdiction encompassed an area of some ninety-two square miles: seventy-nine square miles of land and thirteen square miles of water. We were actually under control and authority of the state, rather than the city.

The police commissioner at the time was Donald Pomerleau, who served in that capacity from 1966 to 1981, having previously served as chief of police in Miami and in Kingsport, Tennessee. A former marine, he was sent by the IACP to investigate the Baltimore Police Department in 1965, during the height of the civil rights movement, following the Watts Riot in South Central Los Angeles. He reported that the BPD was among the nation's most antiquated and corrupt police forces, that it practiced excessive force, and that it had a nonexistent relationship with Baltimore's large African American community. To improve the department and prevent race riots, Maryland's governor and Baltimore's mayor hired Pomerleau with a mandate to clean up the department. In an attempt to fully integrate it, Pomerleau lifted restrictions on African American officers, who previously had been assigned only to foot patrols, quarantined in rank, barred from patrolling white neighborhoods, and given limited specialty assignments.

I was assigned to Baltimore's Northern District, which didn't have the most crime in the city but had its fair share, and certainly enough to keep us busy. The district covered the world-renowned Johns Hopkins University Homewood Campus and some of the city's most expensive homes, where the rich and elite resided (including Police Commissioner Pomerleau). It also covered some very active crime territory, which had its share of robberies, assaults, rapes, and homicides. There were sections where police themselves were at risk if they worked alone.

As a member of the operations unit, I focused on the high-crime areas of the district. The unit worked from 2:00 p.m. to 10:00 p.m. and from 6:00 p.m. to 2:00 a.m. By overlapping the routine patrol shifts of 8:00 a.m. to 4:00 p.m., 4:00 p.m. to 12:00 a.m., and 12:00 a.m. to 8:00 a.m., we eliminated vulnerable time periods that could be exploited by criminals. Because I was a rookie, I worked the six-to-two shift exclusively for the first two years, including all the major holidays, when everyone else was home celebrating with their families. These hours were tough and put a heavy strain on my marriage. I really envied my friends who were off work on weekends and holidays.

ঔঞ

There were some great police officers working routine patrol in the Northern District. They were very aggressive and proactive, they knew everyone on their beat, and they worked very well with private citizens and business owners. They really put in a100 percent effort every day, and I tried to learn as much as I could from and emulate them. There was also a very small number of officers—I called them "problem children"—who were just too aggressive and weren't sensitive to anyone, not even their fellow officers. Those officers were behind the majority of "signal 13" (officer-in-trouble) calls. They were constantly requesting backup for routine car stops after they unnecessarily agitated the wrong citizen. They were regularly involved in vehicle and foot chases, assaults, and shoot-outs. In general, they created more problems than they solved. Our operations unit was always bailing them out of trouble.

During the three years I was assigned to the Northern District, I worked exclusively with the operations unit. Once I received a call for a potential suicide on the roof of the US Public Health Hospital, near Johns Hopkins University. When I arrived on the roof of the five-story building, I found doctors there trying to convince a female mental patient not to jump. Unfortunately, they weren't too convincing. She was perched on the very edge of the roof, and she looked very serious about jumping. I quickly handed my gun belt to another officer—I didn't want the woman to snatch my gun—and so she couldn't pull me over with her, I had the officer hold onto my pants belt while I attempted to grab her. Just as she was about to jump, I caught her around the waist and the officer pulled us both back by my belt. By then both the woman and I were falling in the wrong direction; thank God the other officer had the strength to pull us both back and keep us from falling off the roof.

One of the few times I worked the two-to-ten shift, I was called to a bar shooting. I arrived to find a very gory scene: the victim's head had literally been blown off, point-blank, with a shotgun. The shooter had fled the scene. Within minutes I was told where he lived and that witnesses had reported he had just arrived there. I drove to his residence, talked him out of the house, arrested him, and recovered the shotgun. As it turned out, the person he shot was a well-known neighborhood bully who happened to mess with the wrong person that day. Everyone I interviewed supported the shooter, and I found myself supporting him myself during his trial. He ended up with a much lighter sentence as a result.

I also found myself involved in some funny incidents while on patrol. One time my partner and I were caught up in a long, dangerous car chase. When we finally got the stolen car stopped, we jumped out of our cruiser and approached, guns drawn. Unfortunately, my partner didn't put our car in park—and it was at the top of a hill. It started rolling away, and needless to say, we looked like the Keystone Cops chasing our vehicle down the street. After it hit several parked cars, we were able to catch up and get it stopped. Fortunately, the car thief was too busy laughing to take advantage of the situation and flee. Still, we had a lot of explaining to do when we got back to the district station.

I earned the nickname "Pockets" because I carried a second gun in my coat pocket when I was assigned to a solo foot patrol at night in a high-crime area in the Northern District. I was always having to confront notorious bad guys hanging out on corners or acting suspiciously, so I would keep my hand on the gun hidden in my pocket. It gave me confidence, and more important, it made me look confident when I confronted these guys by myself. I'd decided it was worth the hole in the coat if I ever had to pull the trigger. I never had to, fortunately, but that gun got me through some very scary moments. While working foot patrols I became an expert at twirling my nightstick. I also learned some people skills. I learned I'd better treat everyone fairly, because if I ever got into trouble out there by myself, I might need someone else to call for help.

Smoking was really starting to bother me now, but I just couldn't quit. I was smoking menthol-tipped Kools, and I'd become addicted to them. Sometime in 1972, I switched to smoking a pipe. Though I didn't inhale directly from the pipe, I did somehow get the nicotine satisfaction. Smoking a pipe made me look more sophisticated, or so I thought, and I continued to smoke one for the next fifteen years. I thought it was much healthier than smoking cigarettes, and I felt better as well.

One evening on patrol it occurred to me that I'd been driving for an hour and hadn't seen another patrol car, which was unusual. I finally stumbled upon about twelve of them, all parked together. I asked one of the officers what was going on and he said, "Look up." When I did, I saw a beautifully endowed naked woman deliberately—and most capably—entertaining her audience from a third-story window of an apartment building. The officer told me she put on the same show at the same time every night. She kept it up until someone reported seeing a large number of police cars parked under her window every night. Our internal affairs unit closed down the peep show and reprimanded some supervisors and officers as a result.

Sometimes I found myself at odds with other officers. Once, for example, I was called to a street fight between two black male teenagers. I arrived, broke up the fight, and sent them on their way. I never considered those kinds of fights a big deal; if I had been arrested for all the fights I'd had growing up, I would not have been a policeman. But one of the "problem child" officers arrived and confronted the two fighters as they were walking away. An argument ensued, and he arrested them both. I was a little dubious about what they were being charged with, considering that I had sent them on their way. I was surprised later when I was subpoenaed by their defense attorney to testify on their behalf. The arresting officer drove me and a couple of other officers from the Northern District station house to the downtown courthouse for the trial. Along the way, I told the "problem child" that my testimony was going to conflict with his, but he didn't seem concerned, or maybe it just didn't register with him. He testified, and then I was called. I was very uncomfortable, but I had to tell the truth as I saw it.

The judge at that time was a tall, distinguished-looking black man with the bulk of a linebacker. As I was testifying, I could see that he was getting increasingly upset. After I finished, he stood up and in a very angry tone said, "Case dismissed." He added that if he weren't a judge, he would have been glad to meet the officer in a dark alley and teach him a lesson or two. Needless to say, I had to find my own transportation back to the station house that day.

Another time we received a call for a large altercation on Greenmount Avenue and 27th Street. Of course, every police officer within the sound of that call responded. I arrived on the scene first and began to separate people and calm things down. Just as I got the situation in hand, another of the "problem children" jumped out of his patrol car, arbitrarily grabbed a young kid, and started pulling her by her hair toward the paddy wagon, which was parked about a half a block away. Naturally, the crowd got hostile seeing this officer pulling a screaming girl by her hair. I ran up to help him properly escort her to the police van. He seemed startled when I approached him; apparently he interpreted my help as an insult and an embarrassment, because when I returned to the station house my sergeant met me in the parking lot with his fists clenched. I had to calm him down and explain that I had had the situation under control until the other officer's behavior had reignited the crowd.

I learned from my sergeant that the other policeman had accused me of assaulting and embarrassing him in front of other officers and the citizens on the street. Fortunately he didn't formalize those allegations. This "problem child" was eventually fired for being drunk on duty, wrecking his patrol car by hitting parked cars, and stealing from a warehouse after responding to a burglary call.

◈

One day while working the day shift, I stopped at a local diner for lunch. I got into a conversation with one of the waitresses, who told me that she was once married to an FBI agent but he had died in a traffic accident. This was long before I ever thought of becoming an FBI agent or even thought I might be eligible to become one. Her words startled me, because up until she made that comment I didn't think FBI agents could die from anything that killed us regular mortals. I thought they only died in gun battles with the mob; otherwise they were invincible or died from old age. For some reason, this revelation was upsetting to me, and it continued to bother me for quite a while.

There were still a lot of student demonstrations taking place on college campuses in Baltimore, and our operations unit had received crowd (riot) control training for these situations. The first time our unit was called out to handle a demonstration, it was at Morgan State. Fortunately, I was on vacation. The next time I wasn't so lucky.

Students at the University of Maryland were rioting and engaging in some very aggressive and violent demonstrations that had lasted for days. The campus police couldn't handle them, so the Prince George's County Police and Maryland State Troopers were called in, but the students were still out of control. Finally the governor exercised state authority and called for two hundred Baltimore City police. I was called, as was my best friend, Police Agent Zander Gray, whom I had met on the job.

I envied Gray because he was single, had a Corvette, and had graduated from Morgan State. Because of his degree he became a police agent, receiving a higher salary than the most senior policeman and just a little less than a sergeant. He'd wisely taken advantage of a departmental incentive program to encourage completion of college.

Although we were both assigned to the operations unit at the Northern District, we usually worked different shifts. On evenings when we were on the same shift and if things were quiet, we would pull our patrol cars alongside each other and talk for hours about the job, women, parties, everything. We often hit the nightclub scene in Baltimore or DC—to the consternation of my wife—and compete for the attention of the ladies.

Along with our fellow officers, Gray and I boarded buses, riot gear in tow, and left for the University of Maryland. I remember all the boasting about how we were going to settle the riots once and for all, kick some student butts, and make some good overtime. The ride seemed extra-long.

The bus got awfully quiet when we got our first glimpse of the size of the crowd. You could hear a pin drop and a few gasps. It looked like a million students waiting for us—it was very intimidating, even for hardened police. Students were everywhere.

As we turned onto the campus and found our parking area, it was clear to everyone that we faced a serious confrontation. We knew we were the governor's last hope of restoring order on the campus.

We knew he was counting on our reputation as no-nonsense, "kick-ass," big-city cops to instill fear in the demonstrators and make them turn tail and go home. Though we were greatly outnumbered, we had strong leadership; our colonel seemed to have a real grasp of what we were up against, but he was unfazed. We put on our riot gear and took his lead, standing in front of the students in a very confrontational pose. We stood there for what seemed like hours. The colonel climbed on top of a platform where he could see over the crowd and they could see him, and using a bullhorn, he told them that if they didn't disperse by a set time, the Baltimore City police would take coercive and persuasive action.

While we were waiting and counting the minutes, Gray and I were recognized by some students in the crowd. We'd grown up with them in Baltimore and even partied with them. We started teasing each other about the predicament we were in. The colonel noticed this exchange and jokingly asked us whose side we were on.

As the deadline drew near, many students decided that it wasn't worth getting hurt or locked up. I think some of them believed that we weren't very disciplined and that they risked getting shot by the half-crazed Baltimore City police—and I'm sure the governor was counting on this belief. When the deadline was up, we immediately confronted the few lingerers with tear gas and nightsticks. The students dispersed, leaving only a few brave souls to be arrested. It turned out to be an easy job—no one on either side got hurt. We went back to Baltimore a success, but we never got our overtime pay—just some sandwiches, chips, and soda. I guess that's what it means to be a "public servant." Oh well . . .

Gray eventually left the Northern District for a higher calling as a police recruiter for our personnel division at downtown headquarters. I wanted very much to follow in his footsteps, but I knew the dream of advancing to one of the sought-after jobs in the department depended on my going back to school, and finishing.

CHAPTER 4

▲

THREE SISTERS PONDS

It was majestic, peaceful, and serene,
a sacred place for brief escapes
to extravagant, boundless, and limitless dreams.

I would sit alone on the splintered throne
underneath the sycamore tree.
My mind would roam in this timeless zone
where my thoughts were unshackled and free.

On display was Three Sisters Ponds,
manmade and conjoined for visual pleasure,
embraced by an array of foliage that bonds
this astonishing landscape together.

An occasional oriole, sparrow, or blue jay
would land and perch on my throne.
They seemed to completely ignore my stay,
as if they were focused on dreams of their own.

It was here that I launched my thousand dreams.
Some proved more realistic than others, it seems.

Some were vast and as deep as these ponds.
Undaunted, unfazed, I would successfully forge on.

Whatever happened to Three Sisters Ponds?
I've searched, but it all appears to be gone.
I have new ideas and dreams to launch,
but it can't be done without the throne and magical ponds.

Phil Reid

Part of the operations unit's responsibility was to provide patrol coverage in Druid Hill Park. As I mentioned earlier, I practically grew up in that park: got my first job as a lifeguard there, met my first wife there, gathered there with family and friends to picnic and play tennis and baseball. Some of my fondest memories of my daughter are of times we spent together in Druid Hill Park. It was already a very special place for me, so I didn't mind the occasional assignment in the park.

We provided park coverage either in a patrol car or on a Vespa scooter, known by its call sign, Scooter 8. There was the occasional rape, robbery, homicide, or suicide, but these incidents were infrequent and usually there wasn't a lot to do. When on park assignment I often ran into old friends, and we would get a chance to catch up.

While working there I stumbled upon a special place called Three Sisters Ponds. Located in an isolated section of the park, these conjoined, manmade ponds gave the occasional visitor like me a sense of privacy, escape, and personal oasis. Encircled by an array of multicolored plants and trees and well-manicured lawns and shrubs, and home to various species of birds and the occasional deer, the setting was beautiful, serene, and majestic.

I found a bench there where I could sit facing the ponds, take in the full display of foliage, water, and sky, and daydream. Sitting there, I felt that I could see the world and its challenges more clearly, that I could understand and solve any problem, and that no goal I set was unattainable. The power the place had on me was almost scary.

Whenever I was assigned to the park, either in a patrol car or on Scooter 8, I would find time to ease on over to my "throne" at Three Sisters Ponds to eat lunch and do some serious thinking, planning, strategizing, and, of course, dreaming. While sitting there I had so many epiphanies that I started bringing a notepad along to keep track of them all. They helped me find my bearings and keep me on course.

I thought about my recently failed marriage, about my daughter and our future. In 1972, my wife and I had produced a beautiful girl. I'd named her Maisha Mengi, Swahili for "long and enduring life." Unfortunately, her mother and I separated soon after she was born, but my daughter remained the love and pride of my life—as she still is to this day. When my marriage broke up, I moved back in with my mother on Madison Avenue. Of course, she was happy to have her son back home.

Gazing out over the ponds, I thought about my need to finish college. Though my police salary was comparable to those of my friends with college degrees, I still felt left out. Now that I was single again, I dreamed of traveling around the world and having exciting experiences in other cultures. I wanted the opportunity to have a nice car and home, maybe even a boat. I wanted to have my share of the American Dream. Though my job paid a middle-class wage, I was not satisfied—in part because I didn't like shift work and working holidays when everyone else seemed to be off enjoying themselves. I wanted a more challenging and prestigious job in the police department, with better working hours. I realized I was not happy with my lot, and I knew that none of my dreams had a chance of materializing unless I finished school. Doing that would require a total restructuring of my life.

One Sunday morning, I felt the need to go to the ponds, perch on the throne, and do some serious thinking about my past, present, and future. I had no clue what I hoped to accomplish there; I just knew I needed to go. When I arrived, there were a few other couples sprawled out on the ground with blankets and picnic baskets and other paraphernalia. As I sat there on the bench, I began agonizing over why I had struggled so much trying to read, write, and speak well. Why did I have such trouble learning and understanding things, when everyone else seemed to pick them up far more quickly and easily? Why did I end up having to learn to read and write and educate myself in my own way, on my own terms? Why was learning so difficult for me? Was I lazy? Was I just plain stupid? Or both? Whatever the problem, I had to identify and solve it if I was going to achieve a successful and accomplished life.

I was eating a peanut butter and jelly sandwich and drinking chocolate milk when it hit me: dyslexia. I recalled hearing somewhere about the disorder, which is associated with learning difficulties. At the time there wasn't a lot of information available on dyslexia, but finally I found a pamphlet about it at the Pennsylvania Avenue branch of the Enoch Pratt Free Library—the same library that had saved me a few years back, when I decided that I had to teach myself how to read, write, and do basic math. Though the information in the pamphlet was limited, I felt I'd found a likely explanation for my learning problems. I never sought a formal diagnosis of dyslexia, because I knew I could have been denied promotion opportunities if the disorder had been confirmed by a police department physician. A private doctor would have kept a diagnosis confidential, but if dyslexia did turn out to be the reason for my difficulties, I was afraid I might have convinced myself that I couldn't do things because of it. That wouldn't have been good, either.

This epiphany helped me identify and cope with my shortcomings and, most important, look for ways to overcome them.

Over the years I was able to accomplish many of the goals I set while sitting on that bench overlooking the ponds. I returned there often to set new short—and long-term goals, and I continually updated and revised my strategies for accomplishing them. I also did some of my studying there during lunch breaks or when I was off duty. Even after joining the FBI, I kept going back to the ponds, but they gradually disappeared—whether they were purposely drained or simply neglected, I never knew. My throne eventually disappeared, too. What a loss!

The decision to change my life and actively pursue my dream of a college degree paid off. After doing some checking, I verified that the department would finance my schooling with LEEP funds, and it would even pay for my books. It was going to be difficult both working and going to school, but I knew my mother had done the same thing very successfully under far tougher circumstances—I didn't have four teenage boys to raise and support. Although I realized I was "educationally challenged," I was ready and eager to move forward.

✍

I enrolled in the criminal justice program at the Community College of Baltimore, whose course schedule accommodated students working days or nights. I started out getting Ds, then Cs, then Bs, and finally I got my first A. I earned my associate's degree in May 1973.

Now that I had a degree and three years' experience in the department, I was eligible to take the exam for promotion to sergeant. I studied hard and passed the exam, but didn't score high enough to get promoted. Despite my redoubled efforts in the classroom, I'd never gotten good at taking written tests. So I began looking at other career opportunities within the department, and I was pleasantly surprised at the number of choices I had. Finally, I narrowed the list down to the units that truly interested me: Training, Homicide, Internal Affairs, Recruiting, Criminal Investigation, Vice and Narcotics, Youth Services, and Intelligence. I looked these areas over for several months, asking a lot of questions and, in general, trying to do my homework so I'd make the right choice.

During the summer of 1973, anti-drug graffiti began showing up on the walls of buildings in different parts of the city. The graffiti always targeted the dealers, with messages like "Off the pusher" or "Death to the pushers," and it was always signed "Black October." A significant number of the city's homicides at the time were related to the well-organized trade in illicit narcotics: in other words, pushers killing other pushers. Baltimore was a major market for heroin, cocaine, and marijuana, and I was continually running certain pushers off the street corners on my beat.

For weeks similar graffiti appeared, catching the attention of the public, the media, and police. There was no way of telling whether the Black October threats were a joke or something deadly serious. It was like the quiet before the storm—everyone holding their breath, expecting something to happen. The messages seemed to have an effect on drug pushers, though, because for a while many of them were conspicuously absent from their usual haunts.

It turned out that the pushers had reason to run scared. That became obvious in July with the murder of Turk Scott, a member of the Maryland House of Delegates who had been indicted for conspiracy to transport forty pounds of heroin between Baltimore and New York. A group calling itself Black October claimed responsibility for the murder in a note left near his body. A similar note had been found on the bullet-riddled body of a drug dealer in the Pimlico section of Baltimore a few days earlier.

I believe many Baltimoreans were conflicted about what Black October had done; some probably considered the murders a public service. Our homicide division determined that Black October was a lone individual who had decided to take the law into his own hands and eliminate the drug trade from the streets of Baltimore. And it worked for a while; believe it or not, some of the pushers even asked for police protection. As it turned out, a minister's son—twenty-year-old Sherman W. Dobson—was arrested in connection with the two slayings. He received a lot of community support and even court sympathy and leniency throughout the judicial process.

During the fall of 1973, while I was still researching possible jobs at BPD headquarters, my friend Gray left his job as a recruiter in our personnel division to take a private-sector position with Chrysler Corporation. He recommended to his sergeant that I take his place. I was interviewed by the sergeant and then by the personnel director, and I got the job. They were looking for someone with at least a two-year degree.

That turned out to be a pivotal point in my career because it thrust me into the administrative side of law enforcement. When I look back, I have to give credit to God for making this job available shortly after I got my degree. This is also a perfect example of why you should go out and get your degree, and not just talk about getting it.

Being a recruiter would require a whole new skill set: I would have to learn how to speak in front of groups, talk about my experiences working the streets of Baltimore, sell the BPD, and represent the image of a Baltimore City policeman. This was my new world; these were my new challenges.

CHAPTER 5

▲

RECRUITING FOR THE BPD

I worked as a police recruiter for two years, and I really enjoyed it. I thought it was the greatest job in the world. In those days we were always hiring new recruits, so it was my job to attend state and local job fairs and give presentations to community groups and our public schools. I even wrote recruiting commercials for local radio stations. One in particular was pretty long but read like a poem or song lyrics, and the disc jockeys would play it over and over again and comment on how good it sounded. We hired quite a few former New York City cops who had been laid off because of a budget crisis. We provided testing at police stations in the evenings and on Saturday mornings to give working people the opportunity to apply.

We made a significant effort to hire military veterans, traveling to bases on the East Coast and setting up recruiting booths there. I remember driving through Smithfield, North Carolina, on my way to Fort Bragg and Camp Lejeune to recruit soldiers who were transitioning out of the military, and passing a large billboard with a picture of a fully cloaked Ku Klux Klansman on a rearing horse.

It read, "You are now in Klan Country. Act accordingly." And I said to myself, *Okay!*

Our recruiting effort in North Carolina was a great success. It was also . . . interesting. During one of my trips to Camp Lejeune, I checked into a hotel just outside the base. It was a very hot day, about ninety degrees, and I decided to go swimming in the hotel pool. The pool was very crowded, but I jumped in anyway to swim some laps. As soon as I jumped in, everybody—men, women, and children—jumped out. I was startled at first, but I kept on swimming. I could see everyone standing around the edge of the pool, staring at me, but I was too scared to get out, so I kept swimming laps. They didn't know it, but I could swim laps all day, thanks to the Druid Hill YMCA. After a while I guess it got a little too hot for them, and when it became obvious I wasn't slowing down, they gradually began to reenter the pool. After it looked like everything was back to normal and it was safe for me to exit the pool, I did so very inconspicuously, counting my blessings that I wasn't lynched that day. Recalling the billboard, I guess I wasn't "acting accordingly."

One of my proudest moments as a recruiter occurred the day the department's minimum height requirement of five foot seven was temporarily waived to accommodate Asian applicants. I quickly informed my brother Donald, who was only five foot five and had always wanted to be a policeman. He applied that day, took the test, and was accepted. Within a week the original height requirement was reinstated, so we were very lucky to have gotten him in when we did. Donald graduated from the police academy in July 1973, the third brother in my family to join the department. His colleagues nicknamed him "Walking Small," and ultimately he became the best cop in the family.

On October 10, 1973, I was looking for a parking spot in downtown Baltimore and noticed what appeared to be Secret Service vehicles circling the federal courthouse nearby. All of a sudden traffic was stopped, and we were held in place for more than fifteen minutes. It happened to be the day that Vice President Spiro T. Agnew resigned from office, and he was at our courthouse, pleading *nolo contendere* to corruption charges through an agreement he'd reached with the Department of Justice. (The charges were related to tax evasion.) It was a historic moment in our country's history, and I felt a part of it because I was held in traffic while he was being whisked either in or out of the courthouse.

⁊₰

On July 11, 1974, the Baltimore Police Department went on strike. Earlier that year, Police Commissioner Pomerleau allowed members of the department, for the first time in its history, to join Local 1195 of the American Federation of State, County and Municipal Employees (AFSCME) labor union and establish collective bargaining. I worked very closely with the local labor union president, members of the Fraternal Order of Police, and the Vanguard Justice Society to help bring the department on board in preparation for upcoming labor negotiations. We recruited some nineteen hundred BPD officers to join Local 1195.

Things were going well until the union president decided to call a mass meeting of police union members. The auditorium was packed. Things were calm starting out, but as various officers took to the podium to express their opinions, things got out of hand. There were rallying cries for a strike, which I knew the union president didn't want, and he quickly lost control of the podium, the meeting, and what was being said. Then a couple of officers with a lot of charisma started shouting, "Strike!" All of a sudden the police in the audience took up the chant and ran out of the auditorium. I realized that this wasn't good for anyone.

I had to decide whether or not to go out on strike, and although I had become a very active member of the union, I chose not to. All administrators, managers, and detectives were called to put on their uniforms and report to a district station house, so I reported to work that night to the Central District after it was clear that there weren't many police working in Baltimore City. I had been off the streets for two years. We ended up working twelve-hour shifts for a month, until we could restore order and get most of the officers back on the street.

There was evidence that the striking police had sabotaged communications by pulling radio microphones out of patrol cars. They also set up picket lines at each of the district station houses and were trying to intimidate all the other officers into striking, as well—including my younger brother, who was new to the department and still on probation.

The strike was tied up with other, civilian city employees who went on strike at the same time, including sanitation employees, corrections officers, and employees of the Department of Recreation and Parks and the Department of Education. This caused a citywide crisis. Garbage began to pile up along the streets, inmates in the city penitentiary began to riot, and within hours of the police walking off the job, arson began to erupt, costing the city millions of dollars in property damage and resulting in at least one death.

The strike lasted from July 11 to July 15, 1974. It was the first time since the Boston Police Strike of 1919 that police in a major American city had gone on strike. This was a real strike as opposed to a partial walkout, "blue flu," or work slowdown. It is estimated that nearly fifteen hundred cops went on strike, and those who didn't were called "scabs" by fellow officers.

During the strike, Baltimore was not a safe place. There was looting in the commercial district, the number of fires was 150 percent above normal, and within the first two days of the strike at least two hundred stores were robbed. In areas where tensions already existed, things got worse. An eleven-year-old girl was shot outside her house when a man drove down her street, firing randomly. On July 12, Maryland Governor Marvin Mandel ordered outside police help from 115 state troopers. On July 13, in an effort to stop the strike, Chief Judge Robert C. Murphy threatened to jail striking employees.

On July 15, members of Local 1195 were offered a 21 percent wage increase over two years. Still, hundreds of officers held out, demanding unconditional amnesty—a demand rejected by city and state authorities. Eighty-two probationary officers were fired, including my brother Donald. Fifty-five union members made appeals in court and lost. There were approximately 673 letters of reprimand, 130 disciplinary hearings, and 90 forced resignations. AFSCME lost the right to automatically deduct union dues from paychecks and to act as the police officers' exclusive bargaining agent. AFSCME was fined $10,000, but none of its leaders was sent to jail, which had been a possibility under the law.

Pomerleau, who was a former marine colonel, viewed the striking officers' behavior as a personal betrayal, particularly after he had allowed them to join the union. He immediately announced a deadline for the officers to return to work. As soon as he was able to stabilize police coverage of the city, he initiated departmental disciplinary hearings that went on for years after the strike. The city and state officials maintained a solid front against compromising and refused to make a settlement that gave strikers amnesty. Many officers were fired or officially disciplined. I was so glad I hadn't gone on strike, because it would have affected my career with the department and my future chances of joining the FBI. Donald was not so lucky. He was called before the disciplinary hearing board and fired, along with all other officers who were on probation and participated in the strike. I had to go to bat for him, using all my capital within the department to help him get his job back. He was eventually rehired.

❧

Once I became a recruiter, I re-enrolled at Morgan and started taking night courses to obtain my bachelor's degree in sociology. I was determined to graduate from Morgan and nowhere else. The good news was that the school let me back in again and accepted LEEP funding to pay for my classes and books, even though it didn't have a criminal justice program at the time. I considered sociology a good alternative, as I've always been intrigued by the study of human interaction and the results of those interactions. The bad news was that the many low grades that I had accumulated during my irresponsible years at Morgan immediately dropped my GPA to a 1.7 despite the much higher GPA I brought with me from Community College of Baltimore. My challenge was to bring that GPA up to at least 2.5 by getting nothing lower than Bs. I knew I had to get aggressive to make that happen.

My first two semesters of night school at Morgan went well. I was able to get my studying done during the day, while I was working. Then I reached the point where I had taken all the night classes offered in my major; the remaining forty-three credits hours I needed to graduate could only be taken during the day. These were also the most difficult classes: languages, sciences, math, and statistics. I begged my sergeant to let me handle all the night and Saturday morning testing for the next two semesters, which would allow me to attend class during the day. Fortunately, he agreed.

I almost blew my deal with him when I overslept one Saturday morning and missed administering the test to waiting applicants. My sergeant and the director were very upset and disappointed with me, and they threatened not to let me finish school. I was very remorseful and swore that it would never happen again. They forgave me—and believe me, I kept my word.

I took twenty-three credits the next semester and twenty the semester after that. I even tried to pull off a dream and pledge my favorite fraternity, Omega Psi Phi—but that didn't go so well. Once I started pledging, the fraternity members began denying me my much-needed library time. As a result and with much regret, I quit pledging; I knew I had a very limited window of opportunity to graduate from college. Because I didn't finish pledging, I was designated a Forever Lampado, which I believe makes me only an associate to the Omega Psi Phi fraternity.

I graduated from Morgan in May 1975 with a 2.7, having earned several As and Bs that brought up my GPA significantly. I was proud and very appreciative that Morgan gave me so many opportunities over the years to graduate—the hard way. I have been bragging ever since that I'm a Morgan graduate.

One of my professors at Morgan suggested that I consider a career with the FBI—something I'd never thought about before, simply because it seemed way outside the realm of possibility. But once he brought it up, I never forgot it. You can dream, can't you?

After I received my bachelor's degree, I was promoted to police agent and my salary increased to $15,000. That was a lot of money in 1975! By this time I owned a Corvette—just trying to keep up with the Joneses (or with my friend Gray, in this case). Of course Gray later bought a Pantera and then a Ferrari, which I could never match. So I had accomplished all my goals: finishing school, getting better positions in the police department, earning a higher salary, and even buying a Corvette. *Time to set new goals*, I thought. *But where do I go from here?*

I began looking for opportunities to expand my horizons. I took the sergeant exam again and got an even higher score, but still not high enough to get promoted. Now that I had a four-year college degree, I was itching to do something different.

CHAPTER 6

▲

TEACHING AT THE POLICE ACADEMY

In October 1975, not long after I received my bachelor's degree, I successfully applied for a teaching position at the Baltimore City Police Academy. I knew I needed a change and a new challenge in my life, but if I wanted the position, I had to get the word out that I was interested in it. I received a big help from the BPD's chief of patrol, who would later become Baltimore City's first black police commissioner. He was good friends with Oprah Winfrey, who at that time was only locally known as an anchor at one of the Baltimore TV stations. I did get a chance to meet Oprah; she was introduced to me by a friend who was also in the local broadcast business and went on to star in the HBO series *The Wire*.

The position I applied for at the academy involved teaching traffic law and enforcement to new recruits and in-service training classes for veteran police. As a matter of fact, I wasn't a big traffic law enforcer when I was assigned to street patrol—I despised giving out traffic tickets. But although I knew very little about traffic law and even less about teaching, I needed a new challenge in my life.

I had to become a traffic law expert in a very short period of time because my first new recruit class was coming through soon. I also had to learn how to prepare lesson plans and get comfortable and confident speaking in front of a class.

I taught at the police academy for three years, during which time there was a sex-for-grades scandal. We had just started hiring female police, and they were going through the academy when I arrived. I found out later that some of the other instructors were having after-hours sex parties in the academy pool with trainees. Fortunately, I was never invited. The story was the subject of a media frenzy for quite a while. Ultimately, some of the instructors were demoted and others fired outright.

There were several good instructors at the academy. I wasn't one of them, but I tried to learn as much as I could.

❧

In late November 1975, the director of the academy asked me and a sergeant, who in my opinion was the best instructor there, to attend a weeklong International Association of Chiefs of Police (IACP) hostage negotiation/crisis intervention workshop in New Orleans. This was the first time I had flown anywhere on behalf of the department, and I was thrilled and honored to have been asked. The sergeant and I were good friends, having both patrolled the Northern District early in our careers. We flew to New Orleans together and checked into our hotel just off Bourbon Street, which was where the conference was being held.

After checking into the hotel, we headed for Antoine's, a restaurant in the French Quarter that the sergeant highly recommended. (He had been to New Orleans before and considered himself a connoisseur of fine cuisine and wines.) There was a French restaurant in downtown Baltimore that I liked called Café des Artistes, so I was looking forward to eating at Antoine's. It turned out to be one of the best meals I'd ever had. My appetizer was gumbo creole soup loaded with blue crab meat, oysters, and shrimp, and my entrée included a peppered steak drenched with a sauce that was to die for. We complemented the great food with some great wines. It turned out to be the most expensive meal I'd ever had, too, but I bragged about it for years to come.

The sergeant also suggested that we eat brunch at Brennan's, another very popular (and expensive) eating establishment in the French Quarter—and another winner. After paying the bills at Antoine's and Brennan's, I had to eat breakfast, lunch, and dinner at McDonalds for the next three days, but it was worth it.

The workshop went very well, and we learned a lot about negotiating and crisis intervention, which at that time was a new approach to crisis resolution in a hostage situation. We both received IACP Crisis Intervention/Hostage Negotiation training certificates.

While I was teaching at the academy, I met two FBI agents who were teaching there, and they told me that the FBI was looking to hire former state and local law enforcement officers with college degrees. They convinced me to put in an application.

CHAPTER 7

▲

APPLYING FOR THE FBI

I n early 1976, I applied for the FBI through their Baltimore field office, located in Baltimore County near Social Security Administration headquarters. There I met that office's lead recruiter. He appeared sincerely interested in getting me hired by the FBI and spent a great deal of time explaining the hiring process and what the job of special agent entailed.

The recruiter made it clear that this was one of the most popular and sought-after careers in the criminal justice field, and that the competition was anything but easy. He then explained the most basic requirements for eligibility: a special agent had to be a US citizen aged twenty-three to thirty-six with a valid driver's license, a four-year degree, and at least three years of work experience. A special agent also had to be available for assignment anywhere in the FBI's jurisdiction. I was ready to move anywhere, any time.

He was very clear about the academic, physical, and firearms training challenges that lay ahead at Quantico if I successfully made it through the application, testing, and screening process. There were three programs through which I could qualify to join: Accounting, Law, or Diversified. He said that I would qualify under the Diversified Program because it included law enforcement background and experience.

I was pleasantly surprised to learn that you didn't have to be an attorney or an accountant to become an FBI agent. In fact, I could hardly believe that the FBI was giving my application serious attention, but the recruiter made it clear early on that the bureau was aggressively recruiting candidates with state and local law enforcement experience under the Diversified Program. The FBI hadn't been entirely successful in building strong liaisons with state and local law enforcement agencies in the past, he said, but he believed this situation would improve as a result of this new recruiting effort.

Being a special agent was like no other career I had ever explored, the recruiter said. It was challenging, exciting, and very rewarding, and every day I had a chance to serve my country, as special agents were responsible for conducting sensitive national security investigations and enforcing over three hundred federal statutes. As an FBI special agent, I could work on terrorism, foreign counterintelligence, organized crime, white-collar crime, public corruption, civil rights violations, financial crime, bribery, bank robbery, extortion, kidnapping, air piracy, interstate criminal activity, fugitive and drug-trafficking matters, and other violations of federal statutes.

He certainly had my attention. I was always looking for opportunities to do something different, and I saw the FBI as fertile ground to be able to do just that whenever I needed a change. Perfect!

If I made it through the hiring process I would be put on an applicant list prioritized according to specific critical skills the FBI needed. The recruiter assured me that my skills would put me high on the list. Once a background investigation was complete, I would be placed in a new agents' class, after which I could choose among four career paths: foreign counterintelligence, counterterrorism, white-collar crime, or criminal investigations.

All SA trainees began their careers with approximately fifteen weeks of intensive training at the FBI Academy in Quantico, Virginia, one of the world's finest law enforcement training facilities. Trainees lived on campus and spent their classroom hours studying a wide variety of academic and investigative subjects. The curriculum also included intensive training in physical fitness, defensive tactics, practical application, and firearms. Several tests were administered in these areas to monitor trainees' progress. They had to successfully complete all the training requirements in order to graduate; then they were sworn in and assigned as special agents to one of the FBI's fifty-six field offices, based on the bureau's current staffing and/or critical specialty needs.

I immediately began preparing for the application process, as well as for academy training. I remember being quite concerned about the testing phase of the application process, as well as the academics I would face at Quantico. The first thing I had to do was make sure that I kept my nose clean with the police department and that my performance evaluations were good. I recalled the strike and was again glad I hadn't participated in it—that surely would have knocked me out of the running. I jumped into a cardio and weight-training program to improve my heart and lung capacity and build my upper-body strength. I wasn't too concerned about the firearms testing.

To prepare for the written and verbal exams, I did more reading and practiced my listening skills to enhance my comprehension and recall. I even tried standing on my head to get more blood flow to my brain and taking ginkgo biloba supplements to improve my memory and attention span. By the time I had successfully gotten through all the tests, the interviews, the background checks, and the physical, everyone at the police department knew I was applying for the FBI, although I'd tried to keep it a secret in the event that I didn't qualify. Since so many of my family, friends, and colleagues knew I was applying, I was really afraid of being rejected or not getting through Quantico.

During the application process, the BPD placed a limited freeze on hiring, resulting in fewer academy classes and less need for instructors there. Because the higher-ups assumed I was going to the FBI, I was the first instructor to be sent back to the street as a patrolman. They did give me a choice of district, so I asked for the Northern District because I was familiar with the territory. Except for the strike, it had been almost four years since I had worked the streets, and I was very upset because I didn't know how long it would be before the FBI would call me, or if they would call me at all. I eventually did get the call and was assigned to begin classes at Quantico in October 1976.

The night before I had planned to give my two-week notice to the BPD, I received a panicked, eleventh-hour call from the recruiter, who told me not to resign because my new agents' class had been cancelled. He said the FBI was freezing hiring for a year, after which the testing procedures would be totally changed; I would have to reapply in a year and go through testing and screening all over again. I don't recall the reasons for the overhaul, but I do remember how devastated I was. I began to doubt whether I could survive a new application, testing, and screening process or even stay out of administrative trouble at the BPD now that I was back on the street as a patrolman.

Everyone was expecting me to resign the next day and move to Quantico. I found it embarrassing to continue on with the department, but I had to grin and bear it for the next year. The only thing that saved my pride was that police academy classes were starting to pick up again, and the department continued to let me teach when my area of instruction came up for each class.

⋙⋘

As part of my initial application, testing, and screening, the FBI requested that I clear up my marital status with my first wife. We had been officially separated since 1972, but we were not divorced—we had agreed not to for our daughter's sake. I was told by the FBI that the divorce had to be finalized because then there would be no lingering issues that could surface during my background investigation. When I had to tell her that the FBI was making me get a divorce, it didn't go over too well.

I had also met another woman during this interim year: Bernadette Cook, who would become my second wife. We met through a blind date arranged by Gray and her brother-in-law, another friend of mine. Of course, I had to be sure she could survive the FBI's background screening, which she did.

Over the next several months I repeatedly called the recruiter to find out when the FBI would be ready to hire again. He helped me through the new application, testing, and screening process, and I finally was assigned to another class beginning in October 1977. But prior to my resignation from the BPD, a problem arose with my medical exam: the doctor had diagnosed me with a heart murmur. In order to void that evaluation, I had to get three other doctors to overrule him. I accomplished that, only to be told that my white blood cell count was too high; now I had to get a specialist to disprove this as a health risk. By the time I started class, I was a basket case.

CHAPTER 8

▲

TRAINING AT THE FBI ACADEMY

When I started the FBI Academy in October 1977, J. Edgar Hoover had been dead five years, but his presence, influence, and legacy with the FBI was still strong and omnipresent. The FBI director at the time was Clarence Kelley, who had held that position since July 9, 1973. Before then he had been the Kansas City police chief and had been an FBI agent from 1940 to 1961.

During Kelley's tenure, the FBI made a strong effort to develop a thriving force with more women agents and more reflective of the ethnic composition of the United States. By the late 1970s, nearly eight thousand special agents and eleven thousand support employees worked in the bureau's fifty-nine field offices and thirteen legal attaché offices. Kelley was also instrumental in hiring more law enforcement officers to become FBI agents. My timing was impeccable!

The FBI Academy in Quantico is located in a very remote section of Prince William County, Virginia, and enjoined by a marine base. First opened for use in 1972 on 385 acres of woodland, it is a relatively small government academy. FBI and Drug Enforcement Administration (DEA) agents undergo training courses there.

The main training complex includes three dormitory buildings, a dining hall, a library, a classroom building, a forensic science research and training center, a thousand-seat auditorium, a chapel, administrative offices, a large gymnasium and outside track, and a fully equipped garage. In addition to the main complex, there is a mock city known as Hogan's Alley, which consists of facades replicating a small town; it is primarily used for FBI and DEA training. Behind the facades are fully functioning classrooms, audiovisual facilities, storage areas, and administrative and maintenance offices. Just beyond Hogan's Alley is a 1.1-mile pursuit/defensive-driving training track. The extensive firearms training provided to all FBI, DEA, and other law enforcement officers is conducted at an indoor firing range, eight outdoor firing ranges, four skeet ranges, and a two-hundred-yard rifle range. The FBI Academy is a secure facility and, as such, is not open to the public for tours.

Several units of the FBI are based at Quantico, many of which were added after I graduated in 1978. The units based at Quantico are Field and Police Training, Firearms Training, the Forensic Science Research and Training Center, Technology Services, Behavioral Science Unit, Investigative Training, Law Enforcement Communication, Leadership and Management Science, Outreach and Communications, Physical Training, New Agents' Training, Practical Applications, and Investigative Computer Training. Most of these units are used for developing new field agents, but they are also used to help get other agents up-to-date on new techniques through in-service training.

The FBI National Academy is also located there. This is an independent program for US and international law enforcement executives, focusing on leadership and the administration of justice in state and local law enforcement. The FBI National Academy conducts four ten-week sessions each year.

Once I arrived at Quantico for training, my first stop was the visitor registration desk on the ground floor of the Jefferson Hall dormitory. I'd been instructed to check in there and get my photo identification, which I would keep the entire time I was assigned to Quantico.

Quantico reminded me of a small college campus. You could walk almost a quarter mile, from building to building, and never go outside. The buildings were connected by glass-covered ramps that made me feel like a hamster in a Habitrail. As more buildings were added in the future, they would be connected in the same way. The ramps kept students out of bad weather as they navigated between classes, and they also made campus security tighter, with just a few controlled entrances.

In the halls I found spacious lounges with TV sets, video games, newspapers, and card tables. Some had display cases with samples of elaborate and sometimes beautiful law enforcement memorabilia from around the world, often donated by visiting students from other countries. Small alcoves contained coin-operated washers and dryers and many vending machines, which offered the usual mix of healthy and not-so-healthy selections. The hallways were adorned with artwork, often with a patriotic theme, and a quiet hush was the norm as people moved about.

At two locations along the hallways were shrines to FBI agents and graduates of the FBI National Academy who had given their lives in the line of duty. The Hall of Honor, located near the chapel complex, was the larger of the two. The library, open twenty-four hours a day, seven days a week, offered access to the FBI's vast holdings of thousands of pieces of law enforcement literature.

Within these walls I found pretty much everything I needed to survive the weeks of training, such as a bank, barbershop, pub, thousand-seat auditorium/theater, post office, convenience store, laundry and dry cleaners, first aid station, dining hall, gym, pool, classrooms, administrative offices, and nondenominational chapel. The dorm room where I lived housed two of us; we shared a private bath. The cafeteria could hold several hundred at a sitting and offered a nice selection of food and beverages at no cost. I gained weight easily while I was there.

My new agents class, which started October 3, 1977, was the first to come in under the new application process. It was a comparatively small class—only nineteen instead of the usual forty or so—this, I believe, as a result of some casualties of the new process. The trainees came from assorted backgrounds and experience, with several attorneys and accountants, but also a few former law enforcement officers like me.

Our class counselor was a former Oakland, California, police officer. He was not just very athletic—he looked like a movie star. He was also one of the most intelligent and quick-witted people I've ever met. I formed the impression that all FBI agents were like him, which I found intimidating and even discouraging.

During our first class session, when he gave us an overview of what to expect for the next fourteen weeks, I felt my self-confidence start to sink. He told us not to expect to go home for the first four weekends because we'd need the time to work with our study groups. I had never been a part of a study group, and I became very concerned about failing and having to return to Baltimore and beg for my job back. He then told us to go back to our rooms and change into running gear and meet him on Hoover Road in thirty minutes. He had us run five miles that day.

ↄ⅃ℐↄ

The living accommodations were sparse, with no TV or radio. I shared a dorm room with a Tulane University graduate and attorney from New Orleans. He had a very strong southern accent that I found irritating. But soon after I got to know him, I began to think he had a little "brother" in him: he could sing and dance with the best of them and knew all the Motown songs. In addition, he was one of the smartest, hardest-working, nicest guys I'd ever met.

I had never been away from home that long and hadn't spent much time with white people. I had a lot to learn.

Because I had never lived with white people before, I was surprised to see how hard they worked to get good grades; I'd always thought things came easily to them. I watched them study for hours at night, on the weekends, and in study groups. This really scared me: if *they* had to work this hard, I figured I'd need to work even harder. They often talked about buying homes after they got their assignments. I didn't know anything about buying a home. They also talked about stocks and bonds. Again, this was all new to me. I just listened and learned.

In those days you could smoke in the academy, and my roommate had to put up with my pipe smoke for the entire course. Fortunately, it didn't seem to bother him. I believe I was the only smoker in the class.

I kept hearing about the Board Room, a popular lounge at the academy where you could eat, drink beer and wine, and socialize. I was too scared to even think about having fun until I knew that I had passed the academy. So I stayed away from the Board Room for several weeks.

There was a lot of pressure on me. A trainee had to maintain an eighty-five academic average and couldn't fail more than one major written test. We were also tested for firearms and physical fitness and had to maintain a minimum score for each. About eight weeks into the training, I flunked a law exam with a score of eighty-three; I had to take the make-up test, which I passed, thank goodness. That put even more pressure on me. While I was at the academy, the US Postal Service called to offer me a job as an inspector. I had applied there as a backup, in the event that the FBI job didn't go through. I obviously had to turn it down, and all I could do was hope I wouldn't regret the decision.

About ten weeks into training we were asked to list five Offices of Preference (OPs) in order of priority. Your OP would be your "dream" FBI field office, the one you would want to be assigned to for the remainder of your career, and possibly your life. It was a big decision that required some serious thought and consultation with my future wife, Bernadette.

After discussing it with her, we decided that the Alexandria, Virginia, field office (AXFO) would be perfect as my first choice, and that my other four choices should be close to or south of there. So after Alexandria I listed Norfolk, Virginia; Washington, DC; Richmond, Virginia; and Miami.

During training at Quantico we took a field trip to the AXFO to see how an actual FBI field office functioned. I was impressed by its proximity to Washington, DC, and Baltimore as well as its beautiful setting in Alexandria's Old Town, about a block from the Potomac River. Since both Bernadette and I were from Baltimore, we wanted to be close enough to visit family and friends, but we were not sure we could live there again. We were told that the chance of getting a dream OP were very slim, particularly in the first ten to fifteen years of your career; your best chance was after you'd built up seniority. I didn't think much about it after I turned in my list, because it didn't look like I'd be seeing my OP until later in my career, when I was close to retirement.

✑♪

About two weeks before graduation, when it was clear that the remaining agents in the class (including me) would be graduating, we all received our transfer orders of assignment. My orders were to the Norfolk field office. This happened to be my number-two priority—

how lucky could I be! Oddly enough, all I could think of was the Norfolk State College football chant—"We don't drink, we don't smoke, Norfuck . . ."—and for days I kept repeating that chant through the hallways of the academy. It was all very exciting, and I was on cloud nine.

Once it became clear that I would not have to go back to Baltimore and beg for my old job back, and that I would be graduating and getting my FBI credentials, I decided it was safe to remarry. So the weekend before I graduated, Bernadette and I married in her church in Cooksville, Maryland. Some of my class members were able to attend, and it was great seeing them there.

I couldn't believe that I had made it through and graduated from the famous FBI Academy—it was the proudest moment of my life. Thank God for the LEEP funds and the flexible class hours offered to law enforcement students! If I hadn't rallied to turn my grades around and finish college, if I hadn't learned how to listen in class, take notes, and study well enough to get Bs and As back then, I never would have made it through the academy, and this moment would not have happened. It was a scary thought.

There was a snowstorm the day of our graduation, so my mother and father weren't able to make it. That was a real bummer. I know they really wanted to be there; they were very proud of me.

The day I walked across a stage and received my FBI credentials, I swore I would honor them for the rest of my life, on and off the job. I had a new career as an FBI agent ahead of me, and a new wife, too. I charged out my service revolver from the academy's gun vault, and then I was on my way.

> *I need change*
> *To help me to steadily grow*
> *I need change*
> *To enhance what I already know*
>
> *I need change*
> *To stimulate my boundless imagination*
> *I need change*
> *To keep me in continuous transformation*

I need change
To satisfy my curious soul
I need change
To challenge the bonds that hold

I need change
To keep me forging along
I need change
To ensure that I'm living strong

I need change
To sustain my limitless aspirations
I need change
To ensure I reach my destinations

Phil Reid

CHAPTER 9

▲

FIRST OFFICE AGENT

Bust-Out

New FBI agents aren't called "rookies." When they get their initial assignments, they are referred to as "first office agents," or FOAs. I had to get used to this and a lot of other FBI terminology.

My classmates and I were given a short period of time to report to our first offices of assignment. I sold my Corvette because we needed the money, and then Bernadette and I packed up all our household goods, loaded them into a trailer behind her Mustang, said our goodbyes to family and friends, and drove to Norfolk.

Our temporary quarters were in a hotel in Virginia Beach. When we arrived there, the hotel wanted a month's rent in advance and I didn't have enough funds available on my credit card to pay for it, so I needed the FBI to vouch for me. The Norfolk office sent two agents who helped us get checked in. I reported to the office the next day at noon, but only after the assistant special agent-in-charge (ASAC) had called my hotel looking for me. As it turned out, I was supposed to have reported for work at eight o'clock that morning. My new career was off to a shaky start.

They took me in to meet the special agent in charge (SAC), the ASAC, and my training agent. I was told that because of my law enforcement background, I would be working criminal matters such as bank robberies, fugitives, extortions, and kidnappings. Since I'd screwed up on the first day, I figured I had a lot of work to do to reverse their initial impression of me.

The SAC and ASAC briefed me on the Norfolk division's history, territory, and investigative priorities, and on their own expectations of me. They explained that Norfolk was Virginia's second-largest city, behind neighboring Virginia Beach. It is located at the core of the Hampton Roads, a metropolitan area named for the large natural harbor located at the mouth of the Chesapeake Bay. Norfolk has a long history as a strategic military and transportation point; Norfolk Naval Base is the world's largest, and the world's largest military alliance, the North Atlantic Treaty Organization, has its defense headquarters there. Therefore the bulk of our work was related to the military.

Norfolk is also home to the corporate headquarters of Norfolk Southern Railway, one of North America's principal Class I railroads, and Maersk Line, Limited, which manages the world's largest fleet of US-flagged vessels, from which a significant number of our interstate thefts cases were generated. Linked to its neighbors by an extensive network of interstate highways, bridges, tunnels, and bridge-tunnel complexes, Norfolk is bordered by multiple bodies of water and includes much riverfront and bay-front property. I was happy that I was still so close to the water.

We eventually left our temporary quarters and moved into an apartment. While I was getting settled into my new assignment with the FBI, my new wife was getting settled in, as well. She began looking for a job and finally found one in the accounting department of a Norfolk hospital.

I liked the fact that my new job with the FBI meant working Monday through Friday, even though they were usually ten-hour days. We were off on holidays and weekends—something I had to get used to. I also liked wearing a suit and tie and flashing my FBI credentials. I realized quickly that I was an FBI agent both on and off the job; people were watching all the time. We got so much respect by the public and in court, as well—in those days, our evidence wasn't challenged.

✑

Because I was the new agent in the office, I was given some very old, unsolved bank robbery (BR) and fugitive cases to start with. Most of the fugitive cases involved military deserters.

During my first week in the office, I was looking over surveillance camera photos of unidentified suspects in bank robberies from all across the country. I couldn't believe it when one of them turned out to be a guy I graduated from high school with in 1966. I immediately told my training agent, who asked me to call the BR squad in Baltimore and advise them who it was. This was my first BR solution, though it wasn't a Norfolk case.

I reviewed the old BR and fugitive cases and conducted follow-up investigations. In many cases, I reinterviewed witnesses and retraced some of the escape routes from bank robberies to try to identify more potential witnesses. This was a lot of fun, and I was having quite a bit of success, too. I couldn't believe they were paying me to do this.

My first FBI arrest was a navy deserter who had been on the lam for quite a while. I reviewed his file, developed some new leads about his whereabouts, and caught him in downtown Norfolk, shopping with his girlfriend. We took him by surprise, but he didn't resist arrest; his girlfriend seemed relieved that we had arrested him. I remember thinking, *I must be a real FBI agent.*

I started to *feel* like a real FBI agent when they began assigning me to new BRs I could work from start to finish. The bank surveillance films weren't much help, except in one case in particular. The camera hadn't gotten a good shot of the robber's face, but it did capture a unique, half-moon-shaped scar on his right forearm, so I had that shot enhanced by our FBI lab. Working with a sharp assistant US attorney, I developed a very circumstantial case and arrested our suspect. After the arrest, I noticed the scar on his right forearm and realized it matched the one in the surveillance camera photo.

Still, the assistant US attorney and I were reluctant to introduce the scar into evidence at trial. We believed that if the defense showed the photo to the jury, they would look at it more carefully than if we had introduced it. And we felt that if the jury looked at the photo more carefully, they would be convinced the suspect was the robber. So the assistant US attorney showed the surveillance photo to the defense attorney, who obviously was disturbed by it. In an effort to discredit the photo, he introduced it into evidence himself, trying to convince the jury that it couldn't be a photo of his client's scar. As we had hoped he would, the defense attorney even had the jury compare the scar in the photo with his client's scar. Once the jury saw them both, they convicted the suspect in short order.

I loved testifying in court as a special agent, because judges, juries, and even defense attorneys seemed to be in awe of the FBI. In fact, defense attorneys often seemed too intimidated to challenge our testimony or our evidence. Back then, there was still a lot of respect for the bureau—we could say or do no wrong. Unfortunately, because of missteps over the years, there now is no hesitation to challenge FBI evidence or courtroom testimony. Still, the US attorneys who present and prosecute our cases do an exceptional job of ensuring our testimony and evidence can withstand the harshest of scrutiny.

I worked very closely with local police departments in the Virginia cities of Norfolk, Virginia Beach, Chesapeake, and Portsmouth. The fact that I was a former policeman really endeared me to them.

(Now I understood why the FBI liked to hire former policemen.) It also let those local officers know that, like me, they could apply for positions with the FBI, as well as with other federal law enforcement agencies.

✣

My training agent, the bank robbery and fugitive programs coordinator for the Norfolk field office, was my first FBI hero among many over the years. He was a great investigator: smart, tenacious, and a good athlete. I wanted to be like him. He was a great help getting me started as an effective and productive FBI agent. He led by example, and he gave me a lot of attention and was very patient with me. Heaven knows I needed a lot of attention and patience, and I felt fortunate to be getting it from an agent of his caliber.

A black agent assigned to the Norfolk office, was another hero of mine. But he owned me at racquetball; he was merciless, constantly reminding me that he had no friends on the courts. He and his wife helped Bernadette and me settle into the FBI culture. He had already been in the FBI for a while, and I found him to be wise beyond his years. I listened to him intently as I gradually developed my FBI career goals and plans; he gave me a lot of insight into the various personalities in the office and how to succeed in spite of some of them. He also helped me navigate the process of buying our first house in Virginia Beach, with the help of my training agent's wife, who was our real estate agent.

I really enjoyed working and being responsible for the development of cases that were assigned to me. Whenever I needed help or had questions, there wasn't anyone in the office who wouldn't help me. Once I started working a case, I found it hard to let it go—I found myself working late into the night and even through the weekends sometimes. What I really liked was that my work ethic was recognized and appreciated by the senior agents and management.

After I'd been an agent for a little over a year, the SAC recommended that I become a relief supervisor, the backup who manages the supervisor's agents while he or she is on vacation or on leave. Given my brief tenure, it was a real honor for me to be asked, but after I was given the training, headquarters wouldn't approve the appointment because I hadn't been in the bureau at least two years. As it turned out, there wasn't a written rule to back up this decision, and I was made a relief supervisor. But afterwards a new written rule was established that all future relief supervisors had to have at least two years' experience.

❧

I used to have fun trying to figure out "whodunit." One memorable case involved numerous thefts from a cargo hangar at Norfolk International Airport. The case agent had tried everything to catch the thief, from installing surveillance cameras in the hangar to putting tracking devices in boxes that could potentially be stolen. Nothing seemed to work. I was handling other cases at the time, but I had heard about the case and the problems they were having trying to solve it.

One evening my supervisor called me, saying, "Get your ass over to the airport and solve that damn theft case." I thought that was pretty presumptuous of him, and I also had to concern myself with the sensibilities of the case agent, who might resent an FOA being asked to help solve his case.

I grabbed one of the other FOAs, and we reinterviewed the employees in the hangar. I made sure we asked all the right questions and that they were very clear in their responses. I didn't hesitate to re-ask questions to check their answers. I made sure we had exact details of all relevant employees' movements, activities, and potential motives. My partner and I played good cop/bad cop.

By the time we finished questioning the employees, we had identified the suspect and solved the case—and we had done it all in about two hours. The case was too sensitive to garner high-profile praise, but my supervisor gave me a quiet, heartfelt thank you.

I got my first travel from an FBI case when my training agent and I caught a bank robbery fugitive from Los Angeles in Norfolk and were subpoenaed to testify against him in federal court in LA. When the suspect heard we were in LA to testify, he decided to plead guilty, so my training agent and I had some free time to do some sightseeing before our return flight. We did a blitz of Hollywood, visiting Sunset Strip, Grauman's Chinese Theater, and Hollywood and Vine, and seeing the Hollywood sign in the hills with our own eyes. You couldn't beat that!

On another trip, this one to Boston for another BR case, I testified and then did some sightseeing before I flew back to Norfolk.

In 1978, during my first year in the Norfolk office, Director Kelley resigned and was replaced by William H. Webster. At the time of his appointment, Webster was serving as judge of the US Court of Appeals for the Eighth Circuit. He had previously been a judge in US District Court for the Eastern District of Missouri.

❦

After a year or so of working criminal cases in the Norfolk office, I asked for a change. Believe it or not, I was getting burned out working criminal cases; I wanted to try working foreign counterintelligence (FCI)—spy cases. I was pleasantly surprised when the office supported my request. It turns out we had quite a few military bases in our territory that were major intelligence targets of enemy countries. So I was sent back to Quantico for a month-long FCI training certification course. I had fun working FCI cases, which relied a good deal on surveillance, either fixed-position or moving by car or plane.

One day I was asked to be an observer for one of our pilots who was providing air coverage during an FCI surveillance operation. We went up in his FBI Cessna 182, and as we were circling the target I began feeling a little woozy. I looked around for a barf bag but couldn't find it in time and off-loaded into a monocular case. The pilot was forced to abort the mission because the smell was so bad in the cockpit that he began to get sick himself. Of course we laughed about it for years, and he even let me go back up with him a few times after that.

Some of our surveillance missions lasted for days, and we followed targets in all types of vehicles, including mobile homes. I once brought my wife with me in an RV that we were using to conduct a weekend surveillance. Having her with me provided a perfect cover.

๛

Each FBI office has its "heavies," the go-to agents or squads when a crisis or a big case comes up. Most FOAs aspire to become a heavy, and I was no different. The heavies in the Norfolk office ran 5K and 10K races and even the Shamrock Marathon, and so did I. Most of these guys were on the office SWAT team. I was really surprised when they invited me to join them.

I became a SWAT team "assaulter"—that meant I would be the first to go through a door. It was an exciting time, although I was quickly brought down to earth when I attended SWAT training. It was held on Pawley's Island, South Carolina, where a well-known, affluent family had set aside an area on their plantation for law enforcement agencies to conduct training. I was told that it was a former slave plantation, which made me uncomfortable—a feeling compounded by the black employees' behavior, which to me seemed slave-like. I felt like I had stepped back in time and wasn't sure whether they were going to enforce the Fugitive Slave Act and not let me leave the plantation when training was over.

๛

My daughter, Maisha, stayed with us each summer while I was assigned to the Norfolk office. Since my wife and I were working, we would take Maisha to day camp Monday through Friday, and then on the weekends we would all go fishing and crabbing at the Virginia Beach fishing pier or Rudy Inlet, making a meal of our catch. We would also take day trips to Jamestown, Williamsburg, Busch Gardens, and many other historic sites in the area.

❧

After about six months of working FCI cases, I asked to return to criminal cases. By this time there was a new criminal case supervisor who had a great reputation among his agents, and he had been lobbying for me to return to criminal work.

The new supervisor assigned me several new cases, including a "bust-out" in which person(s) unknown had fraudulently purchased several local travel agencies and then quickly abandoned them, disappearing with the airline ticket stock, which they sold for a fortune. The problem was that seats on various flights were filled, but the airlines themselves weren't getting paid.

I soon discovered that although similar crimes had been occurring all over the country, the majority of the cases were in New York, and the operations there seemed to be well-organized. I ended up reassigning all my other cases so I could focus exclusively on the bust-outs. This investigation was designated a major case by FBI headquarters, which meant that whatever human or material resources were needed would be made available. I established a war room and found myself working around the clock, including weekends, to stay on top of new cases coming in. I sent leads all over the country and even around the world trying to identify who was responsible and build my case. Because I was able to identify stolen tickets, airlines could deny seats to passengers who presented them.

As I worked the case, it became more and more obvious that organized crime was behind it, and that one of the New York mob families was making a lot of money. At that time, the bust-outs constituted one of the FBI's biggest and most important cases. The scheme threatened to bring down the major airlines because their seats—mostly seats on international flights, which brought higher prices—were being filled by passengers with stolen tickets. Braniff airlines may have been driven out of business due in part to this scheme.

Because the case was looking more like a New York field office case than a Norfolk one, the NYO made a strong bid to headquarters to have it reassigned there. On October 1, 1979, I received orders for reassignment to the NYO. It caught me by surprise, because I had been led to believe I would be with the Norfolk office for four to five years. Maybe I was being reassigned there to continue with the bust-out investigation? Oh well, on to New York, the Big Apple!

CHAPTER 10

▲

THE BIG APPLE

Squad M-9

After I had overcome my surprise, I began looking forward to moving to New York. I really liked the idea that I would be working FBI cases there—I couldn't believe they would be paying me to work in New York City. I'm a hopeless romantic; I must have watched *West Side Story* a thousand times when I was a kid, and all I could think about back then was the Jets and the Sharks, and Tony and Maria. I had read about the Harlem Renaissance, and this was my chance to experience it personally. Songs like "Arthur's Theme" and "On Broadway" started running through my head.

My wife and I knew we couldn't afford to live in the city, so we arranged a house-hunting trip, at the FBI's expense, of course, to central Jersey to find a place to live. We fired our first real estate agent because she kept taking us to places where we were too scared to get out of the car, let alone reside. We didn't know what she was thinking.

Our second real estate agent found the perfect house in Fanwood, New Jersey. It was just about to be foreclosed on, but we could see past the bad colors, overgrown shrubbery, and broken front screen door. This house was a diamond in the rough. Plus it was in a family neighborhood perfect for Maisha's holiday and summer visits—a nice, small, tree-lined, quiet community, with great neighbors. Quite a few FBI agents lived in Fanwood or the adjacent towns. The location was ideal: I could catch the train to Newark, take the PATH train to the World Trade Center, and walk from there to the field office in lower Manhattan. On weekends, Bernadette and I could go into the city to catch Broadway shows and visit museums and restaurants.

When I flew into LaGuardia for the first time and my plane flew over the skyscrapers, providing the same panoramic view in the opening scene of *West Side Story*, I almost broke into song: "The Jets are going to have their day tonight . . ."

After the plane landed, I picked up my luggage, hailed a cab, and gave the driver my temporary address in Astoria, Queens. We got into an argument about something along the way, and he deliberately dropped me off at the right house number in Astoria, Queens—but on the wrong street. I didn't realize the problem until I knocked on the door. I didn't know where I was, the neighborhood looked a little hostile, and I had more luggage than arms. Luckily, a little old lady recognized my peril and helped me find the right address, which was the next street over. She even helped carry my luggage. I guess that was my welcome to the Big Apple. Fortunately, I hadn't given the cab driver a tip.

I settled into the apartment, which had been arranged for me by my former Norfolk ASAC and the New York office's deputy assistant director in charge (DADIC), Ken Walton. I would stay there until our house in Fanwood was ready and my wife could give her notice of resignation.

My temporary quarters had been used as a lookout to keep an eye on suspected organized crime or foreign counterintelligence targets.

FBI apartments like this always had extra bedrooms where agents with a higher ranking than mine could stay on the cheap. This one was free, with a short commute to the office.

⚜

When new agents arrive in New York, they typically have to do FBI applicant background investigations or FCI cases for at least two years before getting the chance to work on a criminal investigative squad. I was immediately assigned to a criminal squad and expected to continue to lead the work on the bust-outs. Apparently, the higher-ups were so pleased with my work in Norfolk that they wanted to keep me on it in New York. Both my former Norfolk ASAC and Ken Walton really set me up well and gave me the red carpet treatment when I arrived at the NYO.

I was first assigned to Squad C-10, a general criminal squad that handled theft from interstate shipment, art theft, crimes on federal reservations, and Asian organized crime. The supervisor was a pure New Yorker, right down to the accent. I believe he was born and raised in New York and he appeared to love every minute of it. Because I was a relief supervisor and he already had one, I became the backup to his primary relief supervisor.

Many other agents were given transfer orders to New York when I received mine. And it wasn't just new agents like me who were being moved there—agents who had been in the bureau for years were getting transfers, too, and they were not happy. The reassignments were the result of a study showing that the bulk of the bureau's experienced agents were assigned to field offices in small towns, where the numbers of major and complicated crimes were the lowest. The study had been prompted by the FBI's request for more federal money to address big-city crime. Congress was willing to support the increase provided experienced agents were moved to cities where experienced crime fighting was needed. It was decided that any agent hired before October 1, 1969, who hadn't served in one of the ten biggest field offices was eligible for transfer to a big city like New York, Chicago, Boston, Miami, Detroit, Cleveland, Los Angeles, or San Francisco.

So hundreds of agents were uprooted from their nice, comfortable small-town field offices and transferred to big-city field offices where everything was a little more active and expensive. This became known as the dreaded 10/1/69 Transfer Program. Quite a few agents resigned rather than moving, and many who did move were unhappy about it, although they were generally productive and their experience was very much appreciated.

✑✐

Bernadette had given notice to her boss back in Virginia, and she met me in our new home in Fanwood. I moved out of the apartment and took a week off to get the furniture moved into the house. Within the first two weeks of the move, someone broke into the house and stole some minor items; we had our own ideas about who the suspects were. We notified the police, who completed a burglary report, and then we changed the locks on the doors and had an alarm system installed.

Bernadette settled in very quickly and found a job in the accounting office of a local psychiatric hospital. She even went out one day and came back with a beautiful, newborn, store-bought cocker spaniel we named Lady. Bernadette had grown up with dogs and missed having them around. I'd never had a dog before, except for the black Lab her boss in Virginia had rescued and Bernadette brought home. We had tried to make it a part of our family, but it was an uphill battle, and in the end we had to turn it over to the local animal shelter. But this one looked like a keeper.

Bernadette's father visited us soon after we moved into our new home. He really wanted to go into New York City, and he especially wanted to see Times Square, which he hadn't seen in forty years, so we took him one Saturday afternoon. It was very crowded in Times Square, and Bernadette's father was enjoying the sightseeing, when all of a sudden police cars roared up from all directions, chasing a man on foot. Some of the cars drove up on the sidewalk, causing pedestrians to scatter. The police jumped out of their cars with guns drawn, bearing down on the suspect, who immediately put his hands in the air. Of course we were all frightened, particularly my father-in-law. "Welcome to New York," I said.

✑

As I was getting settled into my new squad, I met the supervisory special agent (SSA) who was supervising one of the FCI squads. He was black and the youngest supervisor in the New York field office. I was pleasantly surprised that we had black supervisors, and all I could think of was how J. Edgar Hoover must be turning over in his grave. This SSA welcomed me to New York and offered any help I needed to get settled in. His offer was much appreciated.

My supervisor assigned me to the New York side of the bust-out case, as well as other pending cases. He also gave me a partner, a very cool Italian-American who was married to the daughter of a famous baseball player. I was under the impression that he and his wife were independently wealthy, because he collected his payroll checks but never seemed to cash them—he just let them accumulate in his desk drawer. They lived with their beautiful daughter in a very nice brownstone in the heart of downtown Manhattan.

My new partner and I became good friends and even spent a couple of days together with our families at his townhouse on exclusive Fire Island, where our wives met for the first time. He was a pure New Yorker, and he knew his way around the city. When we covered our case leads together, he did most of the driving; he thought I was too timid and didn't drive quickly or aggressively enough for New York City traffic. He was a honker and a screamer behind the steering wheel. I loved driving in city traffic, but I was very patient and never saw the need to honk my horn.

In December 1980, a few days after John Lennon was killed outside his apartment building in Upper Manhattan, my new partner and I drove by there to pay our respects and give a salute to a great singer-songwriter. Hundreds of flowers, candles, and other symbolic items lay in front of the Dakota. What sold me on the Beatles was not just their songs, but the fact that they gave credit to a lot of Motown writers and singers for inspiring their careers. They named Smokey Robinson, in particular, as one of the best songwriters of all time.

❧

Once I settled into the NYO, I asked to join the Manhattan SWAT team. That wasn't a full-time assignment—your priority responsibilities were your assigned cases—but you always had to be available for SWAT call-outs, which required dropping whatever you were doing and responding with the team. The NYO had three SWAT teams: Manhattan, New Rochelle, and Brooklyn/Queens. Because I worked out of the Manhattan office, I applied for the Manhattan team. The NYO's three SWAT teams were considered the best in the FBI, and the Manhattan team was supposed to be the best of the three. To my pleasant surprise, I was quickly accepted on the team. Being a former Baltimore City policeman and having already been through SWAT training in Norfolk were a big help.

When I arrived in New York, the Manhattan team was in the midst of a lawsuit initiated by the residents of 91 Morningside Drive in New York City. Agents had mistakenly raided the plaintiffs' apartments during a search for a major fugitive, Joanne Chesimard, who had escaped from a New Jersey prison while serving a life sentence for murder. She was a member of the revolutionary/ criminal organization known as the Black Liberation Army. On May 2, 1973, Chesimard and two accomplices were stopped by two state troopers for a motor vehicle violation on the New Jersey Turnpike. At the time she was wanted for involvement in several felonies, including bank robbery. She and her accomplices opened fire on the troopers, seemingly without provocation. One trooper was wounded and the other was shot and killed execution-style, at point-blank range.

Chesimard fled the scene but was subsequently apprehended. One of her accomplices was killed in the shoot-out; the other was also apprehended and remains in jail. In 1977, Chesimard was found guilty of first-degree murder, assault and battery of a police officer, assault with a dangerous weapon, assault with intent to kill, illegal possession of a weapon, and armed robbery. She was sentenced to life in prison. Then, on November 2, 1979, she escaped.

The residents of 91 Morningside Drive were suing the FBI and each agent individually. This was the first time the courts had allowed individual agents to be sued, and as a result, all FBI agents are now required to carry personal liability insurance.

The Manhattan SWAT team was loaded with heavies. These guys were respected not only for their ability to go through doors and handle risky arrests, but for their investigative, administrative, and leadership qualities. I was in awe of them, particularly my team leader, but I had to keep that contained and to myself.

Most of our SWAT training took place at Camp Smith, north of New York City, near Peekskill, New York. Camp Smith is a military installation of the New York Army National Guard, and it's also where the NYO conducts its required quarterly firearms training and semi-annual physical fitness testing for agents assigned to the Manhattan NYO.

Our SWAT team leader assigned me to the sniper team. My first weapon was a .223 caliber Remington sniper rifle with a scope. Though it was all new to me, we were given a lot of training, time, and ammunition to practice with. I began to feel very comfortable shooting it and got very accurate within two hundred yards, even right after a two-mile run. We eventually switched over to Winchester .308 caliber sniper rifles.

Because Camp Smith belonged to the National Guard, we had a very close working relationship with them. We used their helicopters to conduct rappelling, insertion, and extraction training on and off rooftops.

After each training session we would all head to a local pub for beer with peppermint schnapps chasers and the best chili and onions in the world. We were lucky we were never pulled over for DWI (driving while intoxicated) or for DWF (driving while farting). The chili with onions was great, but the side effects made for a very long ride home in a car loaded with team members.

Going out on SWAT arrests in New York was very different from Norfolk because of all the high-rise buildings. Members of the team would meet within a block or two of the target location and suit up with SWAT gear on the street, which drew a lot of attention. It always felt like thousands of people were watching, but because there were so many high rises and so many people, no one could tell for sure what our target was. The team leader handled all pre-arrest briefings. He was always thorough and well-prepared, so when it was time to go through the door we did so with a lot of confidence. The number of SWAT missions varied from month to month. Sometimes I would go to work and not get back home for two or three days because I had back-to-back call-outs.

ષ۩ρ

After a couple of months in New York, I realized that the bust-out case needed my full-time attention. I asked my supervisor if he could reassign my other cases and give me a quiet room to work in. He wouldn't reassign my other cases, but I did get a private room. I was granted Office of Origin (OO), or lead office status, on the investigation. DADIC Walton would check in with me from time to time for a briefing on how the case was progressing.

Walton was considered a maverick. Agents had a lot of nicknames for him, but the one that stuck with me was "Hollywood." He was considered an agent's agent—he was very supportive of agents, but I suspect he maintained poor relations with his superiors, because he appeared to enjoy challenging authority. He was instrumental in initiating joint task forces with other federal, state, and local law enforcement agencies to address major criminal and terrorism threats, setting the standard for FBI field offices across the country. He was flamboyant, handsome, suave, and debonair, and he maintained a perennial tan. He wore his brown hair in a pompadour, and his nails were always well-manicured. He dressed impeccably. He wore heavily starched, high-collared shirts, he carried a pearl-handled pistol, and he walked through the office with a Sherlock Holmes-style cape draped over his shoulders. Most of the agents found him intelligent and engaging and very much liked his style of staying on top of cases in the office: the FBI's term for it was "management by walking around." He never hesitated to ask an agent for an update, and the agents were always elated when he asked and flattered by his personal interest.

I began working feverishly on the bust-outs, often staying at the office until late at night and through the weekends. I was the first agent there in the morning (I turned on the lights) and one of the last agents to leave (I turned off the lights). I was sending leads all over the world and having agents and legal attachés at various US embassies interview passengers with fraudulent airline tickets to determine where and from whom they had bought them. We were getting closer to identifying the ringleaders when my supervisor abruptly announced that the case was closed. He didn't give me a reason, and I was afraid to go to Walton because I didn't know if he was involved in the decision. I closed up my war room and moved on. I was very upset and frustrated for months, but *c'est la vie*.

Walton assigned me and another agent the responsibility of providing security for FBI Director William Webster whenever he came to New York. At the time there was no permanent security team assigned to protect the FBI director, and although we had fun doing the advance work and then staying with him when he came to New York, the job wasn't without career risks.

My original partner and I got to be very friendly with Webster after getting him in and out of New York on a few occasions. One night we were all eating dinner together in a Times Square restaurant—the director's wife had come with him on the trip—and our waiter asked us if we all wanted to order drinks. I ordered a soda, but to my surprise, my partner ordered wine. The next day he was taken off the detail and replaced by my SWAT partner and good friend. I assumed Webster reported the incident to Walton, who orchestrated the reassignment. My original partner had forgotten that we were still working as security for the director, and he paid dearly for his momentary lapse in judgment.

Walton really tried to take care of me in New York. He gave me the chance to apply for the position of supervisor of an applicant background investigation squad. But my interview during the screening process reflected that I still had a lot to learn before I could supervise a squad. The primary relief supervisor on my squad was promoted to that position instead, and at the time he was certainly more ready than I was. I still came out ahead, as I was assigned to his former position.

❧

One morning, our squad was informed by the assistant director that we would be getting a new supervisor, and that I would be the interim supervisor until a new one was appointed. We weren't given a reason for the change, but we had heard a lot of rumors.

I ran the squad as acting supervisor for about six months, during which there was a reorganization of the NYO's criminal division. My squad became the major case squad, or M-9, which would handle all new major cases for the NYO, including terrorism, fugitives, kidnappings, and extortions. The majority of the heavies on the Manhattan SWAT team were assigned to my new squad; they would be assigned to the major cases but also would handle any SWAT call-outs. Overnight, my squad had become the most elite criminal squad in the FBI, and by chance I was their interim supervisor. You can bet this new squad of agents didn't require a whole lot of my supervision, and I knew some didn't want it from a wet-nosed new agent like me. A couple of them made that fact very clear to me early on. Believe me, I didn't debate them.

Eventually they selected the new supervisor for my squad: the firearms supervisor at our Camp Smith training facility. He was the overall team leader for all three NYO SWAT teams. We called him "the supreme SWAT team commander." He was very well respected in the NYO, and M-9 was formed with his name on it.

✑✑✑

Tuesday, October 20, 1981, started off as just another busy day for Squad M-9. It got much busier when we began to get reports of a Brink's armored truck robbery in Nyack, New York, in which one of the guards was killed. My supervisor asked me to immediately "stand up" the command center with other agents and start capturing information as it came in. We had to identify investigative leads that would need to be covered by our agents and NYPD task force members.

As details flowed into the command center, it became increasingly clear that this was not a typical, isolated armored truck robbery. We began to realize that the crime was committed by members of two domestic terrorist groups that had been dormant since the sixties and seventies. Because we hadn't received credible intelligence regarding their activities, or had failed to connect the dots, we had thought the groups had disbanded, their members having died, gone to jail, or gone legit. But apparently over the years, members of the Black Liberation Army and the Weather Underground had joined forces and begun robbing banks and armored trucks, establishing their own safe houses across the country and leaving no indication that the crimes were part of an organized ring of conspirators.

As more information continued to trickle into the command center, the picture became clear. After six previous and unsuccessful attempts to rob a Brink's truck, Mutulu Shakur and five or six others had succeeded in robbing this one of approximately $1.6 million, killing one of the Brink's guards in the process. They then drove to another location, where they transferred the money to a U-Haul truck driven by Kathy Boudin and her husband, David Gilbert. Boudin was a member of the Weather Underground and had been a fugitive on the FBI's Ten Most Wanted list for eleven years.

The money transfer was witnessed and reported to the police, who set up a roadblock at the Tappan Zee Bridge over the Hudson River in lower Hudson Valley. In the ensuing shoot-out, two Nyack policemen were killed and Boudin was captured, but Shakur and the other participants escaped and became FBI fugitives. The case turned into a nationwide investigation after we were able to grasp the magnitude of criminal activities these groups had engaged in, undetected, over the years. It became known as the NYROB investigation and was initially assigned to my squad.

We developed intelligence information that the armored truck robbery had been planned in a Harlem acupuncture clinic, so we set up a twenty-four-hour surveillance of the clinic from an apartment across the street in order to identify any additional potential suspects. It was a joint surveillance with NYPD officers and detectives, and it lasted about six months. We were able to pick up a lot of intelligence about the robbery and who was involved through informant information and wiretaps.

One night while we were on surveillance in the apartment, we overheard some very excited, cryptic conversations that piqued our interest. We weren't sure whether there was anything to it, but we asked two NYPD detectives who were on standby for vehicle surveillance to drive to a certain location in Harlem and sit there and let us know if they saw anything of interest. They told us later that while they were sitting there, a van pulled up and parked, and out came two of the biggest and meanest looking "brothers" they had ever seen, wearing long dashikis. They looked around, and then out came Joanne Chesimard herself. The detectives got out of their cars and ran toward her, but as they were reaching for their weapons, the two brothers whipped out automatic weapons from under their dashikis and drew down on them, which stopped them in their tracks. They said Chesimard looked them in the eye, laughed, and then walked around their car, kicking their tires in a taunting manner. Then she got back into the van and they all drove off. We were never able to relocate the van or its passengers. That was the last known sighting of Chesimard in the United States; it is believed that she escaped to Cuba and has been living there ever since.

Sometime in late October of 1981, we developed additional intelligence that the BLA was operating a heavily armed urban guerrilla warfare training camp on a farm in Gallman, Mississippi, just outside of Jackson. Because we didn't have a hostage rescue team assigned to Quantico then, as we have today, all three New York SWAT teams were deployed to conduct the raid.

So we loaded up a National Guard C-130 transport plane with the three New York SWAT teams, an armored personnel carrier, and gear, and flew to Jackson. We knew from our briefings that the group was willing to engage us in a fierce firefight and even die if confronted. We also knew to look out for several manmade tunnels on the Gallman farm; the group could use them to attack us from behind. We were all ready to sign wills that night, because we expected that some of us might not make it back home.

We arrived in Jackson very late that night. We were told by members of the Jackson office surveillance team that the BLA leadership was still on the Gallman farm, sleeping in the main farmhouse. Moving quietly in the dark, we surrounded the farmhouse and established inner and outer perimeters of security. We also looked for the tunnels but couldn't find any. We had SWAT agents standing behind the armored personnel carrier in case we needed to assault the farmhouse. When the sun came up, we used a bullhorn to identify ourselves and call for everyone in the house to come out with their hands up. We were expecting an immediate response of gunfire, but nothing happened.

It turned out that the only people in the house were a couple of kids; a woman later identified as Cynthia Boston, minister of information for the Republic of New Africa; and her alleged common-law husband, William Johnson. They all came out with their hands over their heads and gave up without any trouble.

Unfortunately, there was no treasure-trove of BLA members or evidence of the Brink's robbery, and we didn't recover any of their weapons. (Boston was indicted in the robbery, but the charges were eventually dropped because of a lack of evidence.) We had the right place, but our raid was ill-timed. Somehow the BLA members had left without being noticed by our Jackson surveillance team. Obviously we were all very disappointed, considering the resources we'd expended for this operation. But it was nice that we all went home in one piece.

The NYROB investigation lasted for years and yielded some very significant domestic terrorism intelligence and arrests. Mutulu Shakur was eventually arrested in California on February 11, 1986, and was subsequently found guilty of taking part in the armored truck robbery and the prison escape. Prior to his arrest, he was noticed during FBI surveillance giving reverent attention to a very young child. It is believed that the child was his stepson, the late rapper Tupak Shakur.

❦

Several months later, in June 1982, the US Coast Guard requested FBI assistance to resolve a hostage standoff taking place in international waters off the entrance to Delaware Bay, aboard an 890-foot, Liberian-flagged oil tanker named *Ypapanti*. The incident had begun on May 16, when the tanker was denied entrance to US waters due to the lack of required safety equipment aboard. During the next few weeks, twenty-four of the tanker's Pakistani and Indian crewmen mutinied over a wage dispute, seizing control and taking the captain and eleven of the ship's officers hostage.

After a prolonged period of unsuccessful negotiations, they threatened to kill the hostages, set fire to the vessel, and release 290,000 barrels of oil into the ocean unless the ship's owners paid them union-scale wages. The Liberian government made an official request for the United States to resolve the matter before someone got hurt. Because the ship was in international waters, the FBI needed permission from the National Security Council to conduct a hostage rescue. Alexander Haig was the chairman of the NSC at the time, and he convened an emergency session and approved our assistance.

On the morning of June 22, 1982, the Coast Guard flew the three NYO SWAT teams down to Cape May, New Jersey, where we practiced hostage rescues on a similar tanker docked in the area. We then boarded one of the Coast Guard's ninety-foot cutters and headed out to the tanker. The trip seemed to take hours.

As the tanker came into view, it was clear that we had a big job ahead of us. When we finally pulled alongside the tanker, we were intimidated by its sheer size. The seas were also very rocky, which made it difficult to stabilize the planks we would use to walk back and forth between crafts.

The plan was for the Coast Guard captain to renew negotiations, and if it appeared that no progress was being made, he would take off his cap, which would be our signal to board the ship. We maintained a low profile on the cutter, keeping out of sight of the tanker's hostage-takers and ready for a quick assault. We watched and waited, and then the captain took off his cap.

With the boats rocking, we traversed the wooden planks in our heavy SWAT gear and boarded the tanker. It was wobbly, but we all made it across and handled our assignments quickly and with precision. We rescued the hostages, arrested the twenty-four hostage-takers, and secured the ship without injuries. The vessel was then returned to the control of the captain and his twelve officers. The twenty-four mutinous Pakistani and Indian crewmen were removed from the tanker and placed in custody with INS until they could be returned to their homeland.

The very next month, before we could catch our collective breath, Squad M-9 received a call from the Secret Service asking for help with a case they had dubbed CAT. The case involved an unknown male (he called himself "Cat") who was sending letters and making phone calls threatening President Ronald Reagan. The Secret

Service considered the threats serious and believed he was capable of carrying them out. The president had survived being shot by John Hinckley Jr. just over a year earlier, on March 30, 1981.

The unidentified male had also made threats against New York State Senator Alfonse D'Amato, which gave us jurisdiction in the investigation. We discussed the limited information that the Secret Service had on this person with our profiling unit chief (UC), John Douglas, providing him copies of the threatening letters. UC Douglas agreed with the Secret Service that Cat was a real threat to the president, and he suggested that having both agencies working together increased the chances of catching him.

Our problem was that nobody had a clue who Cat was, what he looked like, how to contact him, or where he was calling or writing from. We believed he was from New York, but only because one of the people who had received a call thought he had a New York accent. The calls and letters were untraceable, so we had to rely on Douglas's profile to get a start. He suggested that the next time Cat called, we advise him that we were going to put an ad in the *New York Post* asking him to call a particular phone number. Frankly, expecting the suspect to look for the ad and then call the number seemed like wishful thinking.

In the meantime, Cat communicated that he was going to catch a train to Washington, DC, to kill the president. So we had FBI and Secret Service agents jump on every conceivable moving passenger train from New York to Washington and walk through each car, looking for anyone acting suspicious. The problem, again, was that we didn't even know what Cat looked like.

We did get very lucky with the *Post* ad. Believe it or not, Cat found the ad and called the phone number. A very brief conversation with him ensued, which we were able to record. We traced the call to public phones in the Bronx. We all listened to him talk. He had a very distinctive voice: he sounded like Elmer Fudd.

Not long after this call, President Reagan was scheduled to give a speech to the United Nations in New York. In anticipation of his arrival, we obtained court approval to tap practically every public phone in the Bronx in the event that Cat called back; we stationed a lot of Secret Service and FBI agents in the Bronx, too. He didn't call. As a result, when Reagan arrived at the UN, it was under unprecedented security.

Cat called again sometime later and agreed to meet a Secret Service agent in Grand Central Station; Cat would call the agent once he arrived there. We weren't sure if Cat would show up. Again we received special court approval, this time to tap every public phone in Grand Central Station. We had agents covering every bank of phones in the station, all of which were mapped with numbers.

Cat did arrive at Grand Central Station, and he called the agent. We were able to trace the call to one particular phone bank, and a Secret Service agent approached him while he was still on the line. The agent identified himself and asked the man his name. His first word was "heh-woh"—and we knew we had our man.

He gave us his name—and as our FBI profiler had suggested, he turned out to be mentally challenged. It had taken us almost three months to identify and arrest him, but it was a great joint investigation between the Secret Service and the FBI. I also believe this was one of the first big cases where our profiling unit was of major assistance. In appreciation for our work on the case, I received a tie clasp and cufflinks with President Ronald Reagan's and Vice President George H. W. Bush's names on them.

❧

On September 29, 1982, the first of seven individuals died in metropolitan Chicago after ingesting Extra Strength Tylenol that had been deliberately laced with cyanide. Within a week, Johnson & Johnson pulled thirty-one million bottles of capsules back from retailers, making it one of the first major recalls in American history. My squad became involved because a New York resident sent a letter to Johnson & Johnson headquarters in New Jersey, demanding $1 million in exchange for stopping the murders. We were not able to link him to the crimes, but he was later convicted of extortion and sentenced to twenty years. Our agents were surprised when they visited Johnson & Johnson headquarters and found themselves talking directly to the company's CEO. They found him very forthright and cooperative during the entire investigation.

The Chicago field office case involving the murders remains unsolved, and no suspects have been charged. Johnson & Johnson's quick response, including the nationwide recall, was widely praised by public relations experts and the media, becoming the gold standard for corporate crisis management.

⁂

While assigned to the NYO I had occasion to sit in on an organized crime trial in which the now-legendary undercover FBI agent Joe Pistone testified. He was on the stand for days, and watching him made me proud to be an agent. He had the courtroom mesmerized and amazed by his story and his bravery, although the defendants and their cohorts in the courtroom didn't seem as impressed. I had never seen so many cassette tapes of secretly recorded conversations in my life.

I met Pistone a few years later and told him that I was there in the courtroom when he was testifying. He was pleasantly surprised. The movie *Donnie Brasco* is based on his undercover work.

⁂

One morning when I arrived at the NYO, DADIC Walton approached me and asked what my OP was. I told him I thought it was Alexandria, Virginia. Then he said, "You know you got your OP."

"You've got to be kidding," I said.

He responded, "Do I *look* like I'm fucking kidding?"

I realized then that Walton was very serious—and not happy about it. He asked if I wanted the assignment. I thought for a few seconds. Though I really liked what I was doing in New York, I didn't want to be the agent who had a chance to get an OP out of New York and turned it down. I accepted the OP.

Once the word got around that I had gotten my OP, I took a beating from my fellow agents. Instantly I became the scourge of the office, particularly since I had been in the NYO for less than two years and had been given the red carpet treatment from day one. In addition, I had only been in the FBI for about four years. As I mentioned earlier, it normally takes an agent ten to fifteen years to get an OP—if he ever gets it at all. The other agents, including Walton, were upset because they thought that I had received a special favor from William Webster through my security detail with him. None of the agents would speak to me. I became persona non grata.

My supervisor had been on vacation, and he came back with a vengeance after hearing I got my OP. Once he returned to work, he called me into his office and told me that I was no longer on the SWAT team. He stripped me of my duties as primary relief supervisor (along with the annual monetary bonus and my take-home car) and gave them to my partner and good friend, whom he named as his new primary relief supervisor.

One thing I can always say about my partner: he was a very loyal friend. That take-home car, which was very valuable in New York, just sat in the office garage. He wouldn't touch it out of loyalty to me. I never forgot that.

My supervisor viewed my getting an OP as disloyalty to him, to the SWAT team, and to the squad; he assumed that I had gone behind his back and asked the director for an OP transfer. Of course, I hadn't asked for a transfer, I never knew it was coming, and I didn't know how it came about. Bernadette and I had planned to stay in

New York for years—we loved New York. I was devastated and became very depressed about how I was being treated. After all the time and hard work I had put in at that office, it was amazing to me how quickly some people turned on me without even knowing the facts.

In the meantime, Bernadette and I traveled to Alexandria for a ten-day house-hunting trip, which gave me a break from my predicament in the NYO. I was already aware of how nice Alexandria was, but my wife was pleasantly surprised to see for herself that the field office was located in such a scenic and historic place. She was excited at the prospect of living in Old Town and finding a job there, as well. It was a very expensive place to live, however, and we didn't have a whole lot of money to put down on a detached home, so we looked at condos. We found a recently renovated condominium development that we were very pleased with, just a few blocks from the field office. It was small, so we had to downsize, but we were in Old Town and I could walk to work. We were also just two blocks from the Potomac and a mile from a sailboat marina, and along the river was a running and bike path to Mount Vernon. I remember thinking that this was the way OPs should be, and that I could live there forever.

It took me several weeks to figure out how I had gotten my OP. I considered asking the director if he had had anything to do with it, but I decided that wasn't a smart idea because it could backfire on me if he was insulted at the insinuation that he would violate protocol. It turned out I was just lucky. The Alexandria field office had lost five experienced agents to the 10/1/69 Transfer Program, which meant it was down five agents. I was number forty-three on the OP list for AXFO, but most of the agents ahead of me on the list were ineligible for transfer there for various reasons, so I ended up being number three when they selected five agents for transfer in.

After I explained to my supervisor, the SWAT team members, and the other agents how it all happened, they couldn't stop apologizing. By that time I was very anxious to leave the NYO, put it all behind me, and get to the Promised Land—my OP. The

SWAT team quickly put together a send-off party, for which I was very grateful. They were truly a great bunch of guys.

❧

My final day in the NYO was crazy. As I was trying to leave I got stuck in an elevator for about an hour with a fellow agent, a friend and former Baltimore City policeman who had been working FBI undercover cases. When he offered to drive me home to Fanwood, I didn't realize we would be taking his undercover vehicle, a beat-up Cadillac. Well, we made it halfway through the Holland Tunnel when his car ran out of gas. Unfortunately, it was Friday at 5:00 p.m., when traffic in the tunnel is usually at its worst, along with drivers' patience and attitudes. We were called so many bad names in so many languages—I was just glad we had our guns with us. We phoned for a tow truck, but it was taking forever to arrive. Then, without asking or being asked, a cab driver who was stuck right behind us abruptly started pushing the Caddy out of the tunnel with his cab.

That was my last day in the Big Apple.

CHAPTER 11

▲

MY OP

We waited to move to Virginia until Bernadette was able to complete her last two weeks at her New Jersey job. When we finally moved, we checked into our temporary hotel quarters, where we stayed for a couple of weeks until we could close on our condo. The hotel allowed us to keep our dog in our room, which was unusual. Bernadette quickly found a new job working in the accounting office of a food supply company.

When I reported to duty at the AXFO, I was assigned to a very busy criminal squad full of the office's heavies. I hit the ground running, but it was tough keeping up with my caseload. We had a great supervisor who worked long hours and harder than any of his agents. His door was always open, and he was always cordial. Later on, many of the heavies organized and established an office SWAT team, so I quite naturally joined them. I was surprised that the AXFO didn't already have a SWAT team.

I had been in the FBI for only four years, and I was already in my OP—but I was still sixteen years away from the minimum retirement age. I had to ask myself if I could stay in one place that long. Some agents never get their OP, and certainly it would be rare to get two OPs in a career. The only way I could change offices at this point would be through promotions. So I had to think hard about whether this was going to be my last office assignment in the FBI. In the meantime, I was going to fully enjoy Alexandria.

One of my first cases there involved an FBI headquarter agent's daughter, who was assaulted and raped on the Mount Vernon bike trail. We worked for weeks trying to solve that case, but to no avail. In the meantime, my supervisor began assigning me to bank robbery cases. There were quite a few BRs every day in our territory, and many of the robbers ended up being from the DC area, so we worked closely with the agents in the Washington field office.

One day our special agent in charge came to work and abruptly informed the heavies that he was reassigning a significant number of them, including me, from the criminal squad to the foreign counterintelligence and terrorism (FCI/T) squad. We weren't sure what his motives were because he never explained them. He also shut down the SWAT team and deferred all needed SWAT operations in our territory to the Washington field office. The changes destroyed the morale in the AXFO for years. My supervisor was so miserable that he stepped down as supervisor to work with us as a regular agent on the FCI/T squad.

The FCI/T squad was supervised by a female agent. There were not many female supervisors in the FBI at that time, and she was my first. She had built a strong reputation as an intelligent, very knowledgeable, no-nonsense agent. She had been a firearms instructor at Quantico—you didn't want to make her mad, because you knew she could shoot straight. Her squad was very busy, but not as busy as I was used to from working criminal cases. Suddenly there were no more long hours and weekends.

I remember thinking that this was a Three Sisters Ponds moment. Now I would have time to do things I'd wanted to do for years—train for triathlons, 10Ks, and marathons, and maybe even take up sailing. This could be a life-altering moment for me, and I needed the "throne" to help me think it through. But the last time I had visited the area, the bench and the ponds were gone. I had to make the best of my new situation without their help.

ʊﾉﾚ

At this point I was still smoking a pipe and my weight had ballooned; my health and fitness were in jeopardy. We had just gone through our semiannual FIT test, and I was very unhappy with myself. My blood pressure and pulse were high, and my time for the 1.5-mile run was unacceptable. It was obvious that over the years I had sacrificed my health and fitness for the sake of my casework. I had stayed fit enough to be an effective SWAT team member, but there was significant room for improvement. This was my chance to turn it around.

I joined the local YMCA, worked on my diet, and went on a major weight-loss program. I started running 5K and 10K races, then marathons (I ran the Marine Marathon twice), and eventually triathlons in Maryland, (Baltimore City and Columbia) and Virginia. At my first triathlon in Alexandria, as all the triathletes were getting their gear organized, I lit up my pipe. I must have forgotten where I was, because I got a lot of stares and overheard someone say, "That's curious." I realized then it was time to stop smoking the pipe.

My wife's brother was an excellent cyclist, and so I biked with him through the cold winters in hilly Columbia, Maryland, to get ready for triathlons in the spring. He had been a high school scholar-athlete who went on to graduate from Johns Hopkins University and the University of Maryland School of Law.

I also began to pursue a major item on my bucket list: sailing. After all my trips to Annapolis, Maryland, and a trip to Sausalito, California, and having seen so many beautiful sailboats on the water and in boat shows, I decided to finally buy one. It was a used, twenty-two-foot Catalina sailboat rigged for single-handed racing and cruising. I didn't know how to sail, but I bought it anyway. And of course I named it *My OP*.

The first time I took it out was with Bernadette and her father, who had come to visit us. We had an uneventful launch out of the Washington Sailing Marina, where I'd rented a slip. We got out on the Potomac and headed south. I put up the sails, both main and jib, and I picked up some wind and headed under the Woodrow Wilson Bridge. As we got under the bridge, however, I lost my wind and found a very strong current that relentlessly pushed us into the bridge pilings. I had no clue what to do. There was panic on all our faces. My lack of sailing experience showed quite acutely.

I quickly realized that I had no business being out there, certainly not with my wife and father-in-law. I finally dropped sail, turned on the outboard motor, and got us back to the dock. Needless to say, my father-in-law was neither impressed nor happy. This was the second time he had visited us, and both times something traumatic had happened. I swore that if we returned to land safely, I would not go back out on the water until I'd taken sailing lessons. So *My OP* sat at the dock for a while.

Once I finished sailing lessons, I immersed myself in racing and cruising. I later upgraded to a brand-new, twenty-five-foot Catalina that I named *Quiet Storm*. I raced in regattas on the Potomac and Severn Rivers and in the Chesapeake Bay. The black SSA I had met in the NYO was now assigned to FBI headquarters and living in Alexandria. He became a good friend and a member of my crew. One year, I even raced in the Governor's Cup regatta, an overnight race from Annapolis down the Chesapeake Bay to St. Mary's College, located on St. Mary's River in Maryland.

I did a solo sail from my marina, which was next to Reagan National Airport on the Potomac, down the Potomac River, up the Chesapeake Bay to Baltimore, and back. I traveled the bay's western shore on the way up to Baltimore and its eastern shore on the return. It took me two weeks. I met a lot of nice people along the way and had some memorable experiences; family members and friends met me at certain overnight stops along the way. This was another bucket list adventure, and it was exhilarating.

I raced sailboats for several more years before I finally gave it up because I just didn't have time for it anymore. Meanwhile I was looking at a Corvette at a local Chevrolet dealership, where the salesman wanted to sell me the Corvette and buy my boat, but only if he could also rent my boat slip—a hot commodity in the area. I ended up trading in my boat and my old BMW for a brand-new, 1989 red convertible Corvette. Life in my OP was getting better and better!

During the 1984 Summer Olympics, some of the soccer matches were held at the US Naval Academy in Annapolis. Before our SWAT team was dismantled, we were designated to room at the academy for thirty days to provide security. We stayed in Bancroft Hall, one of the largest dorms on campus. One of the cadets attending the academy at the time was David Robinson, who years later would become an NBA Hall of Famer and an Olympic basketball gold medalist. We saw him on a daily basis in the cafeteria.

While I was there I got the chance to sign out one of the academy's nineteen-foot sailboats to do some sailing in the Severn River and the Chesapeake Bay. What a thrill! I also took advantage of being away from the office and home to try shaving off all my hair. I've been bald ever since. When I returned to the AXFO sporting my new, hairless style, it took the agents there a little time to get used to it. I'm not sure, but I might have been one the first completely bald FBI agents.

❧

I did find time to work FCI/T cases, believe it or not, and many of them had very serious national security implications. The experience of the heavies on the FCI/T squad became a real advantage. Instead of simply monitoring and reporting on potential spies or terrorists, as many agents were used to doing, we knew how to build cases for their arrest or deportation.

Our targets of interest at that time were Libyan students in American universities; we were concerned that the Libyan government would use their students to conduct acts of terrorism in the United States. We were already aware that they were being used as a network to facilitate intelligence gathering here and in other countries around the world. At the center of this network was the People's Committee for Libyan Students (PCLS), headquartered in McLean, Virginia. At the time the PCLS represented as many as twelve hundred Libyan students in the United States. It was supposed to be providing student financial support only, but our investigation proved it was involved in intelligence gathering, terrorism support, and harassing and spying on their own students who were not toeing the line.

For several years during our investigation of the PCLS, we engaged in proactive electronic and physical surveillance of our priority Libyan targets. We tracked them both entering and leaving the United States, and we noticed that their travels back and forth always seemed to include a stop in Malta, an island nation in the Mediterranean Sea, about seven hundred miles from Libya. Little did I realize at the time how important Malta would become to me within the next couple of years.

At one point I was flown to meet one of the PCLS's top-ranking officials, who was moving to McLean to work at the group's headquarters. He was willing to assist our investigation without being paid, by reporting on the activities of other PCLS officials. I already had another Libyan official on the inside. Both men shared anti-Gaddafi views and turned out to be very productive sources of information.

Over the years, the Libyans became aware of our surveillance. They spotted us from time to time sitting in parked cars; sometimes we deliberately let them see us to deter them from committing crimes. We knew that they were always checking to see if their phones were tapped, or if their offices or residences were bugged. One of our major targets would go into a spitting frenzy every time he caught me following him—he would look me in the eye and start spitting in my direction. (I don't think he liked me.) I considered him to be one of the most potentially dangerous members of the group. Although we hadn't connected him or any of the PCLS members to any crimes at that time, we nevertheless were concerned that eventually they would commit an act of terrorism. We knew that he met with members of various US radical groups, gave them money, and even paid for their trips to visit Libya.

❧

One night in May 1985, while we were in our command center monitoring our Libyan targets, I heard another surveillance team in operation on our radio—it was the Norfolk field office surveillance team coming through our territory. It turned out that they were shadowing John Walker, who within hours was arrested for espionage at a hotel in Montgomery County, Maryland. Walker, two family members, and a friend had been selling classified information to the Russians for eighteen years. All of the members of the spy ring, with the exception of his son, Michael, received life sentences for their role in the espionage. The case was run by two agents I had worked with out of the Norfolk field office. One of them, Robert W. Hunter, wrote a book called *Spy Hunter*.

In Florida the Tampa field office developed a foreign counterintelligence case involving an army lieutenant colonel, Wayne Gillespie, and six others who were indicted in Orlando for conspiracy, bribery, and fraud charges in a plot to acquire US military weapons. They were accused of trying to buy 1,140 anti-tank missiles worth $9.1 million and export them to Iran. The seven were arrested August 1, 1985, after an FBI undercover investigation. I happened to be in the right place at the right time; I was asked to arrest Gillespie in Alexandria. It made a big splash in the national media, and I got my first fifteen seconds of fame as an FBI agent. I had family members and friends calling me because they'd seen me on TV.

One of the saddest days in FBI history occurred on April 11, 1986, when two agents out of Miami were killed and five others wounded in a shoot-out with serial bank robbers William Russell Matix and Michael Lee Platt, who were also killed. Despite outnumbering the suspects four to one, the agents were pinned down by rounds from automatic weapons and were unable to respond effectively. This incident led to the use of more powerful, military-style handguns and shoulder-fired weapons in the FBI and police departments around the country.

About a year later, on May 26, 1987, William Webster left the FBI to become director of the CIA. The bureau's executive assistant director, John E. Otto, became acting director, serving in that position until November 2, 1987, when William Steele Sessions was sworn in as FBI director. Prior to that appointment, Sessions served as the chief judge of the US District Court for the Western District of Texas. He had previously served there as a district judge and as a US district attorney.

⚭

In early 1988, we initiated a surveillance operation to record the activities of a newly arrived Libyan. The Libyan student officials assigned to the PCLS appeared very frightened of him and acted subservient whenever he was in their presence. As we began to focus on him, we became increasingly concerned that he had been sent to the United States to do something really bad, but we didn't know what it was. Eventually we established a command center in the AXFO, where we watched him and the other priority Libyan targets twenty-four hours a day. This operation went on for months, using FBI surveillance teams from field offices from all over the country. It was a huge commitment of time and personnel.

Continued monitoring and intelligence reports from other sources revealed that the Libyan was purchasing vehicles with cash and meeting with people not associated with the PCLS. Then through another, very sensitive source, we learned that he was interested in buying weapons, and that his possible target was former White

House aide Oliver L. North because of North's alleged role in US air strikes on Tripoli. President Reagan had ordered the air strikes in April 1986 in retaliation for the Libyan terrorist bombing of La Belle discotheque in Berlin that targeted off-duty US military personnel. That terrorist attack killed 3 people and injured 229, including 79 active military.

On July 20, 1988, because the situation was looking very dangerous, the decision was made to arrest our suspect and the other priority Libyan targets, but he got out of the country before we could act. We conducted searches at the PCLS and at a Washington, DC, travel agency owned by Mousa Hawamda, a naturalized citizen from Jordan. We did arrest five Libyans, including the "spitting" Libyan. Because it was being used illegally to channel funds to support anti-American activities, the PCLS was permanently closed. And Hawamda's travel agency was allegedly a Libyan front: its real purpose was to support and facilitate identification of the American officials involved in the Tripoli airstrikes. We believed the ultimate goal of the operation was the assassination of these individuals. Mousa Hawamda left the United States and became a fugitive. The spitter ultimately pled guilty to the charges against him: conspiracy; illegally diverting Libyan student funds to finance anti-American demonstrations in the United States and conferences of American dissidents in Libya; and violating the US trade embargo on Libya.

This investigation led to the dismantling of the Libyan intelligence and terrorism network in the United States and thwarted the possible assassination of Ollie North and perhaps others, as well.

❦

During this period, my desk mate, SA Lon Heriuchi, became my good friend as we worked together on FCI/T cases. He was a 1976 West Point graduate and a smart, hardworking agent. Though he was young, he was mature and very organized, and I tried to pick up some of his organizational skills. Heriuchi was a major influence in my finally giving up pipe smoking: because he was my desk mate, he complained about it every day. (In those days you could still smoke in the office.) I eventually had to stop just to end the complaints.

Heriuchi was also a good swimmer, and one day my former supervisor asked both of us to work with his son, who had a chance to break his school backstroke record. For an entire afternoon Heriuchi and I worked with him on stroke technique and flip turns, and the next day he broke the school record. My former supervisor was always grateful to us, as was his son, who eventually became an FBI agent.

Heriuchi got engaged, and Bernadette and I attended his wedding. He later became a member of the hostage rescue team (HRT) and was reassigned to Quantico, where he became an HRT sniper. A few years later he was involved in the 1992 Ruby Ridge standoff and the 1993 Waco siege. In 1997, Heriuchi was charged with manslaughter for the death of Vicki Weaver at Ruby Ridge; the case was eventually dismissed.

One of the nicest, most hardworking and unassuming agents in the AXFO was SA Earl Edwin Pitts, who was assigned to our Fredericksburg, Virginia, resident agency (RA) and eventually transferred to New York. In December 1996 I was heartbroken and disappointed to hear that he had been arrested on charges stemming from espionage activities with the Russians while he was assigned to the NYO. His wife, Mary Columbaro Pitts, turned him in.

CHAPTER 12

▲

THE BOMBING OF PAN
AM FLIGHT 103

"The Bananas Are Rotten"

I n mid-1988, the Alexandria field office was closed and consolidated with the Washington field office (WFO). My walking-to-work days were over: I had to commute to DC. As it turned out, this was the best thing that could have happened to me. The WFO worked a broader range of investigative matters and therefore offered many more opportunities than had the AXFO. That meant I had to decide the direction of my career in the FBI and what kind of cases I liked working the most. This was definitely another "Three Sisters Ponds" moment, but of course the throne was long gone.

Initially, the decision about where to work was made for me: I was assigned to the domestic terrorism squad. Once I settled in, I also joined the WFO SWAT team as a sniper—and because I was on the team, I got a take-home car. Life was good!

One day at work I overheard a black female agent talking about her recent return from working a case in London. I told her that I wasn't aware that the FBI worked cases overseas. (I don't know how I'd missed this in my training at Quantico.) She said the bureau conducts extraterritorial terrorism investigations all over the world; whenever an American citizen was murdered, kidnapped, or seriously assaulted in any foreign country, the WFO, which covered the entire world at the time, deployed agents to that country to conduct the investigation. There was a special squad of agents in the office who handled all those investigations.

I was intrigued. I immediately contacted the supervisor, SSA Larry Knisley, and asked if I could transfer to his squad. He said he didn't have any vacancies, but he would keep me in mind. He did ask if I wanted to be put on standby to deploy to another country if he needed the help, and of course I said yes. He also told me to make sure that I had both a US passport and an official government passport if I wanted to travel overseas on these investigations. I quickly obtained them.

On August 10, 1988, not too long after I agreed to international deployment, I was asked to travel with an FBI forensic examiner to La Paz, Bolivia, to conduct an investigation into the attempted bombing of the motorcade of Secretary of State George Shultz by possible narco-terrorists. The information I received was that a remote-controlled bomb had exploded as his motorcade was traveling between the La Paz airport and the city center. No one was injured, but four vehicles, including the one carrying Shultz's wife, were damaged, and the incident raised concerns that a wave of Colombian-style terrorism would follow. According to the briefings that I received, Shultz's visit was intended to promote Bolivia's counter-drug trade efforts, which is probably why the narco-terrorists expressed their unhappiness with his visit.

Before leaving I did some homework about La Paz and learned it had an elevation of 3,660 meters above sea level, making it the world's highest de facto capital city, or administrative capital. (Bolivia's official capital and seat of justice is actually Sucre, but

La Paz has more government departments—hence the qualifier.) The city sits in a bowl surrounded by the high mountains of the Altiplano, and overlooking the city is the towering, triple-peaked mountain Illimani, which is always snow-covered and can be seen from several spots around the city.

It was a long, bumpy flight to La Paz. During one of our stopovers in Sao Paulo, Brazil, a terminal security guard asked me for my passport and tickets, which I provided. He then walked away with them and disappeared. I began to worry because they were reboarding my flight; I started pacing and noticed him watching me. When I finally walked up to him and asked him for my documents back, he just stared at me. Then, while holding the documents in one hand, he stuck out his other hand, indicating that I should give him money. I snatched my documents and ran to my flight, hoping he wouldn't follow me. He didn't.

As our flight approached La Paz, the pilot informed us that because of the high altitude of the airport, they would be dropping fuel. He also told us that because the air was so thin, he recommended that we take it very slow disembarking and minimize any conversation; otherwise we were going to feel sick. At the time I was a marathoner and triathlete and didn't believe I needed to take those precautions. But as soon as I stepped off the plane, I felt dizzy. It got worse when we arrived at the International Hotel in La Paz. Not only was I feeling extremely dizzy, I also had the worst headache that I'd ever experienced. I took some aspirin, but it didn't help. I couldn't sleep at all. I was very worried that I wouldn't be in good enough shape to start my investigation in the morning. This was my first overseas case, and I didn't want to blow it.

I went to the American embassy to meet our FBI legal attaché (or "legat") for a briefing, and just as I stepped into the embassy foyer, I threw up on a large, colorful rug emblazoned with the State Department seal. This wasn't the first impression I was hoping to leave, or a good omen about future official trips overseas. I was immediately taken to the embassy infirmary, where I was diagnosed with altitude sickness. When I told the doctor that I had to conduct a week-long investigation and couldn't afford to be sick, he gave me a portable oxygen tank and told me suck up some pure oxygen any time I started feeling dizzy, and I would be fine. Fortunately he was right, but I had to carry around that silly-looking tank for the whole visit. I was able to get all my work done and put together my investigative summary report. Before I left, I briefed the legat on my preliminary findings. He would pass the information on to our ambassador in Bolivia.

One of our stopovers on the way back was in Rio de Janeiro. As we flew out of the airport there I saw the Christ the Redeemer statue and my first aurora borealis. I couldn't help but think just how lucky I was. When I got back to the office, I didn't mention the altitude sickness because I was afraid it might impact my being asked to go on future trips overseas. Everyone seemed pleased with my report, which later led to an agent being assigned to La Paz full-time for several years to conduct a follow-up investigation.

❧

On August 17, 1988, not long after I returned from Bolivia, SSA Knisley asked me to begin preparations to fly to Pakistan to assist in the investigation of the suspicious plane crash that killed Pakistan's president, General Zia-ul-Haq, as well as everyone else aboard, including some US citizens. I got my visa, but the trip was cancelled. We were never told why. The word was that another agency didn't want us there at the time.

By then my daughter, Maisha, was a student at Howard University in Washington, DC, and working at WFO as a summer hire, which made me very proud. I was getting good reports from her supervisor regarding her performance.

SSA Knisley continued to keep me on standby to support his extraterritorial squad. In December 1988, he asked that I prepare to fly to Germany to debrief American hostages from Beirut, Lebanon, in the event that their captors released them as a goodwill gesture for the Christmas holidays. We were to ask the hostages for information regarding their captivity and captors.

I did receive a call, but it wasn't to fly to Germany. On December 21, 1988, SSA Knisley requested that SA Ed Marshman and I travel to London to liaison with the US embassy and our legat there regarding that day's crash of Pan Am Flight 103 over Lockerbie, Scotland. At that point, no one knew whether mechanical problems or a terrorist act was behind the downing of the Boeing 747 jumbo jet. All I could think of was what a terrible tragedy this was, and I couldn't imagine someone deliberately blowing up a commercial airliner in flight with innocent civilians aboard. Though I didn't realize it at the time, this was the beginning of a series of life-changing experiences that lay ahead for me and for so many others.

To prepare for the trip, I did some reading about London. While I knew it was Britain's largest and most populous metropolitan area, I had no idea it was so diverse. More than three hundred languages are spoken within its boundaries.

Marshman and I rendezvoused at Dulles International Airport the next day and booked a red-eye to London—another Pan Am 747. Because the crew knew why we were flying, they upgraded our seats; it was the first time I had ever flown first-class. It was a very comfortable flight, but I worried a bit that other Pan Am flights, such as this one, were being targeted. Our flight arrived at London's Heathrow Airport on the morning of December 23, 1988. When we landed, it hit me that we were in George Michael territory, and all I could think of were the songs on his album *Faith*. I had finally arrived in London—something else I could check off my bucket list—but I only wished it was under better circumstances.

Marshman and I checked into the Montcalm Hotel, in rooms reserved for us by the FBI legat office assigned to the American embassy in London. It was a very nice, upscale hotel in Grosvenor Square, within walking distance of our embassy. The Montcalm offered reasonable rates to anyone having to travel from the States regarding the downed Pan Am flight; otherwise it would have been much more than our per diem allotment.

The United States Embassy in London is located in the Chancery Building, where it's been since 1960. It is the largest American embassy in Western Europe and the focal point for US-related events in the United Kingdom. This embassy, like many others around the world, is situated on land not owned by the US government. The land is leased from the Duke of Westminster—who, when asked if he would sell the land to the States outright, responded that he would if the US government would return the land that had belonged to his family before it was confiscated during the Revolutionary War. The duke refused to grant a freehold because from his perspective, the American government had stolen some of his ancestors' estates in Virginia. Go figure!

After we unpacked, we walked to the embassy. It was a beautiful, stately place—huge, busy, and classy, and heavily guarded by marines who looked like they meant business.

Marshman and I found the FBI's legat office. For more than six decades, the FBI has stationed agents and other personnel overseas to help protect Americans at home and abroad by building relationships with principal law enforcement and intelligence services around the globe and facilitating a prompt, continuous exchange of information. Today the FBI has legat offices and sub-offices in seventy-five key cities worldwide, providing coverage for more than two hundred countries, territories, and islands. Each office is established through mutual agreement with the host country and is situated in the American embassy or consulate there.

In 1988, our legat office in London focused primarily on Irish Republican Army (IRA) terrorism matters and Muslim extremism that could represent a threat to the States.

We were introduced to our London legat, SA Daryl Mills, and several assistant legats who were also FBI agents. They provided us in-depth briefings on what was known about the Pan Am tragedy. They advised that they were coordinating and working very closely with the CIA, British investigative services, and New Scotland Yard (NSY). The actual cause of the crash was still unknown; they were waiting for the American, British, and Scottish forensics examiners at the scene in Lockerbie to provide that information. We explained that if it was determined that the plane was brought down as the result of criminal or terrorist actions, the FBI would join the investigation.

Legat Mills was cool, suave, and debonair. He reminded me of James Bond with his strong, leading-man good looks. He had been in London long enough to have picked up a slight British accent, although I believe he was originally from New England. He liked his drinks, particularly Grouse, which he was more than willing to share—after hours, of course.

Marshman stayed for a couple of days and then had to return to the States because the case was going to be assigned to him, and he needed to get things organized there. I was to stay on in London and establish coordination between New Scotland Yard, the embassy, and WFO regarding any new developments. I was assigned to work with NSY's antiterrorism branch and to represent the FBI in the Heathrow Airport investigation, should foul play be determined. Mills sent a couple of his assistants to Lockerbie, and the FBI sent explosives experts there, as well as lab experts to assist in the identification of passengers.

❧

Members of New Scotland Yard welcomed me to their headquarters and gave me my own cubicle. The "Yard" is the headquarters of the Metropolitan Police, responsible for law enforcement within Greater London, excluding the square mile that constitutes the City of London, which is covered by the City of London Police.

The Metropolitan Police appreciated the fact that I was a former policeman. There were a couple of police officers from Scotland who were also provided cubicles. Scottish police in Lockerbie had organized their evidence search teams and were slowly working their way through the 845-square-mile debris scene.

The information that we had at the time was that on Wednesday, December 21, 1988, Pan Am 103 had pushed back from its gate at London Heathrow Airport at 18:04 and lifted off at 18:25 to make its transatlantic flight to New York's John F. Kennedy International Airport. It leveled off at approximately thirty-one thousand feet, and at approximately18:56, the aircraft began to break apart in midair. Two-hundred forty-three passengers and sixteen crew members were killed. Eleven people in the town of Lockerbie were also killed by large sections of the plane that fell onto houses.

Each morning I rose early, ran three miles through Hyde Park, had breakfast, and then walked to the embassy for briefings. After that I walked to the Yard, past Hyde Park and Buckingham Palace. I often saw the changing of the guard at the palace, and sometimes I listened to the strange characters at Speaker's Corner in Hyde Park. I would also stop and sit by Serpentine Lake and the River Thames, which I found very scenic and relaxing.

My first week of walking to the Yard was a challenge. At various busy intersections, with traffic coming from all directions, fenced barriers kept pedestrians from crossing the street. Every morning, dressed in a dapper suit and tie and carrying a briefcase, I was forced to leap over these barriers—and there were quite a few of them. By the time I got to the Yard, my clothes were rumpled and I was sweaty. *Boy, this is a tough way for the Brits to cross their streets,* I thought. I finally mustered up the courage to ask one of the detectives about the hazardous street crossings. After he picked himself off the floor from falling down laughing—and, of course, sharing my question with all the other detectives—he explained that pedestrians were supposed to use the tunnels that took them *under* the intersections. The new route made my morning walk much more relaxing and enjoyable, but given the detectives' reaction to my first question, I decided not to ask them about the extra toilet in my hotel room.

I found the Brits' and Scots' accents, humor, and terminology very difficult to understand, as if they really weren't speaking English. But it was clear that they were as concerned as I was that the plane was downed by an act of terrorism. Throughout our initial investigation at Heathrow, with the Yard detectives leading, the focus was always on the possibility that a bomb had been placed on the plane. From the outset, NSY committed most of their available detectives and metro officers to the investigation.

As I was walking to the Yard one morning, I noticed a large demonstration forming on the streets. I took a picture, not knowing what it was all about. I had never seen so many Arabs in my life; I didn't even know that London had so many. I later learned that they were protesting Salmon Rushdie's book *The Satanic Verses*, which had been banned and burned by Muslims. As a result of its publication, Rushdie received death threats that caused him to go into hiding for many years.

☙

On December 28, Scottish authorities announced that a high-performance plastic explosive had been used in the downing of Pan Am Flight 103. I called SSA Knisley immediately with the news, and he asked me to stay in London for a while longer. He advised that the case would be designated a major international terrorism investigation and that the code name would be SCOTBOM. I was to work with NSY and the Metropolitan Police, helping review the investigative reports generated at Heathrow Airport from my desk at NSY, and keeping the US embassy, our legat, and the WFO briefed on the status of the investigation. Knisley would have someone stop at my home and pick up extra clothes, which would be brought to me, along with extra cash. I told him to make sure they were cold-weather clothes because it was very chilly in London. One of the agents heading to

Lockerbie from Washington stopped in London and dropped off the clothes and money.

Once Scottish authorities delivered their news about the bombing, the constables of Dumphries and Galloway, Scotland—333 officers strong—immediately announced that they would be the lead agency in conducting the criminal investigation. I was sitting at my desk in NSY when the announcement was made, and I heard the detectives' outraged reaction to it. Before that moment, I'd assumed that NSY was like the FBI, undertaking national and international investigations for Great Britain. Apparently, that was not true. While the Yard investigated the IRA and other terrorism cases, they had to be "asked" to conduct investigations outside of London. And in this case, they weren't asked.

I ended up staying in London for approximately two and a half months. We all worked seven days a week. We worked through Christmas, Boxing Day, and New Year's. There were times when I didn't even know what day of the week it was.

The Yard detectives were very gracious hosts. When time permitted, they took me on private tours of London that included Parliament, Westminster Abbey, the Tower of London, Ten Downing Street, and London Bridge. They even let me sit in Prime Minister Margaret Thatcher's chair in Parliament. In those days, there was a bar in the Yard that served alcohol to employees. So every evening after work, we would have a few drinks there and then go to a nearby restaurant for dinner. One night two beautiful female NSY officers apparently got a bit too friendly with me in the bar; I assume they were reprimanded by their superiors, as I never saw them again. That was a shame, because they were very nice to me.

As a Scottish officer and I were visiting Westminster, I temporarily lost sight of him, and I finally found him standing solemnly over the tomb of Mary, Queen of Scots. I asked him if he was all right, and in a very serious tone he said, "Those murdering bastards."

After further discussion, I realized that the Scots still haven't forgiven the English for what they did to Mary back in the 1500s.

After it became clear that an explosive device caused the downing of Pan Am 103, a worldwide criminal investigation was initiated, led by the Scottish police. Because the flight was serviced before it left Heathrow Airport by an Irish airlines company, Aer Lingus, investigators explored the possibility that the IRA had helped a foreign terrorist group put an explosive on the plane. That theory was ruled out very quickly. As the investigation evolved, a group that came under close scrutiny was the Syrian-led Popular Front for the Liberation of Palestine—General Command (PFLP-GC), a terror group allegedly backed by Iranian cash.

After I had been in London for about two months, I was feeling guilty about having abandoned Bernadette, so I had the embassy's travel office put together a weeklong European vacation for us. Bernadette flew to London, where we did some touring together. We then took a flight to Charles De Gaulle Airport and rode a train into Paris. We were very nervous with each stop the train made because we weren't sure which was ours. After some serious sweating, we got off the train and of course determined it was about four stops too soon. So we caught a cab to our hotel and proceeded to do the typical tour of the city. We visited the Eiffel Tower; saw the *Mona Lisa* at the Louvre; took a dinner cruise on the Seine; and visited the Bastille and Notre Dame. Then we took the train and saw Amsterdam and Belgium. After we flew back to London, Bernadette returned home.

Meanwhile, the FBI had become very interested in the German authorities' arrest of members of the PFLP-GC terror cell. That arrest in Frankfurt had come on October 26, 1988, two months prior to the bombing of Pan Am 103. The German authorities had recovered Toshiba radio cassette recorders containing the plastic explosive Semtex, similar to what we believed had been used in the Pan Am attack.

Of the eighteen cell members arrested by German authorities, sixteen were Palestinian. It was believed they had planned to bomb Iberia Airlines Flight 888; the Germans were forced to arrest them before they could carry out the plot. There was serious concern that some of the people originally arrested but subsequently released could have been involved in the later bombing of Pan Am 103. The Germans had generated tons of documents as part of their PFLP-GC investigation, code-named Autumn Leaves, and these documents needed to be translated into English and then analyzed. I was asked to return to WFO to coordinate their translation and review them for any evidence that could connect this Palestinian cell to the Pan Am case.

❧

On February 4, 1989, I flew back to the United States. I brought German and Arabic translators to WFO from all over the bureau. The Palestinians looked like the prime suspects in the Pan Am bombing, and we generated many leads from the German documents. At this point we had no information that implicated Libya.

As I focused on the Autumn Leaves material, the team of FBI agents and Scottish, German, and British investigators were already working in our SCOTBOM Command Center to coordinate leads in the United States and around the world. The global investigation was managed using the Home Office Large Major Enquiry System—nicknamed HOLMES—the database purchased by the United Kingdom for use in investigating serious crimes. Using HOLMES, law enforcement could collect and collate vast amounts of intelligence data, prioritize it to identify suitable lines of inquiry, allocate tasks to investigating officers, follow the progress made on those tasks, and turn analyses into graphics suitable for presentation in court. UK police began using the system in 1986 for all major incidents, including serial murders, high-level fraud cases, and natural disasters.

All pieces of evidence recovered and processed from the crime scene at Lockerbie, plus all investigative interviews, were entered into this system. Scottish information review teams generated leads to be investigated, and HOLMES kept track of their status. Because of the way the review teams ran the system, we never lost important investigative leads on the Palestinian terrorist groups or later, on possible Libyan involvement. HOLMES was the real unsung hero of the Pan Am 103 investigation.

I spent the next year assigned to the SCOTBOM Command Center, supervising the translators as they converted the Autumn Leaves documentation from German and Arabic to English for review and analysis. In the SCOTBOM Command Center was a picture of a baby shoe that had been recovered at the Lockerbie crime scene. That picture hung prominently on our office wall throughout the investigation as a constant reminder of what had happened and the urgency of our task.

Also on the wall was a list of all the passengers, crew, and Lockerbie residents who died that day. Of the 270 fatalities, 189 were American citizens and 43 were British. The bombing was the deadliest act of terror against the United States prior to 9/11. Many of the passengers were from New Jersey and New York, students and members of the US military coming home for the Christmas holidays. Syracuse University alone lost 35 students.

We began meeting with victims' family members around the country, trying to keep them briefed on the investigation's progress. We couldn't give them any details, but they understood that.

During one of the meetings, a woman named Joan Dater gave me a photo of a painting by her daughter, Gretchen Joyce Dater, who had been an art student at Syracuse University. Gretchen was coming home for the holidays from London, where she was an exchange student, when she died on that flight. She was twenty years old. Mrs. Dater was heartbroken, and I tried to comfort her as best I could. She asked me to keep the picture with me as a reminder of whom and what had been taken from us. I was deeply touched and honored by this gesture. The photo remained in my wallet throughout the investigation, and whenever I looked at it I knew I had to keep pushing and never give up. I still have that picture.

We meticulously investigated every passenger to determine whether there was anything suspicious in his or her background. Ultimately we were able to rule out witting or unwitting accomplices, although some cases were more difficult than others.

As time went on, the investigation began leading us to the island of Malta, but members of the PFLP-GC remained our priority suspects. Forensics had determined the explosive device was contained in a brown, hard-sided Samsonite suitcase that also contained pieces of clothing. We were able to trace the clothing to Yorkie Clothiers, a manufacturer in Malta. This was a significant break in the case—you can imagine the jubilation among investigators—and some Scottish officers and FBI agents jumped on a plane to Malta to interview the owner of Yorkie Clothiers. The owner was able to tell us from his records which clothing store had bought the items in question.

The store was Mary's Place in Valletta, Malta, and it was owned by Tony Gauci, whom the investigators quickly located and interviewed. He recognized the recovered clothing, and even more amazing, he remembered who bought it: a Libyan man who had made the purchase prior to the bombing of Pan Am 103. While Gauci had quite a few Libyan customers, he said he remembered this customer because the man had seemed to choose various articles of clothing at random, not caring what size they were or even whether they were for a man or a woman. The investigators concluded that the person just wanted some clothes to fill up the suitcase. Gauci gave them a full description of "this Libyan," who had been in the store before. Gauci also thought he could recognize the man if he ever saw him again.

Gauci's description of the Libyan didn't mean much to us at the time, but it proved very significant later in the investigation. An

FBI artist met with him and created a rendering of the person who had purchased the clothing. We assumed, incorrectly as it turned out, that Gauci was using *Libyan* as a general term to indicate someone who was Arabic; we were still looking at Palestinians as our prime suspects, and we saw no real Libyan-Palestinian connection. Tony Gauci's information was one of the first of many major breaks in the case.

It became immediately apparent that there was a lot of work ahead for our investigators in Malta. The objective now was to identify the person who purchased the clothing and determine how and why he, and possibly others, placed the luggage with the clothing and explosives on Pan Am Flight 103.

An investigative team was immediately dispatched to the island. It included Scottish and German police officers as well as FBI agents. With the support of our embassy and the British high commission, the team established a cooperative working relationship with the Maltese police and intelligence services. Our agents were provided office space in the embassy, courtesy of US Ambassador Sally Novetzke, and the Scottish officers worked out of the high commission, which was located across the street. To avoid stepping on the ambassador's diplomatic initiatives—or her toes—FBI agents were ordered to keep her updated about what they were doing. That way, she would also be in position to help as needed.

As the agents in Malta were getting started on the new line of investigation, I continued coordinating leads generated by Autumn Leaves, now reviewing the documents for any Maltese connection.

ঔদ৲

In early February 1990, another agent and I were asked to provide Rev. Jessie Jackson with a threat briefing regarding his planned trip to meet Nelson Mandela after the South African leader was released from prison. I believe we got the assignment because we were both black and working terrorism investigations at the time;

regardless, it gave me a brief break from the exhaustive search of German documents.

We met Rev. Jackson and his wife and sons at a residence in the Washington, DC, area. Given his history in the civil rights struggle alongside Dr. Martin Luther King, this was a great honor. We explained that the FBI had received reports of threats regarding his upcoming trip to South Africa. He expressed appreciation for the information but said he was still planning to make the trip. At least he knew he needed to be a little more cautious.

Soon afterward, Bernadette's mother invited me to speak at her church (the one where we were married), about my role in the Pan Am investigation. I was honored by the invitation, but first I had to get bureau approval because the case was ongoing. Though I was limited as to what I could discuss, I was able to give the parishioners a sense of the enormity of the investigation and the significant resources and time being committed to solving the crime. That same day, Nelson Mandela was released after twenty-eight years in a South African prison. I had the pleasure of announcing this to the audience during my presentation.

✦

After a few months it was clear that the rotation of FBI agents into and out of Malta had become a problem. Because we were not keeping the same agents on the investigation there, we began receiving complaints from the embassy staff and the Scottish and Maltese investigators, who were tired of having to bring each new agent up to speed on the case. The bureau was having trouble finding agents who would commit to staying on the island for extended periods.

In early March 1990, I was asked if I was willing to be the permanent case agent for the investigation on Malta. That meant that I would have to live on the island and work with the Scottish officers and Maltese police and intelligence for long stretches of time. I could return to the States for a break, but then I would have to return to Malta. Although there hadn't been any threats or attacks on the investigators so far, and Maltese law enforcement and intelligence agencies were providing our security, I would be in a potentially hostile environment far from the United States, with no weapon with which to defend myself. The other FBI agents and Scottish and German officers had accepted that risk.

I discussed all this with Bernadette, and we agreed that because 270 people had been murdered and those responsible needed to be found, the risks and personal sacrifices we both would have to make were worth it.

In preparation for my travel, I began doing some reading about the history, culture, religion, politics, and languages on Malta. I learned that the island covers just over three hundred square kilometers in land area, making it one of Europe's smallest and most densely populated countries. It has two official languages: Maltese, a Semitic language derived from Siculo-Arabic and heavily influenced by Sicilian and Italian, and English. Both languages are compulsory subjects in Maltese primary and secondary schools. A large portion of the population is also fluent in Italian, which until 1936 was the national language. Malta gained independence from Great Britain in 1964 and became a republic in 1974, retaining membership in the Commonwealth of Nations. Ninety-eight percent of Maltese are Catholics; as I was Catholic, too, I found this advantageous.

When I arrived in Malta on March 6, 1990, I was greeted by our agents, the Scottish police officers, and their lead detective inspector. They transported me to the Suncrest Hotel in Qawra, where they helped me get checked in and provided me a very detailed briefing on the status of the investigation.

Everyone seemed very serious and focused on getting to the bottom of the investigation on the island. We ate dinner together that night and then assembled in the hotel's piano lounge for drinks. When the pianist asked for suggestions, I asked him to play "Candle in the Wind" by Elton John. He did it so well!

The next morning during a team meeting, I made it clear to the inspector and his officers that I understood they were leading the Maltese investigation, not the FBI. Questions about leadership had been a long-standing problem with the investigation, and I wanted them resolved as soon as possible since I was going to be the lead FBI agent in Malta until we finished the investigation. I assured them that my job was to work closely with them on a daily basis and make available every possible resource that would help identify those responsible for the bombing. Even though we all knew that the United States was the target of the attack, that it was an American plane brought down, and that most of the passengers were American, the crime took place over Scotland, and therefore it was their jurisdiction. We needed to establish a united front for the Maltese and make it clear there was no dispute over the leadership. The fact that I was a former policeman as well as an FBI agent was a big help in my getting along with both the Scottish investigators and the Maltese police and intelligence.

Based on evidence uncovered prior to my arrival, investigators believed that the explosives that took down Flight 103 were most likely hidden in an unaccompanied piece of luggage placed on an Air Malta flight from Malta's Luqa Airport and transferred to Pan Am flights leaving Frankfurt and Heathrow. Our job was to identify the culprits who carried out this atrocity—a difficult task further complicated by the fact that we were conducting the investigation in a foreign country with its own unique history, politics, and culture. To overcome language problems, we were provided translators by the Maltese government. We were fortunate to have the government on our side, but we knew we couldn't take its support for granted.

จๅ๐

Though the dress for the investigators was business casual, I chose to wear a jacket and tie every day to remind myself that I wasn't on vacation. It did get pretty warm and uncomfortable at times. I also rented an Opel Vauxhall Nova with steering on the right side.

Because Malta was a former British colony, the Maltese drive on the left side of the road, which was something I had to get used to.

When I arrived in Malta, a homicide investigation was topping the news: pieces of a man's body were being found all over the island. I took it as a warning that I'd better be careful how I treated the locals.

After I had settled in and received full briefings from the investigators, I made an appointment to meet with Ambassador Novetzke. I explained what she should expect of me, and she filled me in on the do's and don'ts in Malta and pledged her full support for our efforts.

I spent my first week in Malta buying various types and makes of alarm clocks from stores all over the island. I then had them shipped back to the FBI lab in Washington, where agents were trying to determine whether a timing device had been used to set off the explosive, and if so, whether it had been purchased in Malta along with the clothing. I was asked to test each clock to make sure the alarm worked. I tested the clocks in the stores, then packaged and shipped them to the States by way of London. About a week later I got a call from a storage hangar at Heathrow Airport asking me why alarms were going off in the boxes we'd shipped. My amusement was cut short when I realized that in light of the Pan Am disaster, this was no laughing matter to the caller. Somehow the alarms had been accidentally set to ring. I quickly apologized and explained that they were harmless.

During my first stay in Malta, I'd had the pleasure of meeting the owner of Mary's Place, Tony Gauci—a man small in stature but large in his bravery, which we all admired. Early in the investigation, when the Libyans heard we were talking to him, they started a campaign of intimidation, showing up in his shop and just staring at him for long periods, trying to keep him from working with the police. They knew that at the very least, Gauci could identify the person who bought the clothes as Libyan. (And he did, but until further evidence surfaced, we assumed he meant

Palestinian or Arab.) The harassment scared his wife, and we heard that his family members had tried to convince him not to cooperate with us, but he was undeterred. Once when the inspector and I walked into his store, he had scars and cuts on his face and arms, and we suspected he'd been fighting with family members over his cooperation with us. Eventually the Maltese police installed surveillance cameras and alarms around his store to provide him extra security.

∽

I spent approximately two years working alongside the Scottish police officers. Hand-picked from among several constabularies, they were seasoned gumshoes, no-stone-left-unturned cops. They didn't let long hours, weekends, or holidays get in the way of furthering the investigation. They were all far from home and all missing their families, and all their families were missing them. Thanks to their hard work and personal sacrifice, our suspicions about Palestinian involvement in the bombing were finally laid to rest.

We accomplished this by reviewing thousands of records. We examined flight passenger manifests from airlines that had flown in and out of Malta on December 21, 1988, and then we identified or ruled out possible suspects by examining each passenger's immigration and hotel records. In addition, we conducted hundreds of interviews of Maltese citizens in coordination with the Maltese police and intelligence, who required that at least one of their officers be present. Some of these interviews required translators provided by the Maltese or by the British or American embassies. Then all the results had to be coordinated with the HOLMES review team, and the system kept updated.

The inspector was a hard-charging, shoot-from-the-hip lead detective from Dumfries and Galloway Constabulary. He ate and slept the investigation, staying on top of every detail and making sure the rest of us did the same. At the end of each day, after interviews had been conducted and records reviewed, our team would go over what had been accomplished that day and decide whether particular lines of investigation required further follow-up in Malta or other parts of the world. Some of the interviews and record reviews generated further work; others we were able to lay to rest. On some days we seemed to be spinning our wheels; on others we would be jubilant because someone we suspected in the crime was identified as being in Malta around the critical date of December 21, 1988.

We got a great deal of support from the Maltese government, although there were certain protocols we had to conform to while conducting the investigation in their country. We also received a lot of help from Maltese law enforcement and intelligence setting up interviews and reviewing immigration and embarkation records and airline passenger and hotel records.

Each morning the inspector and I met with Malta's deputy police commissioner (DPC) and his second-in-command (SIC). We were not allowed to conduct investigations or interviews unless we had one or two of their people with us. The DPC and his SIC went out of their way to ensure that we had investigators and/or translators with us whenever we conducted interviews of Maltese citizens or had to review government or private-sector records. The DPC was very patient with us, which we greatly appreciated. He understood the sensitivity and significance of the investigation but had to balance it with the political reality that not all Maltese citizens were happy about us being in their country.

We all kept very busy, pretty much seven days a week. When we weren't doing interviews or reviewing records, we were doing a lot of paperwork and scanning documents back to our respective countries.

We tirelessly reviewed thousands of embarkation and disembarkation records in Malta's Immigration Records Office (IRO), a dirty, dusty, damp, sweaty room loaded with several decades' worth of immigration cards. Sometime in mid-1990, with the DPC's approval and after months of reviewing the same cards over and over again as new leads came in, we decided to computerize all the cards for passengers coming from "countries of interest" during the critical time period. Most of these passengers were from Muslim countries—Libya, Saudi Arabia, Syria, Palestine, Jordan, Turkey, Iran, Iraq, Pakistan, and Egypt—but some were from Germany, Switzerland, the United Kingdom, Denmark, or Sweden. We piled up thousands of the designated cards, and I brought in two FBI computer data loaders from the States. It took them two months working around the clock to load all the information onto the computer, but this saved us untold hours of looking through shelves of cards during the rest of the investigation in Malta. Now we could run a name through the new database and determine almost instantly whether that individual was in Malta on a particular day or within a particular time frame, which helped identify and eliminate suspects. Also loaded in the system were the hotels or other places where passengers stayed while in Malta—information that would later be invaluable in identifying the actual perpetrators and their associates. We are forever indebted to those two computer data loaders.

                                          ⁀⁀

Although we worked every day, we did find time to socialize. When we got the chance, the Scottish investigators and I attended embassy parties, many of which were held by marines assigned to the embassy or by the ambassador herself. They were usually well-attended, with plenty of food and music. One of them was for visiting US senators Patrick Leahy, Ron Espey, and Barbara Mikulski. I was one of Sen. Mikulski's constituents when I was growing up in Baltimore. She was always a very vocal activist for her district, and she was very popular in Baltimore. She even knew my mother. I had the opportunity to talk to all three senators, which was a great experience. I explained who I was and why I was there, and they were very supportive.

These parties gave me the opportunity to socialize with embassy staff, which included the translators I used from time to time while conducting interviews with non-English-speaking Maltese citizens.

We were very lucky that most Maltese spoke English, thanks to the years of British influence. We were also fortunate that during our investigation, the Maltese Nationalist Party was in power, as opposed to the Labor Party. The Nationalist Party was more pro-West, while the Labor Party was known to be anti-West and had known connections with Libya.

Libyans had political influence in Malta because they owned homes, office buildings, and hotels there. Located less than eight hundred miles away, Libya played an important role in the island's economy. Libya was an outcast nation, suffering as a result of embargoes by the United States and our allies for its support of global terrorism. These embargoes brought shortages of desirable western goods. Because Malta hadn't participated in the embargoes, Libyans flew there via Libyan Arab Airlines, bought items like tires, washing machines, tools, and food, and had them flown back to Libya in the cargo holds. Malta was also a stopover for Libyans traveling to Europe and other parts of the world. Many Maltese told me they didn't like Libyans, but they liked Libyans' money.

⌘

Being on Malta for the better part of two years, I lusted for any news about the United States, and *USA Today* and the *Herald-Tribune* became very important sources of news from back home. I also watched a lot of CNN International news, and I read several European newspapers that kept me current with world events.

There was a certain time of the year between March and June when storm winds from the Sahara Desert in North Africa would travel across the Mediterranean Sea and dump tons of sand on Malta. It was an ugly sight, and for a couple of days at a time, we had to live with low visibility. When it the winds died down, everything would be covered with sand and had to be washed down with water. The summer weather, June to August, was hot and dry. It was warm and sporadically wet in autumn, and the winters were short and cool, with some rainfall between October and March.

I called my wife every day and sometimes twice a day while I was in Malta. In fact, I was told by my office in DC that I held the record for the highest telephone bill in the FBI's history. I kept our local florist in Alexandria in business because I was constantly ordering flowers for Bernadette. I also brought her gifts like jewelry, perfume, and scarves from some of the countries I visited—anything to keep her happy during my long absences from home.

Speaking of flowers, one day while I was shopping in downtown Valletta, I received a call from the US ambassador's secretary asking me if I would mind picking up some flowers she had ordered from a local shop. Without considering that I was about five miles from the embassy, I agreed. The flowers turned out to be two dozen gorgeous long-stemmed roses—so many that I could barely get my arms around the bundle. As I began the journey back on foot, drivers began honking their horns and people pointed at me and laughed. It took me a few minutes to realize that a macho-looking black man—there weren't too many of us on the island at the time—carrying a huge bouquet of roses through the streets might cause a stir. I picked up my speed and tried burying my face in the bouquet, but the thorns got the best of me. The honking got louder and as the comments became more coherent, I realized they were not all that nice. A cab showed up from out of nowhere, perhaps recognizing my personal crisis, and delivered me and my package to the embassy, none too soon. Whew!

My next challenge was the lingering concern that all the investigators were facing: the probability that our hotel rooms and telephones in Malta were bugged. So we tried to be very careful about what we did and said in our rooms and on the phone.

After a hard day's work, we liked to frequent a restaurant called Peppi's, located on Tower Road in Sliema. It was close to our hotels and had great western cuisine. It was an excellent spot for steaks, Greek salads, and pizza, although the pizza was unlike what we were used to in the States—it came topped with oysters, clams, and shrimp still in the shell.

The manager of Peppi's was quite friendly, as were the chef and all the waiters. We felt very much at home there. Because one of the Scottish officers somehow cut his finger in the restaurant, we began to call the restaurant "Fingers," which caught on.

Because I could never find steak sauce in Malta, I brought my own to restaurants, and one of the Scottish officers commented that I must not like the taste of meat because I smothered it in sauce. (Hey, that's the way I was raised!) One of the waiters was a Palestinian kid who had just been awarded a Rhodes Scholarship and intended to start classes in England in the fall. He always wore a chain around his neck with the Palestinian flag and a picture of Palestine, and he told me that someday he wanted to go home to Palestine. I thought about the Palestinians' long struggle for independence and said to myself, *Boy, that won't be easy!*

♪♫

During my two years in Malta I traveled to Lockerbie a few times, which gave me a chance to pay my respects to the victims and to personally thank the members of the Scottish team that was managing the worldwide investigation.

Lockerbie was an interesting town inhabited by some very resilient people. We toured the crime scene, the local graveyard, and the Thundergarth memorial shed, where there was a sign-in registry. The shed was made of red stone and was located adjacent to the field where the nose cone of the plane had landed. The structure was large enough to hold two adults at a time while they reviewed the names of passengers and Lockerbie citizens who died that fateful evening. I signed the registry book and then, next to my name, I left a message for the people of Lockerbie: we wouldn't stop until we'd arrested the bastards who murdered 270 innocent people.

While in Scotland, and realizing how close we were to Ireland, another FBI agent and I decided to take a week's vacation and travel there. The Scots tried to convince us not to go, saying it was too dangerous. I told them that I grew up in Baltimore and was used to it. We caught a ferry over to Larne, Ireland, and rented a car. I wanted to go straight to Belfast, because I wanted to see firsthand the scene of the riots and resistance to British rule. There was a marathon going on at the time, and British troops were providing security; they were lined up along the course in full military uniform, along with military weapons and vehicles. To go into a shopping mall, we had to be searched the way they search people now at airports. Our car was checked for explosives as well.

We then drove south across the border to Dublin, where we felt obliged to order a few pints of Guinness from some local pubs. When we reached Waterford, I purchased some crystal and had it airmailed back to the States for Bernadette. While we were there we met an Irish gentleman who was very nice and very curious about what was going on in the United States. (He seemed to drop the name "Kennedy" a lot in the conversation.) At one point he paused, stared at me, and then said, "You remind me of a browned-off West Cork man." The remark stunned me at first, but then I realized he was probably talking about the dark-skinned Irish who lived in County Cork, and I laughed.

We then moved on to Blarney, where we toured the castle and, of course, kissed the Blarney Stone. We drove through Counties Cork, Kilarney, Limerick, Galway, Sligo, and Derry, and then back to Belfast. It was a great week.

As we were crossing the border back into Northern Ireland, I started taking pictures of the barracks and the British troops drew down on me and took my film. They explained that they had recently been attacked by the IRA and lost a few of their troops, so they were very skittish about anyone taking pictures of their fortifications. The film was returned to me later at the American embassy in London, before I left for Malta.

During my assignment to Malta, about twenty Peruvian pilots were in flight training on American Airlines passenger jets. Some were staying at the Suncrest Hotel, too, so I got a chance to get to know them. These pilots became very popular with Maltese women and even developed love interests. After they completed their training and said their goodbyes, American Airlines provided them a jet to fly back home to Peru. Unfortunately, the airplane mysteriously ditched into the Atlantic Ocean somewhere between Great Britain and the United States. I don't believe anyone survived the crash or any of the wreckage was ever recovered. I do remember that the Maltese women were devastated when they heard what had happened, and that they remained upset for a long time.

Here was my morning routine in Malta: get out of bed early, take a nice, long run, and then get three cappuccinos at the hotel restaurant. (They had the best cappuccinos in the world.) I tried to stay in the best physical shape possible, but it was a challenge. We ate out almost every night at restaurants around the island—our favorites were Peppi's for pizza and Snoopy's for steaks. There was always a lot of drinking, which I personally tried to hold to a minimum.

The British high commission and the American embassy fielded competing bowling teams made up of commission and embassy staff, including the American and Scottish investigative team. (We Americans called our team the Dweebs.) It was very competitive, and we all had a great time. We played at a bowling alley called the Eden Super Bowl. There were trophies awarded at the end of the tournament, and I got the one for the highest score.

Once every other month I would cook a special dinner for the Scottish officers: spaghetti and meat sauce from scratch, with garlic bread. They, in turn, would fix one of my favorites: haggis (sheep innards) with turnips.

From time to time while traveling to and from Malta, I would stop by the US embassy in Rome to brief our FBI legat on how the investigation was going on the island. His investigative responsibilities included working with the law enforcement and intelligence agencies in both Italy and Malta. On occasion, he traveled to Malta and met with me for an update.

I enjoyed being in Rome, so after my briefings, if I had the time, I did some touring. Over time, I visited Vatican City, the Sistine Chapel, St. Peter's Square, and the Coliseum. I even saw the statue of the *Pietà* in St. Peter's Basilica, even though I was run out of there by a very upset Italian priest for taking a picture of it.

I happened to be in Rome when the city hosted the World Cup. When I visited a piano bar across the street from our embassy to have a drink and listen to music, everyone started asking me if I was Marvin Hagler, the boxing champ who had recently moved to Milan, where he was very popular. After I made it clear that I was not (Marvelous) Marvin Hagler, I sat down at the bar. When I had two drinks and received a bill for $110, I thought it was a mistake. As it turned out, I was charged "World Cup" prices.

A park near the embassy held regular fashion shows, so when I could, I would grab a sandwich and a cappuccino, find a seat, take in the show, and people-watch. The men's and women's fashions were fabulous! It was during my visits to Rome that I developed a taste for Italian clothes and good cappuccinos.

∂♪

I found the Maltese people to be friendly, intelligent, and hardworking; many of them spoke several languages and worked two or more jobs. They were also very family-oriented and religious.

On May 25, 1990, Pope John Paul II visited Malta. It was the first time a pope had ever visited the island, even though it was only a short trip from Rome and the majority of Maltese are Catholic. He was there for two days, and his visit sent the island into a frenzy. Legend had it that the Apostle Paul had shipwrecked on Malta centuries ago and baptized all the Maltese as Catholics. One of its islands, St. Paul's, is named after him.

Special, beautiful outdoor altars were built for the pope, and the island was decorated with "Viva la Pappa" ornaments. When he arrived he was driven through town in his bulletproof "popemobile." Everyone was following or even running behind it, shouting, "Viva la Pappa!"—including me. It was wonderful! It was my first time ever seeing the pope in person. I bought all the pope souvenirs, like everyone else, and attended his outdoor Mass.

Because I was working with Maltese intelligence and they knew I was Catholic, they let me get very close to the pope to take pictures. After Mass, as he was being escorted to his limousine by members of the Swiss Guard and Maltese intelligence and I was standing near the limousine to take pictures, the Swiss Guard rushed the pope to his car and quickly drove away. I didn't think much of it until later that day, when one of the Maltese intelligence officers told me that members of the Swiss Guard were asking about my identity and why I was allowed to get so close to the pope to take pictures. The officer explained to me that they had noticed I was of a different ethnic group, and that I reminded them of the Turkish-born national who had attempted to assassinate the pope several years prior. When they saw me, they rushed to get the pope into his limousine and out of the area.

I wasn't sure if I had captured the incident on film, so I had the roll processed quickly, and of course I had. Someday John Paul II may be canonized a saint—and I have those pictures. Wow!

♪♪

In early June 1990, we realized that we needed to interview some Egyptians who were passengers on another flight leaving Malta on December 21, 1988. Based on passenger manifests, they were sitting next to or close to persons of interest to our investigation, so they could have seen or heard something of value. We knew that trying to get them to recall something a year and a half later was a shot in the dark, but we had to take it. After we located them, we arranged to interview them in Cairo. In order to travel there, I needed a visa from the Egyptian consulate in Malta. When I went into the consulate, the staff treated me like a long-lost African brother; they even gave me an extended visa so I could stay in Egypt as long as I wanted. I guess they weren't used to seeing many "brothers" from the States. We talked a lot about the history of our countries and what was currently happening there, and they kept asking me how I stayed in such good shape. I left the consulate looking forward to my trip to Egypt.

On June 7, 1990, I flew from Malta to Rome, where I would have an eight-hour layover en route to Cairo. I was glad to have the time in the airport to prepare for the leads I would be covering in Egypt.

On the Air France flight to Cairo I was seated next to a young, beautiful Muslim woman dressed in full *hijab*. She couldn't speak a word of English, and I couldn't speak a word of Egyptian, but we both were very anxious to communicate—mostly out of curiosity because we were from two different worlds, but also because we shared the same complexion. We had a good time trying to communicate with hand and body language. It made the long flight not long enough, because she seemed as disappointed as I was when we landed.

I arrived in Cairo in the middle of the day. A call to prayer sounded on loudspeakers throughout the city, which was very crowded with a lot of noisy traffic. In Cairo, everybody blows their car horns. I was excited to be in my first Muslim country and to set foot in Africa, and I was very anxious to see the Nile River.

I checked into the Intercontinental Hotel near the Nile and the American embassy, where I stopped in briefly to talk with our legat. Outside the Egyptian embassy I decided to take a picture and immediately had shoulder weapons pointed in my face by the security guards. I guess I didn't see the big sign that banned photography in front of the embassy—nor had I learned a lesson from trying to take pictures at the border crossing in Ireland. In certain parts of the world, photography is seen as groundwork to planning an attack. I knew better, but I wanted to take pictures to document my travels, and I thought it was worth the risk. (I never said I was bright!)

The legat made arrangements for me to stop by a local police station, which was heavily fortified, to review records related to our case and conduct the passenger interviews. I was driven to the station in an armored vehicle with an armed escort. This was a first for me, and another reminder that I was in a very dangerous part of the world.

The police were quite accommodating. I briefed them on why I was there and gave them the names of the Egyptian citizens who had surfaced as possible witnesses. They would not let me interview them, but they said they would do it themselves while I waited and provide me with results when they returned. The passengers didn't seem very happy when they were marched into the station, and they weren't able to make identifications from the photos I'd brought or recall any incidents of value. I got the impression that policing in Egypt was a little different from in the States. We'd known interviewing them was a long shot, but it was a lead that had to be looked into and laid to rest.

After they briefed me on the completed interviews, I returned to my hotel room and found a hotel porter there. I assumed he was Egyptian intelligence who was going through my things or bugging my room. I immediately ordered him out and checked my room to see what was disturbed and look for bugs, but I couldn't find anything out of place.

I called SSA Knisley back in Washington to bring him up to date on the interviews, trying to talk as cryptically as possible because I wasn't on a secure line. While I was on the phone, my door opened and the same porter came in. I told him I was on the phone and to come back later. Acting as though he didn't understand a word

I said, he proceeded to turn down my bed and fumble around the room. Finally he left. Knisley, who was hearing me trying to get the porter out of my room, was laughing like crazy.

After the briefing I realized I had a free evening ahead, so I decided to go out and walk along the Nile and take some pictures of it. While I was there I met a cab driver who told me that for fifteen US dollars he would take me anywhere I wanted for the whole evening. It was risky, but I wanted to go to Giza and see the Great Pyramids. It was a Wednesday, and the laser light show there was in English.

So I got in the car and we drove to Giza—not the smartest thing I've ever done. I didn't tell anyone where I was going because I was afraid they would say no. If I had been kidnapped, no one would have known where to begin to look for me. The light show was great, though, as was seeing the Sphinx and the Pyramids with my own eyes—I scratched them off my bucket list. The cab driver set me up on a camel ride with some of his cousins and led me to his brother's store, where I purchased an Egyptian robe and a red fez.

I made it back to the hotel in one piece, but it was a long time before I had the nerve to tell anyone back in Washington about my solo excursion. I flew back to Malta the next day and immediately briefed the inspector and provided him a copy of my report about the passenger interviews. He was happy to have that line of investigation resolved, but he wished the Egyptians had remembered seeing or hearing something of value.

One great thing about being in Malta was that whenever we were able to get some breaks from the investigation, which was usually over the weekend, we could get in some beach time on the Mediterranean. I was able to do a lot of swimming and sailing, as I could rent a small sailboat from our hotel. The water was just beautiful, and the conditions for sailing were awesome.

In early August 1990, there were demonstrations in Malta and around the world protesting the first Gulf War and the American invasion of Iraq. Our embassy was on high alert as a result. The ambassador held security meetings and discussed contingency plans, including possible evacuation, in case there was an attempt to take over the embassy. The US Marine Corps embassy guards would provide us weapons, if necessary.

During this period I heard about a mass killing from a car bomb somewhere in the Middle East, and it made me very concerned about getting into my car in Malta. So every day, to start my car, I left the driver's side door open and with both feet still on the ground, I reached in and turned the ignition. I figured if the car blew up, the blast would push me out and away from the car, instead of blowing me up inside with the door closed. I had never received training on how to avoid car bombs—all I could hope was that it didn't happen to me.

✆

In mid-August I flew home for a couple of weeks. Prior to returning to Malta, I expressed my concern to SSA Knisley that the Pan Am investigation was on the wrong track. I explained that the body of evidence led me to believe that Libyans were far more likely to be responsible for the bombing than any of the Palestinian terrorist organizations. He replied that these groups' anti-American threats, their history of carrying them out, and their MO made them strong suspects. He felt that until he was proven otherwise, the investigation should stay focused on them.

I replied that Tony Gauci knew the difference in appearance and language between Libyans and Palestinians, and that he had insisted that the person who bought the clothes was Libyan. I also reminded Knisley that the earlier Libyan espionage and terrorism investigations had revealed Libyan operatives going in and out of Malta en route to the United States. Though we had never directly linked them to bomb attacks in Europe, we had nevertheless observed a connection. I repeated my assertion that, having seen firsthand the Libyan presence and influence in Malta, and being aware of the evidence so far, we needed to pursue Libya's possible involvement. After some hesitation, Knisley requested that I draft a "blind memorandum" outlining my reasons for believing Libyans were likely responsible for the bombing of Pan Am Flight 103.

Although the opinions and suppositions in a blind memorandum are not necessarily substantiated by existing evidence, they can act as a framework for developing new evidence and, ultimately, a shift in an investigation's focus. In my document I stated that Libya's motive was probably revenge for the US bombing of Tripoli and Benghazi on April 15, 1986, which in turn was in retaliation for the Libyan bombing of the La Belle discotheque in West Berlin. At least fifteen people died in the US air strikes, including Col. Muammar Gaddafi's adopted fifteen-month-old daughter, and more than a hundred people were injured. All possibilities had been left open at the outset of the investigation; the Libyans had never been excluded as suspects. And evidence that initially pointed to Palestinian terrorists had recently taken a Libyan turn. I assumed Gaddafi was eager to hit back for the air strikes, but because he now fully understood the consequences, he would do so only if it could be accomplished without Libya appearing responsible.

Five months before the Lockerbie bombing, on July 3, 1988, the USS *Vincennes* had mistakenly shot down Iran Air Flight 655 over the Persian Gulf (the Strait of Hormuz), killing all 290 civilian passengers on board, including 38 non-Iranians and 66 children. In the wake of this tragedy, it was rumored that Iran was reaching out to Middle Eastern terrorist groups, offering a reward of $10 million for suitable retaliation. I felt the Iranians would seek tit-for-tat revenge: the lifeless bodies of American civilian airline passengers scooped up out of the sea in fishing nets.

I surmised that members of the Frankfurt cell of the PFLP-GC had accepted the job but were arrested in the Autumn Leaves operation before they could act. The Iranians then asked Libya to handle the job; Libya agreed to be their proxy, but with the condition that the cover/fall guys would be Palestinian. If the Iranians were involved in the downing of Pan Am Flight 103 and the goal was in-kind retaliation for the earlier air disaster, it went sideways when the plane exploded over Lockerbie instead of the Atlantic Ocean. We have yet to prove Iranian involvement, but I still strongly suspect their complicity in the Pan Am bombing.

◌◌◌

When I returned to Malta on August 31, 1990, the Scottish officers had not returned and were not due back for several weeks. This provided me sufficient time to develop supporting evidence that I could use to persuade them to change their focus from the Palestinians to the Libyans. This turned out to be my most productive period on the island.

I gave a copy of the blind memorandum to my CIA partners in Malta. Although I'd been told by one of my superiors in Washington not to work with the CIA, I did so anyway because it didn't make sense not to. They reviewed the document and wholeheartedly agreed with my conclusions. I requested their help in developing potential leads and Maltese informants in order to support the new theory and get us closer to solving the case. I told them I was going to review my files for any relevant reports in the bombing's time frame, and they agreed to do the same. I also mentioned the need to apply a "Mississippi Burning" approach. They knew exactly what I was talking about.

Mississippi Burning is a film loosely based on the real-life murders of three civil rights workers in Mississippi in 1964. In the film, after the three are reported missing and, subsequently, murdered, two FBI agents are sent to rural Mississippi to investigate. (The film's fictitious Jessup County was modeled after Neshoba County, where the real murders took place.) Frustrated by the lack of cooperation from police and private citizens, the agents use the highly unorthodox approach of kidnapping a local mayor and a KKK member to frighten them into revealing the names of the suspects and their roles in the murders.

Though I wasn't suggesting we use the same tactics on Malta, I did want to begin thinking outside the box. Up to this point our investigative approach had been strictly limited: we conducted subject interviews and relied solely on what we were told. I wanted to know who our interview subjects talked to afterwards and what they were saying. We could find out by using informants and/or electronic surveillance.

I started reviewing and documenting the Libyan presence and influence in Malta. Using public records, I checked what the Libyans owned there and their role in island unions and politics. I focused on Libyan intelligence agents and their activities in Malta over the years, particularly during the period leading up to the bombing of Flight 103.

As I've mentioned, the Maltese didn't seem to like Libyans very much, even though they liked Libyan money. Often when I walked into a store, I would be deliberately ignored until I said something and the clerks realized I was not Libyan.

My CIA partners and I identified all known Libyan intelligence operatives associated with Malta. We then tried to connect the list of names to the relevant dates in the case. One of the names that popped up was Lamin Fhima, whom the CIA identified as a Libyan Arab Airlines (LAA) ticket manager assigned to Malta's Luqa Airport. He had known associations with a Libyan intelligence officer named Abdel Baset Al Megrahi. My CIA contacts said Fhima and Megrahi had been partners in a failed a travel agency in Malta.

This was a very exciting development because it led to the first working hypothesis on how the explosives could have gotten into the Maltese airline luggage system and, ultimately, onto Pan Am Flight 103. If the Libyan intelligence officer had given the LAA ticket manager at Luqa Airport the rigged luggage, he could have applied the necessary tags to send it through Frankfurt and onto Pan Am Flight 103 out of London Heathrow. The ticket manager had access to luggage tags and knew flight schedules, so he could have set the timer accordingly. LAA was a Libyan state-owned airline. We decided this scenario was definitely worth looking into.

⹗⹗

In September 1990, the Lockerbie investigation took another major step forward. It involved the identification of a fragmentary item tagged for evidentiary purposes as PT-35. The Scottish crime lab had recovered it from the blast-damaged Yorkie clothing; it had been blasted into the pocket of a gray Alamo shirt of the same make, type, and color bought from Tony Gauci's shop in Sliema. The fragment appeared to have come from a circuit board, but further identification remained stalled for quite some time.

It turned out later that the Scottish officers were a little slow to allow the FBI to get involved in identifying PT-35. I'm not sure how long they tried to identify the fragment on their own, but the delay cost the investigation valuable time. The Scots had gone to more than fifty companies around the world trying to identify this item, to no avail. They only told us about it after they had exhausted their leads. In fairness, this wasn't just their problem. We were all guilty of trust issues and caught up in the rush to be the group that solved this case.

PT-35 was a piece of debris so small it fit on the end of a man's finger. Both the fragment and its importance would have been missed without the careful and thorough evidentiary review process that was in place.

Once the FBI became aware of this evidence, Tom Thurman, an agent supervisor from the explosives unit, asked if he could take photographs to compare the item with pictures and pieces of explosive devices the FBI and the CIA had recovered from other terrorist attacks around the world. Within a couple of days, Thurman and his CIA counterpart had conclusively determined that PT-35 matched the circuit boards of two timers seized several years before in Togo and Senegal. There were potential Libyan connections in both of those cases.

Etched on the back of the Togo timer were the letters *MEBO*, a name traced to an electronics manufacturing company in Zurich.

The timers were designed to trigger explosive devices. According to the owners of the company, Edwin Bollier and Erwin Meister, the Togo timer came from a batch of twenty ordered in 1985. They were built by an employee, Ueli Lumpert, for Libyan customers. Lumpert immediately recognized the small piece of circuit board as part of a timing device he had built, but he said he was never told what its intended use was and didn't know what happened to the timers after they were shipped. Bollier and Meister had had a long relationship with Libyan government officials, producing and selling them electronic equipment for police, security, and military use.

Tom Thurman called to deliver the good news and told me to keep pushing the Libyan connection to the investigation in Malta, because he felt we were finally on the right track. He advised that there would be further interviews of Bollier and Meister; he hoped they would be able to identify the Libyans who had purchased the timers, and perhaps even the artist's rendering provided by Tony Gauci.

Even though my CIA partners and I had begun to focus our investigation on a possible Libyan connection to the bombing, we still had some Palestinian-related leads to resolve on Malta.

One of our suspects was Abu Talb, an Egyptian-born militant who in December 1989 received a life sentence in Sweden for a series of bombings in Copenhagen and Amsterdam in 1985. He was an alleged member of the Palestinian Popular Struggle Front (PPSF), a known terrorist group. Our investigation had determined that he was connected to Abu Nada, the Palestinian owner of the Miska Bakery on the island. The Miska Bakery was identified as having terrorist Palestinian connections by a number of intelligence sources. Abu Talb visited Nada in October of 1988; other evidence showed Talb was on the island December 9, 1988. We determined through passenger manifests and Maltese embarkation/debarkation records that Talb had visited the island during the critical period around December 21, 1988. We didn't know whether he had had the opportunity to put a bomb on the Air Malta flight that connected to the Pan Am flights out of Germany and London. We were looking into Abu Nada's background, as well.

ଏଡ଼

The Scots returned to Malta in early October 1990 with plans to conduct Miska Bakery-related interviews, which included Abu Nada. I had convinced them to consider looking at the Libyans, but first they wanted to lay to rest all suspicions about the possible role of Abu Talb and Abu Nada. Once documenting that the line of inquiry had been thoroughly examined and discounted, it would satisfy the requirements of HOLMES. If we didn't follow it up to the end, Monday morning quarterbacks would always be able to claim a possible Palestinian connection.

About the second week of October 1990, before we began the interviews of Abu Nada, his family members, and his staff at the bakery, I let my CIA partners know the interview schedule so they could cover Abu Nada's post-interview phone calls from either his business or his residence. I did not expect Abu Nada to tell the truth during the interview, but I did expect him to call someone immediately after we left to report the kinds of questions we were asking—and my CIA partners and I were very curious to know whom that would be. I never asked my contacts about how they would capture the calls or the legality of doing so; I knew the CIA operated with far fewer restrictions than the FBI did. We could not install wiretaps or listening devices in the United States without first getting a court order. That's why I recommended a "Mississippi Burning" approach to solving this case.

The SIC helped us out with the interviews because he could speak Arabic as well as several other languages. After the interviews were conducted, I checked with my CIA partners to ask if Abu Nada had made any phone calls after we left and, if so, whether they had been able to gain anything from them. They said that there were no indications that Abu Nada had made any related phone calls. *Oh well—good try!* I thought.

Everything was progressing well until October 25, 1990, when we were stopped in our tracks. During one of my daily meetings with the inspector and the DPC, one of the DPC's intelligence officers dangled a box with a lot of loose wires in front of me and asked, "Is this yours?"

I asked him what it was.

"You *know* what it is," he said.

"No, I don't," I told him.

Then he explained that it had come from the home of Abu Nada, who found it after having problems making a phone call. I told him I didn't know anything about it and suggested that maybe it belonged to Mossad. The DPC told us the Maltese government suspected that either the British or the Americans had violated their country's sovereignty by monitoring the phone calls of one of their citizens, and as a result, our investigation on Malta was immediately suspended until the matter was resolved on a government-to-government level.

Maltese media was all over the story, which Abu Nada had happily given to them. He claimed he was hearing weird noises in his phone and having trouble making calls, so he went to his outside phone box to investigate and found some unidentified wires in it. When he contacted the phone company, they said the wires weren't theirs.

I went back to my CIA partners, who confirmed that they were a little slow in removing the wiretapping equipment. *Yikes!*

In the meantime I was stuck on the island and unable to work. The FBI didn't want me to leave; they were afraid that if I did, the Maltese wouldn't let me return and I wouldn't be able to complete the investigation. The Scottish officers took off, and I was left all by myself.

The suspension lasted several weeks, until a meeting was arranged in late December 1990. Government officials from the United States, Great Britain, and Malta sat down and discussed the incident. Neither foreign government admitted wrongdoing, but both promised to the satisfaction of the Maltese officials that nothing like this would occur again. I was finally able to leave Malta on December 20 so I could be home for the Christmas holidays. That turned out to be my longest stay on Malta: August 31 to December 20, 1990.

I was exhausted and fell asleep quickly on the Air Malta flight heading home. I was abruptly awakened by a loud noise and the dramatic shaking of the plane. Very much startled, all I could think was, *They got me—the plane's going down*. Fortunately, it was only a heavy thunderstorm. I guess a little paranoia had set in during my extended stay.

❦

I returned to Malta on January 6, 1991, worked there until the end of the month, and then flew back to Washington, DC.

In the meantime, a worldwide, low-profile search for a photo of Megrahi, the Libyan intelligence officer, was initiated. We couldn't use Interpol because Libya was an Interpol member and had access to all requests for information made by other countries; we didn't want to risk tipping our hand. So my CIA partners obtained a picture from one of their overseas counterparts. I picked up the undated passport photograph from CIA headquarters in Virginia, and guarding it carefully, I brought it back to Malta with me.

On February 15, 1991, the SIC picked up Tony Gauci from his shop in Sliema and drove him to police headquarters to view a photo array containing Megrahi's picture. Present for the photo spread were the inspector and other Scottish officers, the SIC, and me. We all knew this was a potentially pivotal moment in the investigation. To my surprise, Gauci seemed overjoyed to see me again, and he brought some levity to the room by calling me "the black Libyan." We all shared a laughed before moving on to the more serious subject at hand.

The photo spread the inspector and I had put together was comprised of twelve numbered photos of men who looked similar to Megrahi, but not similar enough to confuse Gauci. Megrahi was number eight in the array. The lineup was photos only. No other information was displayed—no names, no dates, nothing.

We presented the photo spread to Gauci and asked him to take his time looking at each one and then tell us if he could identify any of them as the person who purchased the clothes in his shop in December 1988. Gauci examined the photos very slowly and thoughtfully, poker-faced. He finally pointed to number eight and said that of all the pictures he had been shown, that one most resembled the man who had bought the clothing in his shop, but that man was about ten years older than the one in the photo. Since the date of the photograph was unknown, it was possible that it was not recent. We did not know for sure, however, as we had never seen Megrahi in person.

My eyes and the inspector's locked in sheer happiness, but only for a second. We knew we couldn't let our feelings show because that could be construed as unduly influencing the identification. Gauci went on to say that the person in the photo had thick hair while the man who had come into the shop was thinning on top, but of all the pictures he had seen, only this one resembled the man who bought the clothing.

We were elated that he had picked Megrahi but concerned by his comment about the age difference. We asked him to tell us what was familiar about the person in photo number eight. Again he said that if the man in the picture was aged about ten years he would be confident that was the person who bought the odd mixture of clothing from his store. We later determined that the passport photo was about ten years old.

I went back to the embassy and told my two CIA partners the good news, which they passed along to their headquarters in Langley. When I called SSA Knisley to fill him in, I was told that a photo spread had also been shown to Edwin Bollier, whose Swiss company made the timing device, and he also had picked out Megrahi's photo. We were more confident than ever that we had identified two of the bombers, Fhimah and Megrahi, but we still had to place Megrahi in Malta around December 21, 1988.

We all got together that night to celebrate at one of our favorite restaurants on the island. We drank a lot. These were significant breaks in the case, and we knew we were on our way to a solution. I thought about the Pan Am victims and their families, and I thought about the La Belle disco victims. They were all going to have justice—we were going to catch the bastards. And maybe, just maybe, we could prove that Gaddafi was personally involved and charge him, too. The morale of the team was very high. We couldn't wait to get back to work the next day to finish up.

Armed with new evidence—the names Fhimah and Megrahi—we used our computerized IRO database to check the suspects' flight histories in and out of Malta during periods of interest; we wanted to know who had traveled on the same flights. We also looked into hotel records to determine where they had stayed and whom they had met or had been in telephonic contact with. Although we could not yet prove that Megrahi was in Malta during the critical time frame, we did confirm that Fhimah was there on December 21, 1988.

✏

On April 18, 1991, we had an incredible stroke of luck: my two CIA partners gave us the location of Fhimah and Megrahi's abandoned travel agency. The office had been deserted for several months, and when my investigative team and I searched it, we found a diary belonging to Fhimah. It contained a reminder Fhima had written to himself. Dated December 15, 1988, the entry read, "Abdel Baset is coming from Zurich with Salvu . . . take tags from the Maltese Airline." The word *tags* was written in English and underlined twice. Additionally, an undated entry on the last page of Fhimah's diary said, "Bring the tags from the airport (Abd al Baset, Abd al Salam)."

The reference to luggage tags was the tip-off. It explained how an "unattended" suitcase loaded with explosives and a timer could find its way onto an Air Malta flight originating at Luqa Airport and then be transferred to connections at Frankfurt and London, with a final destination of New York. Not only did Fhimah have access to the tags he mentioned in his diary, but his knowledge of schedules and connections ensured that the suitcase that entered into the system at Malta was loaded onto Pan Am Flight 103.

I was pleasantly shocked by how careless the Libyans had been—again. Their sloppy work had allowed us to quickly identify their role in the La Belle disco bombing, which had led to the retaliatory US air strike. The fact that the incriminating diary entries hadn't been destroyed made me think Fhimah and Megrahi never expected to be on the receiving end of a full-scale international criminal investigation. If Pan Am Flight 103 had gone down over the Atlantic, as I surmised in my blind memorandum had been the plan to seek revenge in kind, there would have been no crime scene to investigate. No PT-35. No Yorkie clothing. No brown Samsonite suitcase. No evidence to trace back to Malta. They hadn't taken into account the possibility of a premature detonation over land, where evidence could be painstakingly collected, fragment by fragment, and forensically analyzed to identify those responsible. Whether it was a sign of their incompetence or of their arrogance, the evidence trail from Lockerbie led back to them.

We were able to view passenger manifests for every flight in and out of Malta during the critical time frame except for those operated by Libyan Arab Airlines. So our next step was to get access to their records to determine if Megrahi had flown into Malta on an LAA flight. We didn't expect LAA to cooperate, so we asked the DPC for help. With his permission and accompanied by one of his officers, we went into the LAA office at Luqa Airport after business hours and surreptitiously conducted a records search. We were all a bit nervous; if the Libyans caught us, they might retaliate against us or the Maltese government for the incursion. The airline manifests seemed to be in order, but the records for the flights on days of investigative interest were all missing. It was obvious that the records had been deliberately removed to keep us from finding out who was on LAA flights in and out of Malta on the days surrounding the bombing of Pan Am Flight 103.

The last thing the Libyan government wanted known was the fact that the bomber, and perhaps the bomb itself, could be connected to it. When Libyan officials realized that the focus of our investigation had shifted away from the Palestinians, they had no choice but to order the state-owned airline to remove the pertinent flight records.

ↄJↃ

While we worked in Malta to prove that Libya was behind the bombing, forensic evidence and intelligence were being developed in other parts of the world that supported our theory.

Forensics had traced the origin of a fragment of circuit board recovered from a blast-damaged cargo container that had held the suitcase bomb. It came from a black Toshiba cassette radio (model RTSF-16), three-quarters of the worldwide production of which had been shipped to Libya. Along with the MEBO timer device (linked to the fragment named PT-35), that strengthened our case even more. Evidence further established that the plastic explosive Semtex was used to power the bomb, and that it had been secreted in a brown, hard-sided Samsonite suitcase packed with clothing from Tony Gauci's shop (Mary's Place), and put on a flight out of Malta to Germany and then on to London.

As our attention turned solely to the Libyans, our intelligence in Malta indicated that we were being closely monitored by the Libyan intelligence service, who we suspected as having organized and carried out the bombing. I think that initially the Libyans didn't understand what we were doing there, because they were used to military retaliatory responses rather than criminal investigations that gather evidence to take someone to court. Also, in the beginning our investigation had targeted Palestinians. As the Libyans began to realize what we were now doing, they became concerned and began surveilling us and soliciting reports on our activities.

Every once in a while I would look over my shoulder and see someone with Libyan physical characteristics—bearded, with a rounder face and a lighter complexion than the Maltese—following behind us. I didn't know whether these guys planned to harm us or were just providing intelligence back to Libya. In some cases they didn't even seem to care that I had spotted them; maybe they thought they could intimidate me, but it didn't work. I never reported the surveillance because I didn't want to appear paranoid to the Maltese authorities who were helping us.

My two CIA partners briefed me on a known Libyan intelligence agent who frequented Malta and was considered very dangerous. He was an active operative who had been involved in murders, assassinations, and bombings around the world. I'll have to admit that after I received a picture of him, I kept an extra eye out.

In addition, I was advised by my office back in DC that the "spitting" Libyan, one of our major targets arrested in 1988, had been released from federal prison and was returning to Libya. I was concerned for my safety because I knew he disliked me immensely, and if he knew I was in Malta—which he likely regarded as his territory—he would seize the opportunity for some kind of payback. So I had to keep an extra eye out for him, as well.

I had a guardian angel watching my back, too—a homeless Maltese man. I would see him every day, walking the perimeter of the island. He didn't speak English very well, but we were able to communicate. He knew I was an American, and he was further intrigued because I was black. He also knew that I was working the

"Lockerbie case," as he called it. Every once in a while he stopped me on the street, pulling me away from the beaten path to let me know whether he had seen any suspicious people tampering with my car, which I parked every night on the street near the hotel. He also watched me when I ran in the morning and checked to see if anyone was following me. I welcomed his efforts because I was concerned about my personal security, particularly because car bombings were becoming very common around the world at that time. In return I gave him American money, for which he was very grateful.

☙❧

My ex-wife died of cervical cancer on May 30, 1991, so I traveled back to the States on June 4 to attend her funeral. Prior to her death, she had made arrangements for our daughter to live with Bernadette and me, but Maisha had her own plans. She wanted to stay in an apartment with some other female students at Howard University, and so that's what she did. (Maisha is independent-minded, like her dad.) Maisha graduated on time from Howard with a business degree.

☙❧

On my return to Malta, I flew from Dulles to Paris on a red-eye flight. I always tried to sleep during these flights so that I'd be ready to work when I arrived. There was no sleeping on this flight, however, because there were significant thunderstorms across the Atlantic all the way to Paris. Like me, most of the passengers were awake and frightened by the turbulence. Many times during the flight the plane seemed to lose power completely and begin a nose-first plunge toward the ocean, only to recover abruptly and continue on its way.

It was the worst flight of my life; I was sure we were all going to die. I thought about all the unidentified body parts recovered at the crime scene in Lockerbie and how those body parts were eventually incinerated. I considered writing my last name on different parts of my body in the event that the plane crashed, so that investigators would have some chance of piecing me back together again. I also thought about writing my last will and testament.

When we finally made it to Paris, the passengers stood up and gave the pilots and flight attendants a boisterous round of applause. We were told later that the plane had been taken out of the fleet because it had received significant damage during the flight.

Upon my arrival back in Malta, I met with my CIA partners and asked them to review their records and check with their intelligence partners around the world for any known aliases that Megrahi could have used. They asked us for a copy of our computerized IRO database so they could enter into the system any potential aliases they found. We certainly obliged.

In the meantime, my CIA partners' records check had revealed that during the December 1988 time frame, a Libyan double agent working at Luqa Airport was providing one of their CIA case officers reports of the Libyan intelligence service's activities at the airport. The information hadn't meant much at the time, but two and a half years later, one of the reports turned out to be critical. The double agent claimed to have seen Megrahi with Fhimah and two other individuals (one described as a "black Libyan") at the Luqa Airport sometime in late 1988. He couldn't recall the exact date, he said, but he had seen Fhimah take a brown, hard-sided Samsonite suitcase from the luggage belt and carry it through Maltese customs without inspection. The double agent reported the incident because he thought it was strange. I hoped I would get the chance eventually to shake the hand of that CIA case officer and thank him or her for the good work. (Believe it or not, years later, I would get to meet him.)

Based on that report, we decided it was possible that the Libyan double agent witnessed the luggage containing the explosive being brought into Luqa Airport from Tripoli. The problem was, he had since returned to Libya, and the CIA had to figure out how to contact him and convince him to leave that country for a full debriefing.

We got another major break when the CIA was able to come up with an alias for Megrahi. He apparently had used the name Abdusamad in Libyan intelligence operations in other parts of the world. We ran the alias through our IRO database and got several hits. Our review indicated that Megrahi, operating as Abdusamad, arrived with Fhimah in Malta on December 20, 1988, via Air Malta Flight 231, and left for Tripoli approximately twenty-four hours later, December 21, 1988, on LAA Flight LN 147 at 10:26 a.m.

On December 21, 1988, at 7:11 a.m., hotel records under the name Abdusamad indicated that Megrahi made a telephone call from his hotel room to a flat rented by Lamin Khalifa Fhimah. We theorized that this was Fhimah's wake-up call to meet Megrahi at the Luqa Airport; their mission was to get the luggage with explosives on Air Malta Flight KM 180, scheduled to leave at 9:52 a.m. We believed that the Air Malta luggage tags that Fhimah obtained for Megrahi were put on the bomb bag, which was placed on Air Malta Flight KM 180. When that flight reached the Frankfurt airport, the suitcase was transferred to Pan Am Flight 103A bound for London Heathrow, a transfer confirmed by Frankfurt's luggage records. At Heathrow the suitcase was transferred again—this time to Pan Am Flight 103, bound for New York.

We were now able to put Megrahi and Fhimah together in Malta on December 21, 1988, and during other critical periods. Although we had only a circumstantial case so far, it was getting stronger by the day. We had Scottish experts examine the IRO card filled out in the name of Abdusamad; they said the handwriting was the same as Megrahi's.

ঔৡৡ

I had returned back home for a brief period when I was notified by WFO Assistant Director Tom Duhadway that my two CIA partners had contacted the Libyan double agent and convinced him and his wife to leave Libya and travel to Malta, where contact would be reestablished. My CIA partners wanted me to debrief the Libyan in person to assess his value to the investigation. DuHadway told me to pack up and head to the US Navy base in Naples, Italy. The interview was to be conducted in international waters aboard the *Butte*, a navy supply ship assigned to the Sixth Fleet. A team of representatives from the FBI, the CIA, the US Department of Justice, Special Forces, and the US Attorney's office in Washington would be traveling with me.

We traveled to Rome on a commercial flight in early July 1991. I noticed CNN reporter Peter Arnett on our plane; given his reputation for sensational journalism, I knew he would have had a keen interest in our operation. When we arrived at the airport in Rome, I had a more pleasant brush with fame. Actress and dancer Debbie Allen was there with her husband, NBA player Norm Nixon. As we drove to the navy base in Naples, we passed the ruins of Pompeii. It made me think of the movie *The Last Days of Pompeii*.

At the base we checked in through security and settled in at a lounge to await our next move; the CIA was orchestrating the trip with the help of the Sixth Fleet. We were subsequently flown by helicopter to the *Butte*, which was waiting for us in the Mediterranean Sea. I was introduced to the captain, who seemed more than delighted to be of assistance to us. The plan was for me to interview the Libyan in the captain's cabin, which provided privacy and sufficient space for me and the team.

Throughout the trip to Italy and while onboard the *Butte*, I worked on a written list of tough questions for the Libyan; I was anticipating a very contentious interview because he was a trained intelligence officer. I was finally told that he and his wife, who was pregnant with their first child, had made it safely to Malta. The plan was that he would leave her on Malta and would soon meet us on the ship. His cover story for family and friends was that he was going sailing with friends on the Mediterranean.

I was still preparing for the interview when I got word that the Libyan had arrived. My CIA partners brought him aboard and walked him to the captain's cabin, where I was waiting. As soon as he was brought into the room, he looked at me and started crying. Then he ran up to me and gave me a hug that was more of a death grip. I thought, *Who says the FBI and CIA don't work together?* I guessed that my CIA partners had told him about me and implied that I was his friend and benefactor. He continued to cry and kept insisting that he was a friend; apparently he thought we were blaming him for the bombing of Pan Am Flight 103. Then he asked for cigarettes.

After I got him seated and calm, I asked my CIA partners how they had gotten him and his wife out of Libya. They said they told him "the bananas are rotten"—a code they had established to indicate that his secret connection with the CIA had been compromised. Upon getting a message that used that phrase, he was to evacuate Libya with his family immediately. When I asked my CIA partners to stay and help me keep him calm through the interview, I was told, "He's yours now. You're on your own." They then left the ship. *This is going to be tough,* I thought.

I began the interview with some key questions to test his bona fides and trustworthiness. He passed. Then I started asking him about the bomb bag and who had brought it into Malta. From his responses it was clear that he would be a valuable witness in our case. I looked at the DOJ prosecutors in the room and said, "He needs to come with us." They agreed. At that point my job was to convince him to testify in our case, relocate with his wife to the United States, and become American citizens.

We had to get him back to the States quickly, directly from the Mediterranean Sea. That meant using an American military jet, but the closest aircraft carrier was the USS *Forrestal,* which was about two days away from our present position. It was stationed off the coast of Turkey, providing air cover for the Kurds in the no-fly zone that had been established over northern Iraq. In an effort to get there as quickly as possible, the captain of the *Butte* decided to take a shortcut around the island of Cyprus. En route, in the middle of the night, we were awakened by a loud noise and thrown out of our bunks: I knew we had run aground. I remember lying on the floor, waiting for the ship to start sinking. It didn't sink, but apparently there was to be no shortcut for us.

It was a long two days catching up with the *Forrestal*. The Libyan kept accusing me of kidnapping him, saying, "I came here for three hours and you keep me for days." He kept spitting up blood, and we had to feed him intravenously because he refused to eat. I was really concerned for his health. All he did was smoke cigarettes. I reeked of his second-hand smoke, and I worried about my own health from having to continually breathe it in.

When we finally reached the *Forrestal* we helicoptered the team and the Libyan onboard. I met the commander of Carrier Group Six and admiral of the Sixth Fleet, who happened to be black. I was so proud that a brother was at the helm of such an incredibly powerful military asset. He had a tremendous bio, too. *This is not my father's navy,* I thought. I thanked him for supporting our operation and briefed him on what we needed to do and why. Then we exchanged hats and patches and took pictures. It was truly a proud moment in my life.

The Libyan continued to accuse me of kidnapping him, and he also kept accusing us of thinking he was involved in the Pan Am bombing. I tried to convince him otherwise, but my words fell on deaf ears. He desperately missed his wife and was concerned that she didn't know where he was, as he had not seen or talked to her for a few days. We knew that the only way we could get him to eat and calm down was to allow him to talk to his wife, who was in Malta with her parents. He finally acknowledged that if he could talk to her he would feel better, and it would let him know that he wasn't really being kidnapped.

If we were to allow him to contact his wife, however, we had to be careful; we didn't want the call to be overheard by Libyan intelligence. And with exceptional technical assistance from some of our government agencies, we made it happen. The Libyan was happy to talk to his wife, and after the call he began to eat and relax. Suffice it to say, that was a very expensive telephone call.

We arranged for the Libyan to fly back to the United States as quickly and securely as possible. He couldn't smoke during the flight, and I was concerned about how that would affect him. I'm not sure how long it took him to get to the States, but his trip was a lot quicker trip than mine.

We catapulted off the *Forrestal* in a C2 COD cargo aircraft and flew back to Naples. Then we caught commercial flights from Rome to Washington, DC.

When the Libyan double agent arrived in Washington, DC, SSA Knisley code-named him Puzzle Piece, because he provided the missing pieces to the Pan Am Flight 103 investigation.

For the first week I handled the debriefing of Puzzle Piece under the close supervision and support of Scottish investigators, DOJ prosecutors, and the US Attorney's office. They fed me interview questions throughout. It was a grueling process, but we believed that with the intelligence he provided, we now had enough information to indict Megrahi and Fhimah.

After the debriefing was completed, my job was to help Puzzle Piece adjust to life in the United States. That wasn't easy—he was on an emotional roller coaster. But as I learned more about him, I respected him as a devout Muslim and a devoted husband and soon-to-be father. It was clear that he was honest, almost to a fault.

We still needed to get Puzzle Piece's pregnant wife to the United States, so a plan was put in place to fly her safely out of Malta without detection by Libyan intelligence. She did not want to travel alone and insisted on bringing her mother and father along with her. Although this complicated the plans, airline tickets were provided for the three of them to fly from Malta to the United Kingdom. Puzzle Piece and several of us from the FBI and US

Justice Department flew to the Gatwick Airport to meet them. Unfortunately, when Puzzle Piece's wife and family arrived there, we lost them, which sent everyone into a panic. Puzzle Piece became very upset and began blaming us because he thought it was some kind of trick by the American government. We finally found the wife and her parents in a remote section of the airport and reunited them with a delighted Puzzle Piece, whose trust in America was instantly restored.

We put them in a car and chauffeured them to the Highly Manor Hotel in Sussex, not far from the English Channel. The hotel had quite a history. The original Manor of Highly dated back to 1326, and the hotel was known to have ghosts, some of which Puzzle Piece claimed visited him during the night. We planned to stay there for a couple of days to give Puzzle Piece and his wife a chance to be reunited after having been separated for several weeks. A couple of days later, when his wife became comfortable with the situation, she sent her parents back to Malta.

We all boarded a commercial flight from Heathrow Airport to Dulles Airport in Washington, DC. Because of the circumstances, we had to get a special clearance from customs for Puzzle Piece and his wife. Customs was very supportive of the operation, and the couple was cleared for entry to the United States.

⁂

I had to return to Malta to finish out the investigation. I knew that the inspector would be upset with my Mediterranean excursion, and if the Maltese ever found out about the operation I could be arrested for violating their territorial sovereignty. For all I knew, the Libyans might try to snatch me up, too.

As I had guessed, the inspector was not happy with me. I explained to him that I couldn't tell him about Puzzle Piece and the plan to spirit him to the States because it was too sensitive. I understood why he felt betrayed. We all had grown very close and had learned to trust each other unconditionally; we always kept each other informed. After we wrapped up the investigation, we took photos with each other, and then I packed up our equipment in the US embassy and said my good-byes. The indictments were scheduled to be announced within the next few days, and I wanted to be back in the States when that happened.

One of my CIA partners had already departed—he had decided to leave the agency and work in the private sector. So we had a going away party for him in absentia. We symbolized his presence at the party with items reflecting some of his quirks. These included rotten bananas, an American flag, his sunglasses, the Maltese flag, and a terrorism poster. There was also a coffee cup and sugar, which he always made a mess with and never cleaned up.

I returned to DC on November 7, 1991, after closing down my office in Malta. I flew back on one of the last Pan Am flights—the airline was going out of business. When we landed at Dulles, there was no docking space for the plane.

The announcement of the indictments of Megrahi and Fhimah was made on a grand scale. A press conference was held at the Department of Justice with major media in attendance. Robert Mueller, who would later become FBI director, was the lead DOJ attorney at the time, and he went through the details of the investigation and the evidence uncovered leading up to the indictments. The only problem was that Megrahi and Fhimah were now in Libya, and the only way we could get them to trial was through diplomatic channels.

I received a financial incentive award from FBI Director William Sessions for my contributions to the Pan Am 103 investigation. Agents receive these awards when their contribution to a major investigation is considered significant, the degree of significance determining the amount of the incentive. I was very pleased with the award. Little did I know how my path and that of William Sessions would cross, and what fate had in store for both of us down the road.

I had spent three years of my life totally committed to identifying those responsible for bombing Pan Am Flight 103. It had been an exhilarating, life-altering experience, but I was happy that it was behind me, and ready to move on.

I had been in my OP for nine years and enjoyed every minute of it. And although we could have chosen to stay there until the end of my career, Bernadette and I decided that we needed to start thinking about a change. The question was, What should come next?

Where was Three Sisters Ponds when I needed it?

CHAPTER 13

▲

THE OFFICE OF PROFESSIONAL RESPONSIBILITY

"There but for the Grace of God Go I"

As it turned out, that question was answered very quickly. I received a call from my good friend and former supervisor in the AXFO, now a supervisor in the Office of Professional Responsibility (OPR) at FBI headquarters. OPR is the FBI's dreaded internal affairs unit that investigates misconduct allegations against FBI agents and professional support personnel. He congratulated me on the indictments and asked if I was interested in a promotion—to supervisor in OPR. I knew this would be a significant salary raise, and I was ready for a new challenge in my life.

This was one of those "God intervened" moments.

Without hesitation, I told him that I was very interested. OPR was a highly respected department in the FBI, and only very select agents were placed there. I was honored even to be considered. I was interviewed by the department's deputy assistant director (DAD) and got the job. I was promoted to supervisor and assigned to headquarters.

As I'd hoped it would, OPR turned out to be a challenge. The caseload was tremendous and very hard to stay on top of. Our unit chief (UC) was a tough taskmaster. There was a lot of report writing required, and he reviewed every word, correcting grammar, sentence structure, and spelling. I felt I as though I were back in grade school, as did the other OPR supervisors. We were all somewhat insulted by the UC's editing, but he was the boss. I remember his first preliminary performance evaluation of me, and it was ugly. If things didn't improve, I'd miss the yearly raise or maybe even get booted out.

I believed he was a fair man, and I also knew my report writing was a serious issue. I asked him what I needed to do to turn around my performance. He said that he had grown tired of correcting the same mistakes in my reports and needed to see significant improvement. He then gave me a set of recommendations and a deadline by which to make them happen.

I followed his instructions and did even more than he asked. He was impressed with how quickly I had improved and how quickly I was turning around my cases. To accomplish this I had to work plenty of nights and weekends. I copied all his corrections and made sure those same errors didn't show up again. I ordered Tony Roberts tapes to improve my self-image. I got writing books "for dummies." I started taking ginkgo biloba again and standing on my head in the mornings before work to improve my memory and recall.

I knew I had to make major adjustments in my life if I wanted climb further up the FBI career ladder. Though the other guys in the unit continued to complain about the chief's corrections, I stopped complaining. I knew I needed to improve—not only to pass muster with the unit chief, but to advance in the FBI.

After I moved to OPR, I received my first letter of censure, a written reprimand for violating conduct policy. In this case I was reprimanded for leaving classified documents out of the safe in my office at the American embassy in Malta. Many times while I was in the process of reviewing classified documents, the ambassador or someone from her staff would call me and I would drop what I was doing and go running. The marines assigned to the embassy found the material out of the safe and reported it to the State Department, who forwarded it to the FBI for their review. You might think that would have been a problem or at least embarrassing to someone newly assigned to OPR, but it was actually a badge of honor to have received a letter of censure while working on the bureau's largest criminal investigation at that time. The DAD handed me the letter with a laugh.

About six months later, my UC told me he was astonished how much I had improved my report writing, as well as my verbal briefings. He immediately assigned me to a major OPR matter in our Merrillville, Indiana, resident agency (RA). I was honored that he would assign me such a complicated investigation. Because of its enormity, I had to put together a team of OPR supervisors as well as supervisors from various field offices to fly to Merrillville to assist. The investigation involved numerous allegations of sexual harassment and workplace hostility; it then blossomed into additional allegations of retaliation and intimidation. I had planned for it to be a weeklong investigation, but because of the additional allegations, the investigation lasted two weeks. The Merrillville RA had more than fifty agents and support employees who had to be interviewed. By the time we completed the assignment, we were calling it the "Merrillville Massacre" because of the numerous disciplinary actions that were eventually taken against its employees.

We opened numerous investigations alleging sexual harassment during the years I was assigned to OPR, and we always addressed them as if the victim were a family member. But our initial task was determining whether the allegations had merit.

I was surprised to learn that we didn't have a statute of limitations on certain types of allegations, such as misuse of bureau vehicles or conducting personal business on FBI time. Some of these alleged incidents occurred years before they were reported. We would receive these charges from spouses in the middle of divorce and sometimes even from children, most likely prompted by a disgruntled parent. But we had to investigate them all; no matter how long ago the incident had occurred.

Most the allegations made against agents and support employees were never substantiated. Some of them came from other employees, such as subordinates, or from private citizens. My feeling was that the FBI was not in the business of making people happy, so if you were truly a hardworking agent, you were going to attract the occasional complaint or allegation. I sometimes felt sorry for the subject of an OPR investigative process. I always tried to treat the agent or support employee with fairness and dignity, because in most cases this was the most embarrassing, humiliating, humbling moment of his or her career. My philosophy at the time was "There but for the grace of God go I."

On July 11, 1993, we received allegations that an FBI agent assigned to the Baltimore office had been sexually abusing his two daughters over a fourteen-year period. As part of an agreement with prosecutors, the agent pleaded guilty to two counts of second-degree sexual offense and two counts of child abuse. In exchange for his plea, the state dropped eighteen other counts against him. This case was assigned to another OPR supervisor, which was fortunate because I'm not sure I could have handled the agent fairly or objectively.

Other cases included the rape of a female agent by a peer, who was subsequently arrested, prosecuted, and sentenced to jail. I also inherited a case in which an agent pleaded guilty to manslaughter for killing a female informant with whom he had had "an inappropriate emotional and sexual relationship."

Working in OPR was an eye-opening experience. I never realized that any of our agents—albeit a very tiny minority—could engage in such despicable behavior.

The most high-profile case we were assigned to at OPR involved Director William Sessions, who along with his wife was alleged to have used bureau personnel and the resources of their protective detail, such as government cars and planes, for personal use. The charges came from members of the director's personal security detail, who were FBI agents.

These were tense times for my unit. We were conducting the investigation of a sitting FBI director whose office was just down the hall at FBI headquarters. We eventually requested that the matter be reassigned to the Department of Justice's OPR, because we were too vulnerable to intimidation.

On July 19, 1993, Sessions was removed from office by President Bill Clinton, who appointed Deputy Director Floyd I. Clarke as acting director. The president noted that William Session's most significant achievement was opening the FBI to more women and minorities. Louis J. Freeh was sworn in as director of the FBI on September 1, 1993. Freeh had served as an FBI agent from 1975 to 1981. In 1991 he was appointed US District Court judge for the Southern District of New York, where he served until he was nominated to be director of the FBI.

In April 1992 I received a case alleging that one of our agents assigned to the McAllen Texas RA had assaulted an officer in the US Border Patrol. According to the officer, he and the agent had disagreed about how a joint agency investigation was to proceed, and the agent shoved him in the chest and threatened more of the same if the officer didn't back down. I was asked to fly to Texas and conduct the OPR investigation. Based on the report from the border patrol officer, I envisioned our agent as big and mean, and I expected him to be uncooperative.

When I got to the office and met him, I burst into laughter. He was short, with a slight build, and about as unintimidating as it gets. After I got control of myself, I began interviewing the agent and found him very cooperative. His version of the altercation was very different from that of the border patrol officer. He said he had shoved the officer only because the man had moved aggressively toward him. There were no other witnesses or videos to confirm what had actually happened, so the allegations were considered unsubstantiated and the matter dropped by both agencies.

As I was leaving the border patrol office, one of the officers told me to look at the TV, because the FBI, after a fifty-one-day siege, had just burned down the Branch Davidian's compound in Waco, Texas, and killed eighty people, including children. I was stunned by the scale of the tragedy. After I left, I remember thinking about what the border patrol officer had said and the way he had said it. Clearly there was a lot of anti-FBI attitude floating around that office, although I wasn't sure what had caused it other than professional rivalry.

Not long afterwards I was asked to speak to a new agents' class at Quantico about OPR and what we did. I was honored but nervous. I put in a lot of time preparing my presentation, and as insurance I swallowed an extra dose of gingko biloba before showtime. Once I got going, I wasn't nervous. I did feel as though I spoke longer than the class counselor expected, but overall I thought it went very well.

After working at FBIHQ I realized I wasn't a "headquarters" type, and I knew I'd never be promoted any further if I stayed there. I didn't have the academic pedigree to survive FBIHQ politics and compete head-to-head. Even among black agents, I wasn't one of "the talented tenth," as W. E. B. Dubois called it. I was a former cop who had gotten his degree through night school. I stood a better chance of advancing through field office promotions.

Having been a supervisor at FBI headquarters for three years, I was eligible to start applying for supervisory positions in field offices across the country, because I had never been a field office supervisor. I needed the support of my unit chief, which I had. As soon as I started looking, I noticed an open position in Hawaii for a criminal squad supervisor. It was the last day of the job posting, but I took a chance and put in for it anyway because I felt perfect for the position. I was a former cop, had worked criminal cases in New York, was SWAT-trained, and had worked in OPR. That last experience ensured that I knew how to handle sensitive personnel problems and could assist in office management.

Rumor had it that the previous supervisor had stepped down because it was difficult to manage the strong personalities on his squad. I immediately faxed my bio and résumé to the Honolulu Division career board. I later heard that when they received my résumé they were already looking hard at another person, but when they saw my background, I was chosen instead. This was another one of those "God intervened" moments.

I couldn't believe they were going to pay me to move to Hawaii and live there. My wife was elated, too. I needed to think through how to become a successful squad supervisor, but Three Sisters Ponds were gone. My substitutes had become the Atlantic Ocean when I was assigned to the Norfolk office, the Hudson River in New York, and the Potomac River in Alexandria. Sitting beside those bodies of water helped center and calm me, but oh how I missed Three Sisters Ponds.

CHAPTER 14

▲

HAWAII

"Paradise with a Caveat"

My wife and I took a ten-day trip to Honolulu in October 1994 to find a place to live once I officially reported there. We felt a bit guilty because the US government was footing the entire bill for our first-ever visit to Hawaii. We stayed at the world-famous Hilton Hotel in the Hilton Hawaiian Village. We had an oceanfront room with a view of Diamond Head. It was awesome!

We found a home we liked in Ewa Beach, on the west end of Honolulu. It was a two-story townhouse with a two-car garage in a gated community. We took a little time for some touring, but we kept it low-key, as this was intended to be a business trip. After completing our ten days in Hawaii, we flew back to Washington, DC, but we were very excited about returning to Hawaii to live there, at least for a while.

When we returned to the mainland, we packed up all our household goods and shipped them and our vehicles to California, where they were placed on a barge and transported by sea to

Hawaii. We left for Hawaii in December 1994, in the middle of a typical Washington snowstorm. Our timing couldn't have been more perfect.

On the plane I thought about how suitable Hawaii was as a replacement for my OP. We stayed at the Hilton Hawaiian Village for the ninety days we were allowed for temporary quarters. This time we stayed in a condominium, another oceanfront with a view of Diamond Head. It was first-class.

The squad I was assigned to was being managed by an acting supervisor. Before reporting to the office, I met with him at our hotel to get a briefing on what to expect. He was of Polish and Asian descent, and I found him to be a hardworking and intelligent agent. He gave me a very thorough overview of the squad members, the work, and the problems that had caused the previous supervisor to step down to become a regular street agent. The squad was split into A and B teams, and the acting supervisor led one of them. It was clear that he wasn't comfortable running the whole squad and was glad I had arrived.

I realized I would have my hands full, but it sounded like my job was to unite a squad full of heavies into an effective, cohesive team. Fortunately, I had a little time to consider my strategy: I wasn't due to report to the office for another week because Bernadette and I were finalizing the paperwork on our new home and arranging to move in.

Our office was located in the federal courthouse building in downtown Honolulu. On my first day in the office, the acting supervisor introduced me to the SAC, the ASAC, the other supervisors, and the members of my squad. He showed me my new office and continued to brief me on the types of cases worked on the squad and the status of those cases. I was very impressed with him. We then left the office to go to lunch, and I was surprised when I realized he had taken me to eat a strip joint. Was this some sort of a setup because I had just left OPR, or was it normal protocol for agents in Hawaii? Or did he think going to strip clubs was a "black thing" that would make me feel more at home? After getting to know the acting supervisor, I realized he meant nothing by it and probably just thought it might be entertaining—and it was, somewhat. But at the time I couldn't get out of there fast enough.

There were ten agents assigned to the criminal squad, which was responsible for violent crimes and major theft investigations. The violent crimes investigations covered bank robberies, kidnappings, gangs, extortion, and crimes against children. The major thefts included theft from interstate shipments and art theft. The squad had a special operations group (SOG) that handled physical surveillances and included two surveillance planes and pilots. A technically trained agent, a telecommunications specialist, and two electronics technicians supported our criminal investigations. Our territory covered the Hawaiian Islands, Guam, Saipan, and American Samoa.

I was surprised by the number of bank robberies that occurred in Hawaii each year, considering there aren't a lot of places to hide on the islands. While the squad had a high solution rate, its case files were in disarray and needed immediate attention. In addition, it was obvious to me that several agents on the squad weren't working in a manner commensurate with their experience level. I had serious conversations with them and gave them performance plans for improvement. I reviewed every case and provided direction on how each was to be brought up to date.

The squad began to gel and eventually became an effective unit.

❦

The great thing about living on Hawaii was that I didn't have to wear a suit or tie to work; the only time I wore a tie was when I had to make a court appearance. Everyday dress in Hawaii was slacks with an Aloha shirt. I ended up with a great collection of those shirts. The best place for variety and price was Hilo Hattie, which had stores centrally located on all the islands.

I really enjoyed Hawaii, and for months I still couldn't believe I was living there. I was a long way from Baltimore, but I was right in line with the dreams and goals I'd launched from that bench at Three Sisters Ponds in Druid Hill Park. I had traveled to Europe, South America, and Egypt. I had gone from being a street cop to a supervisor at FBI headquarters to a field office supervisor in Hawaii. I had sailed solo from Washington, DC, down the Potomac River, up the Chesapeake Bay to Baltimore, and back. I even had my red convertible Corvette. I firmly believe that in America, every dream is possible!

My wife was adjusting very well to Hawaii. In the past when we moved, she would spend the first couple of months getting the house in order, and then she'd start looking for a job. It took her over a year to start looking for a job in Hawaii because she was too busy enjoying the beaches, weather, scenery, and shopping. She eventually found a job with the American Hawaii Cruise Line, which offered seven-day island cruises. The good news was that we were able to take free trips. One night we cruised around the Big Island's Kilauea Volcano and watched bright red lava cascading down the mountain into the sea, which created billowing clouds of steam. That was another experience I'll never forget.

My taste in food changed while we were living in Hawaii. I learned to like sushi and sashimi—and I'll have to admit, before I moved to Hawaii, I would never have considered eating anything raw. We learned to eat sticky rice at every meal, including with eggs for breakfast. Spam was very popular in Hawaii, where people ate it with rice or eggs and in soups. (Back in Baltimore we called Spam "welfare ham." Oh well!)

You can't live in Hawaii without developing an interest in sumo wrestling, and the Hawaiian-born Akebono (real name Chad Haakeo Rowan) was a very popular sumo wrestler when we lived there. We prepared for his matches as if they were football games, with food and beverages in place.

Even though I was unable to attend professional football games while living in Hawaii, I did see the pro bowl games held there. They offered a great opportunity to see the best professional football players, past and present, all at once.

The planes assigned to my squad, two Cessna 182s, were used for aerial surveillance in support of the SOG team. The pilots were very experienced agents with military backgrounds. Every once in a while they would have me fly with them during surveillances or required training flights.

The pilots took me up on one training-day flight from Honolulu to Maui. While over the Pacific between the islands, we saw a pod of whales breaching and diving all in unison, as if they were moving to music only they could hear. On another occasion we flew low over Pearl Harbor, and the pilots told me to look down. I could see the sunken and damaged *Arizona*. "This was the view that the Japanese had when they bombed," one of the pilots remarked. I was speechless. I thought about the "date that will live in infamy," and all the lives lost. It was an experience to cherish because not everyone is allowed to fly into this sacred airspace, and certainly not at such a low altitude.

While in Hawaii I became very interested in the war in the Pacific, especially the Japanese military atrocities. Of course, I visited the USS Arizona Memorial several times. During one of my visits to Guam, I went to the World War II Museum there and became very angry at what the Japanese military did to the citizens of Guam during the war. After that museum visit, I felt a strong need to see Hiroshima and the Japanese peace park.

From Guam I continued on to Osaka, Japan, flying into Kansai International Airport, which is built on an artificial island. (It's my understanding that a system of hydraulics compensates for rising and lowering tides.) I had made reservations to spend the night in the Osaka Hilton before heading to Hiroshima, so I caught a cab from the airport and asked the driver to take me there. He did not speak any English, and we were going back and forth with each other, almost getting into an argument. I couldn't get him to understand that I wanted to go to the Osaka Hilton Hotel. He kept saying "Hilton Osaka," and I would say "Osaka Hilton," and meanwhile I wasn't sure exactly where I was and I was afraid that he was taking me to the wrong place. This exchange went on for at least half an hour and I was getting into a real panic, when suddenly I looked up and I saw the Osaka Hilton. We both laughed, realizing that he did understand me after all. I gave him a good tip and checked into the hotel.

I checked out the next morning and caught a cab to the train station. I had reserved a luxury seat on the Shinkansen, Japan's bullet train, to Hiroshima. It was a smooth, fast trip. I walked through the town and was surprised at how modern and developed it was considering what had happened there forty years ago. It was a very clean city with upscale stores, and it even had a baseball team and a stadium. The only evidence of what had happened there were the remains of a domed building whose steel girders had melted. I took pictures with some Japanese students who were in the area. (They thought I was Michael Jordan.) Then I visited the Peace Memorial Museum and was surprised to see that the exhibits did not mention why we bombed Hiroshima—only that we killed innocent Japanese children.

After World War II, Hawaii became the final home for the USS *Missouri*, on which the Japanese military surrendered. To see it permanently docked close to the Arizona memorial, representing the beginning and end of that terrible war, was a sight to behold.

෴

Soon after I returned to Hawaii I was approached by US Attorney Steven Alm, who asked me to assist in the apprehension of a group of Hawaiians who wanted to see a sovereign and independent Hawaii and were considered dangerous militants. Known as the Nation of Hawai'i, the group was led by Dennis "Bumpy" Pu'uhonua Kanahele. They wrote up their own "subpoenas" and began serving them on Hawaii's federal judges. The purpose of the subpoenas was not clear, but Bumpy was indicted on August 2, 1995, on charges of interfering with Honolulu police officers while they attempted to arrest a federal fugitive in January 1994. Bumpy was also accused of harboring the fugitive and obstructing a US marshal's attempt to arrest him two months later. Alm took the group's "subpoenas" as a threat to the safety and security of the federal judiciary. I was asked to help the US Marshals coordinate the arrests of Bumpy and his group on federal obstruction charges.

I was concerned that their arrests would generate a lot of publicity and hostility throughout Hawaii. I flew my SOG team to Maui, where Bumpy was at the time. The team began reporting on his movements and determined that he was planning to fly Hawaiian Airlines back to Honolulu that day with his lieutenants/bodyguards. We asked Hawaiian Airlines to dock the plane in an isolated area of the terminal upon landing in Honolulu. In the meantime, the SOG team boarded the flight from Maui with Bumpy and his men. After the flight landed at the Honolulu International Airport, the SOG team arrested them without incident and turned them over to the US Marshals.

Once the media became aware of the arrests, they had a field day. I was pleasantly surprised and impressed by Bumpy and his men, who were very cooperative with us.

Initially Bumpy contended that the United States had no lawful jurisdiction over him, but he eventually pleaded guilty to the felony charge of obstruction. In 1998 he was sentenced to four months in prison; the judge gave him credit for the three and a half months he had spent in prison without bail. The judge also fined him $500 and ordered him to spend another four months under electronic monitoring at his Waimanalo home. In 2002 Gov. Benjamin J. Cayetano granted Bumpy a full pardon. Bumpy vowed to avoid all violence, choosing instead a Gandhian path of passive civil resistance.

I had a great SOG team. They loved supporting investigations with surveillances and being involved in arrests. They had the best of all worlds: they got a piece of all the action without having to do all the paperwork.

One night we received information from a mainland FBI office that was helping local law enforcement track down a couple of fugitives wanted on an armed home invasion warrant. They believed the fugitives were somewhere in the Waikiki area of Honolulu. We were allowed to help local law enforcement as long as there was an existing warrant, so we were faxed a copy of the warrant and were given descriptions, but not much else. We did have a cell phone number for one of suspects and began to trace his location through a system called Trigger Fish, which triangulates cell sites to pinpoint a call. At the time this technology was all new to us. The fugitives were eventually located in Waikiki and arrested without incident by the SOG team.

In 1996 a US citizen assaulted two other Americans at McMurdo Station, a federal research center in Antarctica. I knew I was responsible for the FBI's criminal investigations in the Hawaiian Islands, American Samoa, Guam, and Saipan; now I learned in a call from headquarters that I was also responsible for McMurdo Station, and I was ordered to send a team of agents there.

The United States operates three year-round research stations in Antarctica, as well as two research vessels and numerous seasonal field camps in the summer. Federal law extends special maritime and territorial jurisdiction to cover offenses committed by or against American nationals in Antarctic. Because Hawaii was the closest federal presence to Antarctica for jurisdiction and prosecution, I was tasked to send my SOG team there to investigate and arrest, if necessary.

A special deputy assigned to McMurdo Station detained the suspect, and under my direction and that of the US Attorney's office in Hawaii, he secured the evidence and placed the suspect under continual observation until my SOG team could assume control of the situation.

It was a long trip for the team, and we had to make sure that when they arrived in Christchurch, New Zealand, appropriate cold-weather garments were waiting for them. Obviously, living in Hawaii didn't require them to wear warm clothing—or even own it. When they arrived in Antarctica they conducted the investigation, arrested the suspect, and transported him back to Hawaii, where he was prosecuted. I'm sure the SOG team will never forget the experience.

✦✦✦

Thank God the FBI has a culture of health and fitness. When I arrived in Honolulu, I had a growth on my neck that the physician at headquarters had told me to have checked right away—and that was six months earlier. I stupidly waited until I got to Hawaii and got my squad in order before I went to a doctor; I didn't want anything to get in the way of my transfer. I'd taken a big risk, but fortunately the biopsy was negative. The bureau requires semiannual physicals and fitness tests, and they are lifesavers. (Although many agents may not realize that fact during their careers, they will certainly appreciate it by the time they are ready to retire). A good number of agents keep in shape, mostly by running.

I was invited to go to Tokyo to attend an organized crime conference sponsored by the Japanese national police. The conference covered the Japanese branches of the Yakuza and Triad criminal organizations and their impact on Asian Pacific Rim countries. I brought Bernadette along with me. We were invited to the Imperial Palace, where we had access that the public doesn't normally get. While Tokyo had American fast food staples like McDonalds and Denny's, we also enjoyed traditional Japanese fare. When we dined out with our hosts, they were amazed at how well I used chopsticks, but I had gotten a great deal of experience with them eating Japanese food in Hawaii.

Some things did take a little getting used to. For example, all the buttons and switches in our hotel seemed to be set lower than they are in the United States, I guess because of the height difference between Japanese and Americans. And the cab drivers in Tokyo all wore white gloves and surgical masks to prevent picking up germs from us tourists. But the Japanese scenery and culture were fascinating. Seeing Mount Fuji was a great experience for us, and Bernadette bought a Japanese kimono that was beautifully embroidered with very rich colors. When we got back to our residence in Hawaii, we hung it on one of our walls, because it was just as pretty as a picture.

Hawaii was an expensive place to live, and many of our new agents were struggling to make it on the bureau's entry-level salaries. I was fortunate enough to be there on a supervisor's salary, boosted by a 20 percent cost-of-living increase. With Bernadette working, too, we were very comfortable financially.

I spent three of our five years on Hawaii attempting to qualify for the Big Island Ironman competition. I began doing two-a-days, training in the morning before work and at night with a triathlon team. The first two years, just as I got close to the qualifying date, I ended up with ruptured discs that required back surgery. During my third attempt I fell off my bike near the sandy beach at Barbers Point Naval Air Station, not far from my home. It became clear that doing the Ironman wasn't in the cards for me, although I had managed to complete a couple of Olympic-distance triathlons in Honolulu. I was ready to try something new—and as it turned out, change was just around the corner.

ৡৢ

In October 1996, FBI headquarters received complaints from the CIA that the Honolulu office wasn't properly conducting the criminal terrorism extraterritorial investigation into the March 8, 1995, assassination of two US Consulate employees in Karachi, Pakistan. The Honolulu office was responsible for all cases in which Americans were victims of murder, kidnapping, or serious assault in Asia or the Pacific Rim. The investigation was being handled by a squad responsible for foreign counterintelligence as well as applicant background investigations, and its supervisor didn't have sufficient terrorism or criminal investigative experience. Headquarters was also unhappy with the status of another high-profile investigation in India involving the kidnapping and assumed murder of five foreign tourists, including one American.

Deputy Director (DD) Bob "Bear" Bryant asked our SAC, John Shiman, who was aware of my extraterritorial investigative experience, to ask me if I would be interested in forming a new counterterrorism squad in Honolulu that would include an extraterritorial terrorism (ETT) program. This was another one of those "God intervened" moments. I was ready for a change, and I had truly missed working ETT cases. Shiman said my first priority would be to straighten out the two major cases in Pakistan and India. Bryant, meanwhile, asked me to send him a proposal to justify the establishment of an ETT program in Hawaii. Realizing that these cases required the use of a significant number of experienced agents, he said I could draw personnel from other field offices, if necessary.

I couldn't wait to get my teeth back into ETT cases and to have business cards that read "Counterterrorism Supervisor." I hand-picked agents for reassignment to me from the foreign counterintelligence squad, and after interviewing each one personally, I made case assignments. I knew that not everyone wanted to travel overseas because of family constraints. It was also very dangerous work, and I had to let them know that fact up front. *I'm living in paradise, but I'll be working in hell,* I thought. *I guess this is paradise with a caveat.*

For the most part, headquarters and the SAC gave me free reign to choose who would be on my squad. My aim was to create a squad of heavies, if possible, as they would be tasked with an important mission. The squad I formed consisted of seventeen agents and eight support staff. Everyone assigned to the squad had to have an official passport for international travel. Our responsibilities included domestic and international terrorism investigations, ETT investigations, and civil rights investigations. I would serve as the crisis management coordinator for the division.

I was asked to review and update the investigations in India and Pakistan, and to do it quickly. I had to study up on those countries' history, culture, religions, languages, and geography. I had to be particularly careful because I would be bouncing back and forth between India and Pakistan, which were at war with each other. I needed the help of both nations, and I had to be careful what I said and did so as not to offend. I also knew both countries would be running their intelligence agents at us. I assembled a war room in the office so I could post information and maps on the walls. I'm a very visual person; if I can see something up on the wall, I get better clarity than if it's tucked away in a file.

I reviewed both investigations and was not satisfied with the quality and thoroughness of what had been done—I fully understood why the CIA was upset with us over the Karachi case. I decided I needed to travel to India and Pakistan, conduct reinvestigations, and bring those files up to date to give us a better chance of identifying those responsible. Two of my best agents and I traveled to New Delhi on October 21, 1996.

♪♪

Our investigation in India concerned the July 4, 1995, kidnapping of six foreign tourists by Al-Faran, a terrorist organization located in Srinagar (Jammu/Kashmiri), India. The six victims, who were kidnapped while trekking through the Himalayans, included two British tourists, Keith Mangan and Paul Wells; two Americans, John Childs of Simsbury, Connecticut, and Donald Hutchings of Spokane, Washington; a German, Dirk Hasert; and a Norwegian, Hans Christian Ostrø. A note released by the kidnappers a day later read, "Accept our demands or face dire consequences. We are fighting against anti-Islamic forces. Western countries are anti-Islam, and America is the biggest enemy of Islam."

John Childs managed to escape and was rescued four days later. He was able to provide excellent intelligence on his captors. For several months attempts were made to negotiate with the guerrillas, but without success. We believed the guerrillas grew tired of moving their captives from camp to camp and eventually killed them. Ostrø was beheaded by his abductors; his body was found near Pahalgam on August 13, 1995, with the words *Al Faran* carved onto his chest.

The kidnappers demanded the release of Pakistani militant Maulana Masood Azhar and twenty other people imprisoned by India. Several national and international organizations issued appeals to Al-Faran to release the tourists, and representatives of the embassies of the victims' countries also visited Kashmir frequently to seek their release, again without success. In December 1995, the kidnappers left a note that they were no longer holding the men hostage. Mangan, Wells, Hutchings, and Hasert have never been found and are presumed to have been killed.

In May 1996, a captured rebel told Indian investigators and FBI agents he had heard that all four hostages had been shot dead on December 13, 1995, nine days after an Indian military ambush killed four of the original hostage-takers, including the man said to have been their leader, Abdul Hamid Turki.

The kidnappings were widely covered by western press and helped bring terrorism in Kashmir to the attention of the international community.

Donald Hutchings' wife, Jane Schelly, made repeated trips to the region to get answers, but in vain. By the time I became involved in the investigation, the hostages were already believed dead; my job was to work with Indian authorities to locate their bodies and return them to the families, and to identify and apprehend their murderers.

We remained in New Delhi until October 25, 1996. While there, I met with the American ambassador to India, Frank G. Wisner, as well as CIA representatives, and we reviewed and copied the case files our agents had maintained in the embassy. We left with the intention of coming back to New Delhi after we had consolidated that information with the information we already had on file in Honolulu. This would bring the case current and put us in a strong position to reinvestigate.

✼

We flew from New Delhi directly to Karachi, the largest city in Pakistan and its main seaport and financial center. It is also a major hub of higher education in South Asia and the wider Islamic world.

The US consulate in Karachi is a tempting target for Islamic fundamentalists because of its prominent position downtown, next to the Marriott Hotel, and because it is accessible from two side roads. I found Karachi a scary and dangerous place. Americans are not much liked by the Pakistanis, who believe the money we give their country gives us control of whoever is running the government, civilian or military.

The US consulate general sent an armed escort to pick us up at the Karachi airport. You couldn't just land there and catch a cab—that was too dangerous. The vehicle that picked us up was a Chevrolet Suburban that had been converted into an armored tank. It was accompanied by two truckloads of Pakistani officers wearing body armor and carrying full automatic shoulder weapons. They took us to the consulate, where I met with the consulate general and explained my plan for action in Pakistan. He and the diplomatic security officer briefed me on threats to American safety in Pakistan and on precautions that we should take if we wished to stay alive there. We then checked into the Sheraton Hotel, about two blocks from the embassy. Pakistan was the only country that allowed the FBI to carry weapons within its borders, although that was not official policy. Our weapons were maintained in the consulate, and we carried them while working in Pakistan.

Under investigation were the March 8, 1995, murders of two American consular officials who worked for the CIA and the Department of State: Jackie Van Landingham, a thirty-three-year-old secretary, and Gary C. Durell, a forty-five-year-old communications specialist. A third consulate employee, Mark McCloy, was injured in the attack. The victims were riding to work in the consulate shuttle bus on a busy highway when gunmen leapt from a stolen taxi and opened fire.

After I checked into the Sheraton I began feeling sick, so I asked for the closest pharmacy, which was across the street from the hotel. I walked there and was standing in line when I noticed that everyone was staring at me. Then I remembered I'd been told not to leave the hotel because I could be killed or kidnapped. I began to sweat, and one of the Pakistanis in line told me it was unsafe for me to be there and to get back to the hotel. I waited until I got my medicine and then made a quick dash back. That was scary—and dumb.

We remained in Pakistan for about a month, traveling back and forth between the consulate in Karachi and the US embassy in Islamabad. We interviewed witnesses, reviewed files and records, and even visited the crime scene to redo the investigation there. That last trip was very dangerous, but the Karachi police provided security while we rephotographed and reprocessed the scene.

One night during one of our trips to Islamabad, I broke down in my hotel room, trembling and crying uncontrollably because I was so upset at how screwed up the investigation was. I felt we had really let down the CIA, as well as the victims' families. I became even more determined to get the investigation on the right track, whatever it took.

After about a week and a half there, we were able to produce a comprehensive investigative report with a great deal of detail on the murders. In the report we identified new, critical information that could lead to the identities of those responsible. The report also identified potential groups and individual suspects who could have played a role in the crimes, and it laid out a substantial number of promising investigative leads that needed to be pursued. When I briefed the CIA's assistant station chief on the findings, he became very excited and started to make phone calls to his boss in Islamabad and to CIA headquarters. I asked him to hold off until I'd had a chance to brief his boss, as well as the ambassador.

We flew to Islamabad and briefed the CIA station chief and the ambassador, Thomas W. Simons Jr., regarding our updated report on the murder investigation. Both were very pleased. What they liked about the report was that it clearly summarized what had happened (including crime scene photos), it uncovered evidence of preplanning by the attackers, and it identified potential suspects. It also explained the promising new leads and where the investigation was heading. The men also liked the fact that I could give them a copy of the report. I faxed the document back to FBI headquarters and they were happy with it, too. I had used what I had learned from the Scottish officers and their HOLMES system to organize the investigation and the report.

While in India and Pakistan I was introduced to "New Delhi belly." People living in those countries have a higher tolerance to bacteria in food than we do. To avoid getting sick I tried to eat at the embassies or at places the embassies recommended. But one morning I threw caution to the wind and ate some porridge served at our rooming house in Islamabad. I got sick immediately and ended up hugging the toilet for hours. Fortunately, the pharmacists had some medicine—"miracle medicine," we called it—that cleared up the problem quickly.

When I briefed Ambassador Simmons on the status of our investigation into the Karachi murders, he told me about the Taliban in Afghanistan. At that time he was the ambassador responsible for both countries. He said he was in talks with the Taliban leadership and that they were okay to deal with, but they needed to change the way they treated women, which was not only wrong, but also terrible PR for them. Little did we know that we would be at war with the Taliban just a few years later, as a result of their support for Al Qaeda and the 9/11 attack.

The CIA station chief was happy with the report because he finally had solid information to convey to headquarters and to the family of the slain employee. He invited me and my team back to Langley to personally brief the desk monitoring the case. He said they would also fill us in on CIA capabilities in the field.

We still had a lot of investigating ahead of us, but at least now we had a sense of direction, and our customers, the CIA, were satisfied. I sent my two agents back to Honolulu for a well-earned break, while I remained in Islamabad to continue the investigation. At that time I was staying in a rooming house not far from the embassy.

On the morning of November 7, 1996, I went outside to get my newspaper and found the streets abandoned and eerily quiet. The newspaper was also late, which was unusual. I found out later that there had been a coup d'état in Pakistan: President Farooq Leghari had dismissed Prime Minister Benezir Bhutto's government and persuaded the military to assist in seizing control of the country. They placed Prime Minister Bhutto under house arrest and jailed her husband, who they suspected was involved in murder and theft. Apparently the military had waited for the prime minister's husband to return to Pakistan before they took action against both of them.

I was afraid this could have negative consequences for the ongoing investigation in Karachi. When I returned to the embassy that day, I talked to the deputy ambassador and our CIA representatives, who referred me to the military attaché assigned to the embassy. We all agreed that in order to keep the Karachi police behind the investigation, the military would have to encourage them.

Our military attaché arranged a meeting with Mahmud Ahmed, a directorate major general for the Pakistani military intelligence, to discuss the need for military support. I was escorted by heavily armed soldiers to meet with him at a fortified military base in a very remote part of Pakistan. The major general was a very distinguished-looking man with a handlebar mustache, and he was fluent in several languages. After I briefed him on the status of our investigation, he contacted law enforcement in Karachi and ordered them to provide meaningful cooperation. He said he was very interested in the American Civil War, so I told him about Ken Burns's excellent PBS series on the war, and I promised to send him a set of the videos when I returned to the States, which I did. I also invited him to come to Quantico and provide briefings to our agents on the status of Pakistani military support of our investigation, saying that while he was there he could tour some of the major Civil War battlefields. He, in turn, gave me a copy of *War Above the Clouds* by Martin A. Sugarman, a pictorial history of the war between Pakistan and India fought in the mountains separating the two countries. I thanked him and told him I would always treasure his gift.

Upon my return to Karachi I contacted the police, and we met in one of their station houses to discuss my investigative needs. I told them I wanted to interview several Pakistani citizens, and they made those people available; our consulate provided translators. I also asked the Karachi police to re-advertise the $2 million reward for information leading to an arrest in the case, and they did. We had a few walk-ins, but no one who had information of value. Before I left Pakistan I purchased some rugs and a traditional Pakistani dress called a *shawa kamese*. My wife wore it to some of our office parties.

✌

I returned to Honolulu on November 21, 1996. I had been gone for a month but now had to leave again because we wanted to take the CIA up on their invitation to visit their headquarters in Virginia. When we arrived at Langley they gave us the red carpet treatment and provided great briefings on their high-tech information analysis systems. We were also invited to FBI headquarters to update the ETT unit on the murder case in Karachi.

Over the next couple of years, the ETT cases kept me very busy. I was able to take the occasional vacation with Bernadette, although it's hard to say that with a straight face considering I was living in Hawaii. But I couldn't really get away from work because my agents were constantly calling me with briefings from India and Pakistan.

I traveled to Guam several times because we had agents assigned to FBI offices there and in Saipan. I also taught international terrorism classes to representatives from law enforcement and intelligence agencies from countries in Asia and the Pacific Rim, such as Japan, Singapore, Hong Kong, Taiwan, the Philippines, Malaysia, South Korea, Pakistan, India, the Republic of China, Australia, New Zealand, and the Commonwealth of the Northern Mariana Islands. It was a great experience and provided strong contact possibilities for when we needed to travel to those countries. Of course, my presentations dealt with my experience working the Pan Am Flight 103 case, which was a subject of great interest to my classes.

When we traveled to India or Pakistan, we always had stopovers in either Hong Kong or Bangkok. We were usually in Bangkok for a few days waiting for our visas to enter Pakistan, or in Hong Kong for a few days waiting for a connecting flight to New Delhi. This gave us time to do a little touring. Tiger Woods was world-famous by then, and the fact that his mother was Thai had been widely publicized. Several times the flight attendants on Thai Airlines mistook me for Tiger. I told them that I wasn't Tiger, but I wished I had his golf game and his money. They were usually embarrassed at first, and then they laughed.

Before I started taking these trips with my agents, I wondered why they liked Bangkok so much. It didn't take me long to find out on my first visit. It was a beautiful place, the people were very friendly, and the US dollar went a long way there. The food was exceptional, and I felt very safe, which allowed me to relax. I found an Indian tailor who could take a few measurements and make suits, sports coats, cotton shirts, ties, and slacks from scratch. His prices were very reasonable, and he mailed the finished garments back to the

States. My agents also enjoyed the Bangkok nightlife, and they especially liked the strip clubs, whose stages were loaded with young, beautiful Thai women dancing seductively. At about ten or eleven at night, the shows would really begin—those women could do extraordinary things with their bodies.

During one stopover in Bangkok I had a couple of days to kill, so I decided to take a day trip to the bridge on the River Kwai, which was well known from the movie of the same name. It was a very enlightening tour. I took a bus from the hotel to the train station and rode a very old train through the Thai countryside. It was interesting to see the rice paddies and farmers using oxen to plow their fields. When I got to the bridge, a major tourist attraction with several pavilions in the immediate area, I saw some of the biggest elephants I have ever seen. The tour covered the history of World War II, the Japanese imprisonment of Americans and British soldiers, the bombing of the bridge, and the slave labor used to rebuild it.

Our stops in Hong Kong were also enjoyable; the people there were friendly, and the food was good. We managed to get some sightseeing in while we were there. One interesting thing about Hong Kong was landing at its airport: it was a scary approach, and particularly so at night, because the airport was downtown and the plane had to safely navigate through the skyscrapers, just barely missing them before touching down. On one trip I took the tram up to the top of Victoria Peak, a mountain overlooking Hong Kong's Repulse Bay; we also took a boat tour on the bay. Both Bangkok and Hong Kong reminded me of some of the old Jean-Claude Van Damme kickboxing movies, because a lot of the scenes were filmed there.

✺

On January 22, 1997, after completing the review and reinvestigation of the case in India, I flew from Honolulu to New Delhi with two of my agents to complete the report. There were still documents in the embassy file cabinets that needed to be reviewed and interviews that needed to be conducted to bring the report fully up to date and identify leads requiring follow-up. Over the course of two weeks, we fused all the investigative information into a cogent report. Throughout our investigation in India, the wife of one of the captured hostages stayed in constant contact with my case agent to keep abreast of new developments.

The Indian intelligence service arranged for us to conduct a couple of interviews with Kashmirian dissidents in one of the service's facilities. According to one of my agents, as he was seated at a table, interviewing a dissident, he felt something hit his leg. He looked under the table and found a recording device that had come loose. He taped it back in place. Obviously, Indian intelligence was just as interested as we were in what the dissidents had to say. There was no need to protest the incident; we were in their country and had to expect to be surveilled and recorded by them.

I briefed the ambassador and his deputy, explaining that the remaining work was in Kashmir and that I needed the help of police in that area to locate the bodies of the victims and arrest those responsible for their murder. I was told that there was a newly elected governor in Srinagar, the summer capital of the Indian state of Jammu and Kashmir, and that an appointment would be made for us to meet him and solicit his support.

So I flew to Srinagar with the ambassador's deputy to meet with the governor. As we made our landing approach, I looked out the window and saw military tanks circling the airport, as well as bunkers manned by heavily armed soldiers. Until that moment I hadn't realized what I was getting myself into.

I had planned to take pictures after we landed, but that plan came to a sudden end when airport authorities searched my bags and confiscated the camera batteries. There was a war going on between India and Pakistan, and Kashmirian rebels were fighting for independence. Batteries were not allowed in Kashmir because they could be used to trigger explosives, so no cameras or picture taking was allowed there. When we went through customs, we were searched so thoroughly that I felt I'd been physically and sexually assaulted.

After the search gauntlet, we were met by the governor's security detail. Wearing masks and black uniforms, they carried shoulder weapons, side arms, grenades, and extra ammunition. Several military vehicles loaded with soldiers waited for us, covering our front, flank, and rear, and we traveled in a convoy to the governor's mansion. I was surprised by the quaintness of the mansion, but it was heavily guarded. I had to wonder why someone would want to be governor and have to live under such tight security. It didn't look like being governor of Kashmir was much fun.

As we entered the mansion we were met by the governor himself. He was very pleasant and receptive, taking us into a conference room, where he served us tea and pastries. The assistant ambassador explained why we were there, after which I introduced myself and made a personal appeal for his support to help locate the bodies of our victims and round up the Kashmiri rebels responsible for their kidnapping and murder. He pledged his full support, and he seemed serious and sincere.

After completing the session with the governor, our next step was to meet with the leadership of the police in the area and give them the same briefing, but that could not occur for a few days. We had reservations at the Welcome Hotel in Kashmir. The wall of my hotel room was riddled with what looked like bullet holes that appeared to have originated from outside. They tracked down the wall at bed height. I called the reception desk and asked them to send hot water bottles up to my room. I figured the safest place for me to sleep would be on the floor, on top of hot water bottles—and below the line of bullet holes.

Because of the delay, we found time to tour the area. The Himalayas were not far from the hotel, and at the foot of the mountains was Dal Lake. It was filled with large houseboats where I assume trekkers and visitors to Kashmir stayed. It was a shame that such a beautiful place was in a war zone and couldn't be safely enjoyed.

With bodyguards provided courtesy of the governor, we were taken to areas of Kashmir where Genghis Khan and his troops made camp during his campaign to conquer the world. It was an amazing experience—major-league ancient history—and a long way from that "bench of dreams" in Druid Hill Park. We also went into the town of Kashmir, where we bought jewelry, paper-mâché dolls, and carpets that we had shipped home. I enjoyed the food there, particularly the breads and various dal recipes. Later in the week we met with the chief of the Frontier Police and briefed him on the status of the investigation. He promised to be responsive to any requests for assistance.

Through our investigation, we were able to identify and indict nine rebels who we believed were involved in the kidnapping and murders. We passed some of those names on to the Frontier Police, hoping they would arrest the suspects so we could interview them about the location of bodies and other investigative points of interest. Unfortunately, most of them were killed during gun fights as the Frontier Police closed in on them. We reached the point where we were reluctant to give the police the remaining names. By the time I left the case, we had only one living suspect left.

After we flew back to Islamabad, I read in the English-language newspaper *Dawn* about attacks against our bodyguards that resulted in a number of fatalities. Of the ten bodyguards assigned to us, I believe half of them were killed by guerrillas within a week of our leaving Kashmir. It was really sad. The written account of the attacks were quite dramatic: in relating that someone was killed, it would always say, "He had breathed his last."

I returned to India for the final time to introduce my new case agent to the embassy staff and to finish an update to the report. I was also trying set up a visit to see the Taj Mahal, another bucket list item for me. My Indian driver was ready to take me, but I ended up canceling at the last minute because it was taking me too long to complete the update and fax it to FBI headquarters. I was also on deadline, as I had to catch a flight to the Philippines. Missing the opportunity to visit the Taj Mahal has become one of my major regrets.

On the flight to the Philippines, the pilot announced that we were now flying over Vietnam, and I thought of the many American lives lost during the war there. When we landed, I was greeted by our Manila legat at the airport.

At the hotel we were joined by one of my agents, who had flown in from Honolulu, and the three of us drove to the embassy. Once there, I explained to the legat that I wanted to bring all our pending ETT cases in the country up to date. This included several murders and kidnappings. I also wanted to talk with the CIA agents assigned to the embassy.

I met with the CIA station chief to brief him on my intentions and solicit his assistance. After a couple of days reviewing the files, I flew back to Honolulu, leaving my agent responsible for the Philippine casework.

༄

Over the next few months we returned to Karachi to continue that investigation. The original assistant CIA station chief had moved on, and the agency was in the process of selecting a replacement. The person they ultimately chose was female. Initially we had our doubts that a woman could function successfully in a Muslim country because of how women were treated and the role they played in the culture. But this CIA agent turned out to be very effective in operating sources and getting things done in Pakistan. She was a tremendous help in our investigations in Karachi. Again, I returned to Honolulu but left the case agent there to continue his work.

In mid-June 1997, I received information from FBI headquarters that there was a plan in place to arrest Mir Aimal Kansi in

Pakistan. If I had any agents there, they said, I should pull them out immediately because there could be a backlash. Kansi was wanted for the January 25, 1993, murders of two CIA employees near the entrance of CIA headquarters in Langley. I had my agent in Karachi return to Honolulu.

On a return trip to New Delhi with my SAC, we stopped over in Hong Kong, where we had dinner with members of FBI staff from the embassy. This was three days prior to July 1, 1997, when Hong Kong was due to be transferred from British to Chinese sovereignty. I was hoping to stay there long enough to witness the handover, but we had to continue on to India; however, I was able to pick up a few souvenirs from the event. While I was there Chinese troops had started taking their positions on the streets of Hong Kong, replacing the British police officers. The transfer was done very smoothly and quietly.

We arrived in New Delhi on June 26, 1997. My SAC and I met with the US ambassador and personally updated him on our investigation in India. The ambassador was appreciative of the briefing and pledged his continued support of our investigation. We returned to Honolulu the next day.

∽♪∾

On November 12, 1997, four United States citizens and their Pakistani driver were ambushed and killed when gunmen opened fire on their vehicle in Karachi. The four Americans were employees of Houston-based Union Texas Petroleum.

I contacted the consulate in Karachi and advised them that I was bringing a team of agents there to conduct the investigation. I also talked to our Drug Enforcement Administration contact at the consulate and asked him to conduct a crime scene investigation with Karachi police, preserving the evidence until we arrived. Though this wasn't the responsibility or jurisdiction of the DEA, whose agents were assigned to the consulate to address international drug investigations, I knew the agents were excellent general criminal investigators and could protect our interests at the crime scene. They were always very helpful to us in Pakistan. They lived there; we didn't.

The fear at the time was that the real purpose of the shooting was to lure the FBI to Karachi, where its agents could be attacked—this as payback, because two days prior to the shooting, Mir Aimal Kansi had been convicted of the murders of the two CIA employees at Langley. I briefed my agents on the safety concerns, and we took all possible precautions, but we had to go. It was our job.

We arrived in Karachi on November 15, 1997. We were briefed by the consulate general and the DEA supervisor: the DEA had recovered AK-47 shell casings from the crime scene. This was the same type of weapon believed used in the consulate shuttle attack on March 8, 1995. We weren't clear why the car carrying the four oil company contractors was chosen as a target. It could have been a random opportunity to kill Americans, but the gunmen also might have thought they were CIA agents. I assumed the Pakistani driver was killed by accident; in the consulate shuttle attack, the perpetrators deliberately avoided shooting the driver. No group or person had claimed responsibility for the latest murders.

Despite the fact that we had arrived there just a few days after the crime scene was processed, and knowing how risky it was, I asked to see the scene myself so I could begin the investigation.

We set up a war room in the consulate, where we had brainstorming sessions with the DEA to identify potential leads that needed to be followed. We had the full support of the Karachi police.

I asked our lab in Washington, DC, to compare the shell casings from the shuttle bus shooting to the casings found at the scene of the second Karachi attack. Soon the report came back: all the shell casings had been fired from the same weapon. So we were able to connect the two cases.

The DEA agents assigned to the Karachi consulate had been the first responders at both shootings, conducting the initial interviews and preserving the evidence until we arrived. Without their help, our investigations would not have been as successful.

During our investigation of the later shooting, we asked the Pakistani law enforcement agencies to advertise a reward we were offering for information leading to the arrest and conviction of those responsible for the murders. If the Pakistanis were contacted by any of their citizens, the agreement was they would send them to our consulate, where we would interview them, and that we would share any resulting information with them.

I recall one person who walked into the consulate claiming to have relevant information. We interviewed him, but I thought he acted suspicious, and it occurred to me that he was a plant by Pakistani law enforcement to test whether we would actually share information. After the interview I immediately called my Pakistani contact and briefed him on what this person had told us. I think he was surprised by the call, but from then on he seemed to trust me. We received a lot of extra support from Pakistani law enforcement after that. On November 29, 1997, I returned to Honolulu, leaving my team in Karachi to continue the investigation.

❧

It wasn't all hard work and serious business in Hawaii. My squad was responsible for security at all major events held in the state, including the 1998 Miss Universe contest. We took advantage of the opportunity for photo ops with the most beautiful women in the world, including Brook Lee, a Hawaiian who had been crowned Miss Universe 1997. As it happened, just minutes before I took a picture with her she cut her long, pretty black hair very short, with no explanation. It was a stunning turnaround, and I wasn't sure if she was trying to match the length of my hair for the photo op or staging some sort of personal protest. She cut off her hair right before going on stage to turn over her crown to the new Miss Universe. I know it had to be a surprise to the contest organizers.

After five years in Hawaii as a supervisor, I decided it was time to consider moving on with my career. Though I found Hawaii a paradise, there was a caveat—I had to travel to some of the scariest places in the world. I had put my future dreams on hold for three years to work ETT cases, and I was ready to resume work on my career.

By then I had completed all the field office inspections necessary for me to be considered for an assistant special agent in charge (ASAC) position. Conducting field office inspections was a requirement for further career promotion; they provided opportunities to understand how each field office is supposed to be managed according to the FBI's guidelines and procedures. Through conducting these inspections, you learn all this and how to enforce it, as well. I had already participated in the inspections of our offices in Kansas City, New York, Little Rock, Jacksonville, and Washington, DC.

I was lucky because the required number of inspections was being increased from five to seven, and the last thing I wanted to do was another field office inspection. They were a lot of work in a short period of time, and very stressful. Because I had an OPR background and knew how to write up the relevant reports, I was usually assigned the dirty work of going after someone with a performance problem. I could have applied for positions at FBI headquarters, but I'd already established that I wasn't a headquarters kind of agent. I was most productive and effective in field offices, where the real cases were.

I took a look at the most viable ASAC openings around the country: Miami, Quantico, and Anchorage. I asked my wife to choose this time, and she chose Anchorage. I had to admit that I was ignorant; I thought you had to live in an igloo in Alaska. But Bernadette and I Googled Alaska and liked the homes we saw. They were the same type homes that we were used to.

I applied for the Anchorage opening and was interviewed by telephone by SAC George Burtram. He asked some great questions, which he delivered in a strong Boston accent. I felt I had bombed the interview, but I got the job—another "God intervened" moment. I think Burtram liked my work history, and I don't think there was a lot of competition. Not everyone was willing to move their families to Alaska, or even to Hawaii, for that matter. Those offices are a long way from the mainland.

The housing market in Hawaii was not good at the time. Our home had lost $100,000 in value over the last five years due to the devaluation of the Japanese yen. Our saving grace was a federal program that guaranteed to make up the difference in the sale price of your home if a military base closed in the area at the time of your transfer—and Barbers Point Naval Base, which was within a mile of our residence, was closing down at the time. There was a lot of paperwork required to apply, but it was worth it.

We were very anxious to get to Alaska. Again, I could not believe the FBI was paying us to move there.

CHAPTER 15

ᐃ

ALASKA

Operation Arctic Heat

We made our first visit to Alaska in the spring of 1998, to conduct another ten-day house-hunting trip. Though it was very beautiful there, it was indeed cold. We found a piece of land in the Rabbit Creek section of the Chugach Mountains in Anchorage and had a home built on it. Just as I'd had a Honolulu address in Hawaii, I wanted an Anchorage address in Alaska.

When we got some free time from house hunting, we took a train to Whittier, Alaska, and a boat trip to see glaciers. We also visited the Anchorage field office to meet with the employees and my new boss, SAC George Burtram.

Later I returned to Anchorage permanently to begin work, while Bernadette remained in Hawaii to give her employer sufficient notice. I stayed at a rooming house that had been recommended by an agent assigned to the Anchorage office. It was a log cabin with an Alaskan flair that I knew I had to get used to: mounted moose heads, bearskin rugs with heads still intact, and various species of salmon and other fish mounted over the large fireplace. There were four other guests at the rooming house and we all shared the same bathroom, which I didn't like. I had to stand in line every morning to use the facilities. We all ate breakfast together, and they were some hearty meals.

On my first day of work in the Anchorage field office, I checked in with Burtram, a very tall, smart, imposing, and intimidating man. He briefed me on the office environment and priorities; our federal, state, and local relationships with other law enforcement agencies; and what he expected of me. One thing he made clear was that this office had the reputation of being good only for fishing and hunting, not for generating good cases. He wanted that changed, and changed quickly.

My wife eventually showed up and didn't like the boardinghouse arrangements, so we moved into a hotel that became our temporary quarters until our house was finished.

One of my first assignments was to give a "just say no" to drugs speech at a local mall—it was part of the Red Ribbon Program for school kids. I prepared the speech, assuming I would deliver it in a conference room in the mall. As it turned out, however, I was supposed to stand on the third level of the mall, speaking to people on all three levels as they shopped. Of course no one was listening as I braved through my speech. That was my initiation to Alaska. It was like my first day in Hawaii when I was taken to lunch at a striptease joint—just as awkward, but not nearly as exciting.

In Anchorage, as in Hawaii, I was eligible for a 25 percent cost of living adjustment to my salary. In addition, once I was a resident of Alaska for a full year, I became entitled to dividends from the state's oil revenues, which in some years amounted to more than $2,000 for every man, woman, and child in Alaska. There was also no state income tax there.

The Iditarod dog race had its ceremonial start each year down the street from our field office, and I was very eager to see the spectacle. It was scheduled on a Saturday, so I went into the office first and did some paperwork and then walked down to where the race was to start. It was a treat to see those well-trained, athletic dogs raring to go. And what characters the sled racers were!

After standing around for a while, I realized I was in the midst of a physical crisis. My feet, hands, and face were getting numb. I slowly started back to my office, but I soon picked up the pace, making it back just in time to avoid frostbite. I guess I was in denial, thinking I was still in Hawaii. It happened to be ten degrees outside that day. I was better prepared for subsequent races.

I quickly found out that Aloha shirts don't cut it in Alaska. You have to wear clothes in layers. We were given a clothing allowance to buy designated emergency items in case we were ever stranded in a snowstorm—one was a pair of snow boots designed for weather seventy degrees below zero. That was scary!

One day my wife and I had left the grocery store and were sitting in our Jeep, just barged in from Hawaii, and we noticed that the car's temperature gauge read minus twenty-five degrees. Welcome to Alaska! I had my convertible Corvette shipped to Alaska, as well. While in Hawaii I never had the top up; in Alaska I can remember only a couple of days when I had it down.

While Anchorage was the smallest FBI field office, it had the largest territory to cover. At that time there were about thirty-five agents and twenty-five support staff assigned to it; we also had two agents assigned to the Fairbanks RA and one assigned to the Juneau RA. We had a SWAT team and an SOG team with a 280 Cessna plane, and we partnered with several federal, state, and local task forces.

When I arrived in Alaska, I was surprised to see so many blacks there. I later found out that 15 percent of the population of Alaska was black, a result of the military presence in the state. Military personnel who retired from the service in Alaska tended to stay on there to raise their families, plus they could find lucrative jobs there. Even the mayor of Fairbanks, James C. Hayes, was black. There were a large number of Hawaiians and Samoans in Alaska, too, which seemed odd because it was so cold.

We eventually moved into our home in a newly built community called Golden View, on Rabbit Creek Road. The two-story home was built on a quarter-acre of land. The builder had apparently encroached on the easement with the front porch and had to scale it back, which made things a little cramped, but we got used to it. Overall, we were very happy with the new house. We paid someone to finish off the entrance and the side and backyards with planters, walkways, trees, steps, shrubs, and flowers. It was looking good. And then, in short order, we had a problem.

Something was eating our expensive flowers and trees late at night. After this went on for a while, I decided to stay up and see if I could catch the culprit. About 2:00 a.m., a small herd of moose descended on our property and began eating our plants and trees as if they were a free late-night buffet. When we mentioned this to our neighbors who had had the same problem, they suggested a spray containing animal blood, sold at local lawn and garden shops. We bought it and sprayed it, and it worked! It was a little expensive, but worth it. The theory behind the product is that when moose smell blood, they think there are bears (their main predators) in the area with a fresh kill, so they stay away.

In our neighborhood we would see moose, brown and black bears, bald eagles, Dahl sheep in the mountains, and lynxes. It was like living in a zoo. Our house happened to be alongside an animal trail down to a river, so we had to be careful whenever we walked outside. We never knew if we might be confronted by bears or moose. One day I looked out my living room window and saw a black bear with her three cubs trailing behind her. Every once in a while we would see a lynx running by our house. They were beautiful cats with pretty eyes, and very fast.

I remember seeing our first aurora borealis since arriving in Alaska—Bernadette and I were eating dinner one night, and one of our neighbors called and told us to go to the door and look outside. There was the most beautiful array of colors dancing in the sky. We would see many more during our four years in Alaska.

Because the North Pole was in my territory, I had family and friends with kids send me Christmas cards, and I would have my agents in Fairbanks drop them off with Santa, who would send the cards back to the kids with a North Pole postmark.

Within the first few months of moving to Alaska, we made some friends who were planning a Caribbean cruise. Because we were living in Alaska, a Caribbean cruise sounded like a great idea, so we decided to join them and booked a trip. While we were on the ship I found out about an excursion to St. Martin, where match races featuring former America's Cup twelve-meter yachts were being held. One of the yachts was the famous *Stars and Stripes*, sailed by Dennis Connors to win back the America's Cup in the 1980s. I bought a ticket to get on that yacht and bribed the guide to let me skipper it during the match race. We won, and I had a picture taken. I couldn't have been prouder or happier.

Ever since the indictments of Fhimah and Megrahi in 1991, I had been monitoring the efforts to bring them to justice. Col. Muammar Gaddafi initially refused to turn the men over for a trial unless it took place in an Arab country. In spite of three UN resolutions and the imposition of strict economic sanctions, the accused bombers remained out of reach in Libya. Congress and two presidential administrations had done what they could, to no avail. In the meantime, the FBI had named them among their Ten Most Wanted Fugitives.

On April 5, 1999, after eight years of diplomatic negotiations, including help from Nelson Mandela, the Libyan government finally agreed to release Fhimah and Megrahi for trial in a specially convened court in the Netherlands, with Scottish judges. The agreement stipulated that any person found guilty would serve his sentence in Scotland.

I was elated at the news—and I couldn't wait to put the word *Captured* on the men's FBI Ten Most Wanted photos.

In early January 2000, SAC Burtram was promoted to a larger office in Columbia, South Carolina, and I became acting SAC in the interim. This was a "Don't wait for it to happen—make it happen" moment. I applied for his position, even though I didn't think I had a chance.

On February 13, 2000, I received a phone call from FBI Director Louie Freeh's deputy director, Tom Pichard, informing me that I was the new SAC in Anchorage. Getting promoted in place, from ASAC to SAC, doesn't happen often in the FBI. The normal procedure is to do additional field office inspections and spend a couple of years at headquarters as a section chief prior to becoming an SAC—a requirement of which I was absolved, thank goodness.

Less than nine years after becoming a supervisor in October 1991, I was promoted to SAC. I had skipped the standard career path back to FBI headquarters for unit chief, section chief, and inspector positions, which could take additional years. I had made it to the top in the FBI: I was running my own field office, even though it was the smallest and one of the most remote. It was an incredible honor.

The SAC of an FBI field office becomes the bureau's representative within that field office's territories, with full responsibility for all investigative operations and programs. The SAC is considered one of the top federal officials in his or her area of operations, and depending upon the population density, he or she may be responsible for an entire state or group of states. Accordingly, SACs often meet with governors and other top state officials, US senators and representatives, members of local business communities, and frequently the media. They are often in the public eye in their state or region. For these and many other reasons, the position of SAC is often called the best job in the bureau.

I received congratulations from agents from all over the country, including a very nice congratulatory note from SAC John O'Neill from the NYO. I recalled that my first meeting with O'Neill was when we were standing side by side at urinals in a restroom at FBI headquarters, during a break in my briefing to convince headquarters to establish an ETT squad in Honolulu. O'Neill had been in on the briefing and picked this awkward place to tell me that if I wanted to get my wish I needed to provide stronger justification. I returned to complete the briefing, heeding his advice, and we got the approval and support for the new squad. I believe that he was a section chief in the terrorism division at the time.

In 1999 I received an e-mail from the Department of Justice about the trial that was being planned in the Netherlands: I needed to fill out some forms and then fly to Scotland for trial preparations. I traveled to Edinburgh and met with the trial attorneys, as well as one of the Scottish police investigators I had worked with in Malta. He was great to work with—always serious, committed, and totally focused on the investigation. He had spent a lot of time in Malta on the case, and apparently the separation had taken a toll on his relationship with his family. I told him I needed to go back to the sign-in book in the Thundergarth shed/memorial in Lockerbie to follow up on the promise I had written in 1990. So he drove me there, and when I opened the book, I couldn't write it fast enough: "We got the bastards."

♪♫

On April 10, 2000, I received a witness citation from the High Court of Justiciary of Edinburgh, Scotland, to testify at trial in the Netherlands.

The trial started May 3, 2000: eleven years, four months, and thirteen days after the bombing of Pan Am Flight 103. In mid-September 2000, I flew to the Amsterdam airport and caught a cab to my hotel in Utrecht. I met with the DOJ and FBI teams as well as the Scottish investigators. Media and victims' family members were there as well. We were in a waiting room where we could monitor the proceedings over closed-circuit TV.

I wasn't called to testify during the first two weeks, so I made arrangements to see one of my former CIA partners, who had been assigned to Malta during our investigation. During the weekends, I would join a good friend of mine, Dick Marquise, and cruise the Rhine River in Cologne, Germany; we also took a train to Brussels and Brugge, Belgium. At that time Marquise was the Oklahoma City SAC and had been unit chief at FBI headquarters, providing leadership and oversight of the investigation at its inception. He was at the trial in case Puzzle Piece testified.

I was finally called to testify on October 23, 2000, regarding the admissibility of Fhimah's diary, recovered in his abandoned travel agency in Malta. The defense was hoping the diary was illegally obtained and therefore could be thrown out as evidence. But because we were in the travel office legally, and had received the proper approval from the property's legal representative, the court ruled it was legally obtained and could be entered as evidence. I had testified in what is referred to as "the trial within a trial." I was honored at this opportunity, and it was certainly a rare experience. After completing my testimony I continued to wait in the event that I would be called again.

When I was given the okay to leave, I returned to Anchorage worried about the verdicts. I was not confident in the Scottish court system and would have preferred the trial had taken place in the United States. But it was all out of my hands now. I had to put the case behind me, because I had many other challenges as the special agent in charge of the Anchorage field office.

In January 2001, I was faced with my first high-profile civil rights case in Alaska. It involved a series of premeditated, racially motivated drive-by paintball shootings. They took place on a Sunday night and targeted Alaska Natives in downtown Anchorage. The attacks generated attention not only by state media, but by national media, as well. We opened a hate crimes investigation that led to the arrest of two juveniles and one adult, all residents of Eagle River. They had videotaped the attacks and used frozen paintballs against the defenseless Alaskan Natives. The nature of the injuries sustained by the victims was never substantiated, but it was obvious from the videotapes that they were assaulted.

According to statements captured in the video recordings, the three males had traveled into Anchorage for the sole purpose of locating "Eskimo" pedestrians, particularly those whom they believed to be intoxicated. In one part of the videotape the assailants were seen posing as tourists from California and interrogating a fifty-two-year-old Nome man—to wit, asking whether he was drunk. Satisfied by the man's frank admission that he was "always drunk" and had struggled with alcoholism since age fourteen, they promptly shot him in the face. The adult perpetrator was sentenced to six months in prison, a $6,000 fine, and three hundred hours of community service. What penalties the two juveniles ultimately received remains unclear.

The incident inspired Governor Tony Knowles to appoint a fourteen-member Commission on Tolerance, which reported back to him with more than one hundred recommendations for improving race relations in the state of Alaska. This list included more new hate crime laws, increased funding for schools in rural villages, and even adding new verses to "Alaska's Flag," the state song, to recognize the contributions of Alaska Natives.

ৡ৪ৡ

In the early morning of January 30, 2001, I received a call from Dick Marquise telling me that the three judges in the Pan Am trial were going to announce the verdicts the following day at Kamp

Ziest. We needed to catch flights that day if we wanted to be there when verdicts were read.

We arrived there in time and sat down in the courtroom to await the judges' announcements. The guilty verdict for Megrahi came first, then an acquittal verdict for Fhimah. I was floored. There was no way Megrahi could be convicted without also convicting Fhimah. Without Fhimah's access to Air Malta luggage tags, his connection at Luqa Airport, his ability to get the luggage on the Air Malta flight to connect with Pan Am 103 out of Heathrow, and his knowledge of the airline luggage system and flight schedules, Megrahi couldn't have pulled it off. Granted, the case was circumstantial, but I thought it very compelling. We had Fhimah dead to rights providing the luggage tags and being at the airport at the time the bomb bag was put on the Air Malta flight. Fhimah was recruited for the mission because of his knowledge of and access to the airlines. I couldn't believe the Scottish court acquitted him. In my opinion, on the same evidence he would have been convicted in the United States.

I suspected that somehow, in all the years of wheeling and dealing to get the two men to trial, a deal had been reached between the Scottish and Libyan governments that the court would release Fhimah and only convict Megrahi. They eventually released Megrahi as well, less than ten years later. I've often wondered whether the Scottish or British government made a deal with Libya for private business industrial oil rights. At any rate, I couldn't believe there wasn't worldwide outrage when Fhimah was released.

I flew back to Anchorage but made arrangements to meet with my other CIA partner back in Washington, DC, where he was on temporarily assignment. It was great seeing him again, and the timing was right, so soon after the finish of the trial. We had a lot to catch up on. This man was a straight shooter, which was one of the reasons I really liked working with him; I always knew where he was coming from. He was very serious, intelligent, focused, and sincere.

We had struggled initially in our working relationship. He had generated a communication that got me in a little hot water with my office, and that temporarily damaged our mutual trust, but we worked it out. We both knew what was at stake, and it was bigger than both our egos. After that we had a deal: we would review each other's communications related to Pan Am 103 before they were sent, and we kept each other briefed and conspired on different aspects of the case. It had all worked out in the end.

♪♪

In March 2001, Alaska hosted the World Winter Special Olympics, and we shared security responsibility with our law enforcement partners in the state. There was a great deal of security advance work done ahead of the games, in part because many members of the Kennedy family were there. It was interesting to hear Arnold Schwarzenegger speak during the opening and closing ceremonies; it seemed to me that he was practicing to become a politician, which of course he later did, winning the governorship of California.

On April 21, 2001, United Airlines Flight 857, with 231 passengers on board, was three hours into a trip from San Francisco to Shanghai when it was diverted to Anchorage International Airport because Crystal and Cynthia Mikula, twenty-two-year-old identical twin sisters from Buckley, Michigan, had fought and tussled with each other, brawled with flight attendants, and threatened to open the cabin doors in flight. The twins had to be restrained, and once the plane landed we arrested them and charged them with interfering with a flight crew, a felony that carries up to twenty years in prison.

The incident made international news, and for the next day or two I was interviewed on various TV and radio stations, including *Good Morning America*—although because of the time difference, host Diane Sawyer interviewed me at midnight Anchorage time for the morning show.

ঞ৲

In June 2001, Director Freeh decided to leave the FBI for a position in the private sector. I don't think he and the new US attorney general, John Ashcroft, were getting along that well. We had just had a change in presidential administrations, and a change in attorney generals came with the territory.

A few months later, President George W. Bush picked Robert S. Mueller III, a former US attorney in San Francisco, as the new FBI director. He was sworn in on September 4, 2001. I knew Robert Mueller when he was the DOJ prosecutor on the Pan Am 103 case. His mandate as the new director was to upgrade the bureau's information technology infrastructure, to address records management issues, and to enhance FBI foreign counterintelligence analysis and security in the wake of the damage done by the former special agent and convicted spy, Robert Hanssen.

Robert Philip Hanssen was an FBI agent who spied for Soviet and Russian intelligence services against the United States for twenty-two years, from 1979 to 2001. He was arrested on February 18, 2001, and charged with selling American secrets to Russia for more than $1.4 million in cash and diamonds. On July 6, 2001, he pleaded guilty to thirteen counts of espionage in the United States District Court for the Eastern District of Virginia. He was sentenced to life in prison without the possibility of parole.

Hanssen's crimes have been described as the worst intelligence disaster in US history. He is currently serving a life sentence at the Federal Bureau of Prisons Administrative Maximum Facility in Florence, Colorado— a "supermax" prison in which he spends twenty-three hours a day in solitary confinement.

As a result of Hanssen's spying activities, the bureau began administering a polygraph test to every new FBI agent and requiring a new background investigation every five years throughout an FBI employee's career. Historically the FBI hadn't used polygraphs on its own personnel unless it was conducting an administrative inquiry or criminal investigation. The new polygraph testing started with SACs and went down the ladder. At that point I had been in the FBI for twenty-five years without having taken a polygraph.

✒

Within days of Mueller taking over, the 9/11 attacks changed everything for him and the FBI forever.

On that morning, I was getting dressed for work when my wife yelled to me that a commercial airliner had crashed into one of the two World Trade Center towers in New York. As I ran to the TV, all I could think was, *What a tragic accident.* Then a news flash came on that said another commercial airliner had crashed into the other tower. At that point I knew this was no accident. I got dressed and rushed to the office.

On my way in, I received calls from FBI headquarters, the governor's office, Anchorage's mayor and chief of police, and other Alaskan law enforcement officials requesting a joint command center be established to protect Alaska's people, property, and critical assets—especially the oil pipeline. Fortunately, we had recently created and trained our Joint Domestic and International Terrorism Task Force. So we set up a command center with representatives from that task force in my office.

Within an hour of setting up our command center, we were faced with our first major crisis. Soon after the attacks, a call went out for all planes to return to their airports of origin—or if they did not have enough fuel, to land in Canadian territory. Korean Air Flight 85 was en route to Ted Stevens International Airport in Anchorage when the September 11 attacks occurred. While discussing the day's events, the pilot of Flight 85 included the letters *HJK*—the code for "hijacked" in an airline text message. After the pilot transmitted it, the text messaging service company, Aeronautical Radio, Inc. (ARINC) noticed the code. Worried that the Korean pilots might be sending a message for help, ARINC officials notified North American Aerospace Defense Command (NORAD).

Taking no chances, NORAD scrambled two F-15 jets from Elmendorf Air Force Base to intercept the 747. Meanwhile, Alaska air traffic control (ATC) asked the pilots coded questions. Civil airline pilots are trained to answer these questions in a coded way if hijacked. The Korean pilots, instead of reassuring ATC, declared themselves hijacked by changing their transponder signal to the four-digit universal code for hijack, 7500.

Governor Knowles, who was in contact with our command center and concerned that a hijacked plane might strike a target in Alaska, ordered the evacuation of large hotels and government buildings in Anchorage. At nearby Valdez, the US Coast Guard ordered all tankers filling up with oil to head out to sea. Lt. Gen. Norty Schwartz, who was in charge of Elmendorf Air Force Base and the NORAD planes that scrambled to shadow Flight 85, had been on the phone with the White House and was given the green light to shoot down the plane, if necessary, before it could attack a target in Alaska.

With NORAD telling Anchorage ATC that it would shoot down the airliner if it came near any potential targets, the controllers informed Flight 85 to avoid all population centers and head out of the country to Whitehorse, Yukon, Canada. The pilots eventually cooperated, and with an F-15 escort, the 747 was forced to land in Whitehorse. Thank God that Schwartz's pilots used good discipline, judgment, and admirable restraint. The texting turned out to be a matter of miscommunication, but it could have resulted in the unnecessary death of hundreds of civilians. I was on the phone with the Anchorage mayor throughout the crisis, as we were considering evacuating certain areas of the city.

We also had a prominent local Muslim leader try to exploit the 9/11 situation by claiming that his business had been vandalized because of his religion. We ascertained that he was actually trying to get insurance money, and he was eventually arrested and charged with vandalizing his own property. The Muslim community in Anchorage was not upset by the arrest, as I had anticipated they would be.

The Anchorage command center was operational 24/7 and lasted several weeks. We had teams of people from federal, state, and local agencies, plus members of the military and the US Coast Guard, running down leads as soon as they came to our attention. We responded to more than 650 tips or leads from local citizens, as well as leads from other FBI field offices. We established statewide protocols for handling anthrax-related calls because we had private citizens bringing suspicious powders into state troopers' precinct houses, potentially contaminating the offices. We reached out to Arab communities across the state to allay their concerns and let them know that any type of retaliation or threats against them would not be tolerated, and that the FBI and the DOJ would aggressively investigate and prosecute violations of federal hate crime laws.

Our command center worked with the governor and assisted in the coordination of his homeland security initiatives. We also worked with security officials from the oil industry and the CIA. Our priorities were to protect Alaska's citizens as well as its infrastructure: the oil industry; emergency and government services; military and missile launch facilities; public utilities (power plants, water supply, telecommunications and transportation systems, and information and communications systems); and banking and finance systems. We were connected to the Alaska Department of Public Safety, the State Emergency Coordination Center, and public health officials.

I was deeply saddened to find out later that former New York field office SAC John O'Neill had died while attempting to evacuate tenants from the World Trade Center. He had retired from the FBI and become head of security for the WTC just prior to the 9/11 attacks. I remembered his kind letter when I was promoted to SAC, and the help he gave me when I was requesting approval to establish an ETT squad in Honolulu. He was a good man.

As the weeks wore on, things began to quiet down in Alaska. Gradually we trimmed down the numbers of agencies and personnel working in the command center, and eventually we disbanded it completely.

❧

When I became the special agent in charge of the Anchorage field office, I realized I would have to do on-camera interviews, generate press releases, and hold press conferences. I was also responsible for handling any requests for speeches from the community, including social clubs and charitable organizations that wanted to hear about the FBI or what it was doing in Alaska. This was a new challenge for me. Although I never considered myself a good public speaker, I tried to improve my performance with each speech. I always made sure I was more than adequately prepared. I spoke to graduates of the Alaska State Troopers Academy, the NAACP, the Lions Club, the Kiwanis Club, and school groups, among others, and I conducted many interviews with TV stations and talk shows around the state. Some of my speeches were good and some not so much. But all in all, I really liked being asked to speak.

On November 30, 2001, I was proud to present the FBI Director's Community Leadership Award to the founding pastor of the Eagle River Missionary Baptist Church in Eagle River, Alaska. I delivered the national award during a gathering to commemorate his sixteenth anniversary with the church. He was a tireless voice in the fight against racism in Anchorage and chair of the city's very active Minority Community Police Relations Task Force, of which I was also a member. My wife and I attended his church, and he and his wife became mentors for us while we were in Alaska.

One of the most anticipated events for me in Alaska was the visit of my daughter and grandchildren. My wife and I rented an RV, and we all took off a week at the beginning of the summer solstice and traveled Alaska's "great circle route," which included Fairbanks and the North Pole. It was wonderful to see the grandkids' reaction to Alaska's wildlife, waterfalls, snowcapped mountains, and glaciers.

The fact that it was June—and eighty degrees on the North Pole—didn't deter them from sitting on Santa's lap and letting him know what they wanted for Christmas.

My wife got a job in the business office of an Anchorage fitness center, so I received free privileges to the club. I stopped there in the morning before work to swim laps in their pool, although it was really cold during the winter months.

I also tried running in my neighborhood before work, but it was too dangerous because I kept running into moose that didn't like being startled. We had brown and black bears in the area, too, so I would go to Elmendorf AFB to run in the mornings because I felt it was safer; the FBI had base privileges there. Sometimes I would meet Gen. Schwartz, who was also running. He eventually became head of the US Air Force.

ↂↇ

One of my priorities as SAC in Alaska was to establish strong working relationships with all the federal, state, and local law enforcement and military agencies to address any potential terrorist threats. I had a lot of help from Philip E. Oates, the major general of the Alaska National Guard. Together, we worked very hard to bring the leadership of these agencies together to discuss how to solidify our relationships. As a result, ideas began to emerge regarding the need for a Field Training Exercise (FTX) that would help identify the role each agency would play in a terrorist threat, and what equipment and training we needed.

Our original plan for the FTX, code-named Arctic Strike, involved a scenario in which the pipeline was attacked by terrorists and we would respond collectively, in a very coordinated fashion. The oil from this pipeline represented 25 percent of all the oil consumed in the lower forty-eight states. It also fueled a significant portion of our military. As a result, the pipeline had national security implications. Up to then, the only pipeline incidents involved locals getting drunk and firing at it with high-powered rifles—in some cases actually penetrating the pipe, causing leaks. The culprits were usually arrested by the Alaska State Troopers and Alyeska Pipeline security agents.

Plans were for the Arctic Strike exercise to last a day. It was organized by one of the best FBI agents, male or female, I have ever met. She was one of the best agents in the office—and maybe one of the best in the FBI. Whenever there was a major incident in Alaska, she was the go-to person, and she had the respect of all the members of Alaska's law enforcement community. She was indeed a heavy.

Our plans happened to coincide with the air force's need to have a similar training exercise and the bureau's desire to participate. So we decided to combine the exercises, which turned out at the time to be one of the largest, most complex terrorism training exercises ever held in this country. It lasted an entire week and covered the full length of the United States, Alaska, and Canada.

The combined FTX was code-named Arctic Strike/Amalgam Virgo 02. About fifteen hundred people took part, including the FBI, the Royal Canadian Mounted Police, the Federal Emergency Management Agency, NORAD, Transport Canada, the Transportation Security Administration, the Federal Aviation Administration, the Vancouver Airport Authority, and Delta Airlines. (Part of the joint exercise focused on possible threats in US-Canadian airspace; a commercial hijacking scenario was created involving a Delta jet.) The FTXs went well for all agencies involved, but we were certainly exhausted by the end of the week.

The Arctic Strike part of the exercise included a response to an attack on the oil terminal in Valdez, on Prince William Sound. We were tasked with protecting the pipeline and the terminal where oil was loaded onto tankers. There was also a chokepoint in Prince William Sound where a sunken ship could prevent tankers from making their deliveries.

The US Coast Guard gave me a personal boat tour of the area where the Exxon oil spill disaster occurred in 1989. It was still a sight to see: the impact of the spill on the fishing industry and the wildlife there was a shame. At that time, the Exxon case was still in litigation.

Then BP and Alyeska took me on a flight along the entire eight-hundred-mile pipeline, from Prudhoe Bay to Valdez. I sat in the cockpit of a 727 to see the pipeline: four hundred miles of it is above ground, and the rest is below. I had lunch at the pipeline's Prudhoe Bay facility, which had a cage covering the entrance/exit. It was called a polar bear cage because it allowed the employees to see if there were bears around before they stepped outside. The food there was excellent; this was a remote outpost, and food was something the employees really looked forward to. Overall it was a great experience.

Within months of the FTX, I was fortunate and delighted to receive a public service commendation from Coast Guard Commandant Rear Adm. J. W. Underwood. On the first anniversary of 9/11, I was given the Alaska Legion of Merit Award from the governor of Alaska, Tony Knowles, and Maj. Gen. Phil Oates of the Alaska National Guard. Later that month, Anchorage Mayor George Wuerch designated September 20, 2002, "Phillip B. J. Reid Appreciation Day."

One of the pleasant ironies that came out of building a strong, coordinated working relationship with all the agencies in Alaska was that it included the CIA. When I reached out to the agency to request their increased involvement in Alaska, I found out that I would be working with someone who also happened to have worked in Malta at the time of the Pan Am 103 bombing. I'd seen his name on reports at the time, but I never had a chance to meet him. After we realized what we had in common, he flew to Alaska and we had a great exchange. We got his agency's support in Alaska, as well.

During my stay in Alaska, there were always meetings and conferences to attend. We had a strong working relationship with the Royal Canadian Mounted Police (RCMP), and because the state is adjacent to Canada, we found ourselves working joint operations. We had had meetings together in Juneau, so now it was our turn to attend a meeting in the Yukon. I was flown by the Alaska State Troopers to Dawson City, Yukon, Canada. After our meeting, the RCMPs invited us for drinks and dinner at a local hotel.

Dawson City is an interesting town—it looks much like it did a hundred years ago. One of its attractions is a five-dollar drink served at the Downtown Hotel called the Sourtoe Cocktail, containing a human toe. As the story goes, two brothers were traveling back and forth from Dawson City to smuggle rum into Alaska, and one night their toes got frostbite and fell off. While those original toes are gone, the bar maintains a stock of preserved human toes that are added to the drink (one toe per cocktail). People who drink a Sourtoe Cocktail are awarded certificates, and their names are added to the official log book. (There is apparently a heavy fine for swallowing the toe.) I did not sample this drink.

In Alaska we had to get used to earthquakes and tremors, which happened any time of the day or night. Buildings swayed, the ground rumbled, and it was scary because there was no way of telling whether this was "the big one."

While I was assigned to Alaska, a good friend of mine, Glen Geoffrey, was murdered, and the person who shot him committed suicide. An Alaska Native, Geoffrey was the commissioner of the Alaska Department of Public Safety—a well-known, popular public figure. He was also the highest-ranking state law enforcement officer in Alaska, and was being considered for a lieutenant governor position. His death shook all of us in the law enforcement community because he was such an important part of what we were trying to accomplish in Alaska.

When you're an SAC at an FBI field office, one of your responsibilities is to develop relationships with the governors and US senators in your field office's state(s) of operation. You regularly brief senators on any threats and your overall crime-fighting goals and accomplishments in their states, with the hope of maintaining or gaining support on legislation that affects the FBI—such as your field office budget. You do the same for your governor(s), holding meetings to explain how you are working with state law enforcement agencies to keep the citizenry safe.

In Alaska, I found Republican senator Frank Murkowski tough to work with; he seemed to have a very bad attitude regarding law enforcement, particularly the FBI. I tried to brief him on the efforts we were making in addressing the drug problem in Alaska, but instead of voicing his support, he acted very doubtful about our progress.

On the other hand, I found Sen. Ted Stevens (also Republican) very easy to work with and very supportive of law enforcement. He was like a saint in Alaska, and he was certainly known to bring home the bacon. Alaskans joked that if he died, they would stuff him and pretend he was still alive, to keep that bacon coming.

Alaska Gov. Tony Knowles was very supportive, as well. National Guard Maj. Gen. Phil Oates set up my meetings with him.

I felt really proud when our office hosted a black history luncheon for the NAACP and the general public. It was well-attended, with great food, entertainment, and speeches. When it was my turn to speak, I commented that J. Edgar Hoover was probably turning over in his grave to see this many black people in an FBI office who weren't under arrest. Everyone broke into laughter.

After the ceremonies were over and everyone had left, I returned to my office and closed the door to reflect on what had just happened—a black history luncheon held for NAACP members and the general public in an FBI office, hosted by me, a black FBI assistant special agent in charge. I recalled the much-publicized adversarial relationship Hoover had with Dr. Martin Luther King Jr. and the NAACP. *Wow,* I thought. *Has the FBI come a long way, or what?* This was another of those moments when I missed Three Sisters Ponds.

When I joined the FBI, I wasn't naïve enough to think I wouldn't encounter various forms of racism, the likes of which could have been found in any workplace in the United States at the time. I never observed racism in the police department or the FBI as sanctioned policies, but there were individuals—some in high-ranking positions—whose attitudes jeopardized those organizations' progress toward racial tolerance. I always believed my responsibility to my heritage was to keep my eyes open, fight prejudice with a grin and hard work, and never let it get in my way or slow me down. I had my goals to pursue, and only my own limitations were going to prevent me from reaching them.

Over the years, while working as a police officer and then as an FBI agent, I had hoped someday to join the National Organization of Black Law Enforcement Executives (NOBLE). After I became a special agent in charge, I applied and became a proud member.

As a new SAC, I had to develop my own management style—although I must admit I adopted one element of that style from DADIC Ken Walton from the NYO. That was "management by walking around"—a great way of staying in touch with agents and professional support employees and keeping up with the work they were doing. It allowed me to give timely suggestions and support if they needed it.

I was always proud to be a card-carrying member of the International Association of Chiefs of Police; I enjoyed being connected to other police officers from around the country. I was also glad that whenever there was an IACP conference, there would be an SAC conference in the same venue, and the FBI director would be a keynote speaker. When I mentioned my police background to any member of a law enforcement agency, no matter the country, it created an instant bond that got me whatever investigative help I needed.

❧

One of the things I did in Alaska was ask all my employees to attend sensitivity training provided by the Alaska Native Heritage Center. I wanted our office to be more involved in investigations that supported the safety of all Alaskans, including Alaska Natives. In order to do that, however, we needed to understand their culture, history, problems, and languages. In my opinion, the more interest we demonstrated and the more we interacted with them, the better our chances of success. But it was a two-way street: I also asked the Alaska Native Heritage Center to host a training session to help Native Alaskans understand the FBI's mission and culture. The training was held in two sessions, and all my employees, both agents and support staff, attended.

Alaska has 231 federally recognized native tribes, almost half the total number in the United States. While assigned to Alaska, I had the privilege to meet many Alaska Natives and visit many of their museums around the state. They have an incredible history and contribute significantly to Alaska's growth and vitality. Whenever I had the opportunity to meet with leaders and elders to discuss the FBI's role in Alaska, they always welcomed me with open arms. They also shared their communities' issues and concerns, which included drug and alcohol abuse, suicide, domestic violence, and child abuse. In Anchorage there were a lot of homeless native Alaskans (male and female), often with drug or alcohol problems, and there was an annual prayer vigil for native Alaskan victims of violence. I regularly attended community forums regarding the plight of Alaska Natives, as well as the annual conference of the Alaska Federation of Natives. In the process I learned a lot about these wonderful people, and I wanted to make sure that the FBI wasn't ignoring their problems and would be part of the solution.

❧

As SAC I was responsible for covering the entire state of Alaska. It was so vast and unspoiled that the only way to get around was to fly. I either took commercial flights or rode with the Alaska State Troopers, the National Guard, the Coast Guard, or Alyeska Pipeline security. Traveling around Alaska was a great experience for me; I never tired of seeing the wildlife, the beautiful, flowing streams, and the snowcapped mountains. Dealing with the summer and winter solstices in Alaska were a challenge, though. In winter there were only three hours of daylight and in summer only about three hours of darkness. Around the winter solstice, daylight hours were from around 11:00 a.m. until 2:00 p.m. The rest of the time it was dark. I found the best way to survive the winter solstice was to make sure I kept a very busy schedule through the day, so I could hold off going to sleep until the late evening—otherwise I found myself going to sleep far too early and waking up in the middle of the night with nothing to do.

Obviously, Alaska was not for everybody. We shoveled a lot of snow, installed special outlets to keep our engine blocks warm, and used remote-controlled ignitions so we could warm our cars before we got into them. One day on my way home from work in the middle of a snowstorm, I lost control of my vehicle and ended up in a ditch. I didn't know how I was going to get out. A Good Samaritan who happened to be driving by in a truck quickly threw me a rope, had me tie it to the front of my car, and proceeded to pull me out of the ditch. Before I could thank him, he had unhitched the line and driven off. This happened not long after we first arrived in Alaska, and that act of kindness had a lasting effect on me.

One of my best FBI agents in Alaska was my SWAT team leader. A young, intelligent man, he was a triathlete and a black belt in karate. He was responsible for our environmental crimes investigations and was a very aggressive and hardworking agent. He also was married with children. So I was very surprised when he came into my office, closed the door and sat down, and then advised me of his plans to change his sex. He made it clear to me that this was something that he had been agonizing over for many years, and that he would not be happy or satisfied unless he became a female. He told me that nothing and no one could change his mind.

There hadn't been any indications up to that point that this was on his mind. And as far as I knew, this was the first time the FBI had ever been confronted with this particular situation, so I knew it was very important that I handle it with sensitivity. I had to consider the impact it was going to have on the office, and I realized that everyone, including me, would need additional sensitivity training. I called FBI headquarters for help.

The SWAT team rebelled immediately and said that they didn't want him on the team any longer because he would be a distraction. Fortunately, he decided on his own to resign from the SWAT unit, because I couldn't ask him to do it.

He understood as much as I did the impact his decision would have on the other employees, and he was a big help in allowing them to adjust. He shifted from male to female clothing gradually, to minimize the shock. Most of his apparel appeared unisex and was not controversial. He also agreed to use the restroom in our adjacent building at first, rather than using the women's restroom in the main office. Eventually most of the office personnel adjusted and accepted his desire to change genders, and this agent continued to be a great FBI investigator. I'm not sure if he ever had sex-change surgery, because I was soon promoted to a larger FBI field office.

♪♫♪

Metlakatla is the only federal Indian reservation in Alaska where the FBI has exclusive law enforcement jurisdiction. Located about fifteen miles south of Ketchikan, it is only accessible by boat or plane. It is about three and a half hours by air from Anchorage.

The Metlakatla Indian Community operates its own tribal court system, including juvenile and appellate courts. The community also regulates commercial fishing in its waters, where salmon, halibut, cod, seaweed, clams, and waterfowl are important subsistence food sources.

When I was SAC in Alaska, the reservation had significant problems with bootlegged alcohol. It was supposed to be a "dry" community, and bootleggers were making a fortune bringing alcohol in and selling it at very high prices. The alcohol was having a serious negative impact on the community, fueling high rates of addiction and contributing to domestic violence, rapes, child abuse, suicide, and thefts.

Though the reservation was very remote, we began working with the state Alcohol Control Board, the Alaska State Troopers, and the ATF to run sting operations on the bootleggers. We identified the purchasers and some of the liquor stores where the alcohol was being purchased, and as a result we were able to initiate arrests and convictions. I'm not sure, but these may have been the only bootlegging cases the FBI was working at that time.

∽

One morning I arrived at work and received a briefing from our drug task force supervisor about the tremendous amount of heroin showing up in Alaska—an amount that seemed disproportionate to the state's population. This supervisor was another heavy in the office—one of the go-to agents when there was a crisis or a big case to pursue. We had been doing "buy-busts" for years, attempting to work our way up the leadership chain of the known drug gangs, but to no avail. And the problem appeared to be getting worse. So I asked the task force to try a "Mississippi Burning" approach and consider using wiretaps to build their case. Initially I received some resistance, because cases developed through wiretaps take a lot of time and effort and are without quick rewards.

Using the new approach, we were finally able to identify the largest drug operation in Alaska's history and connect it to operations in California and Kansas. We discovered that Alaska had become a major heroin distribution point for a ring that had been operating in the state for more than fifteen years. The drugs were shipped to Alaska inside vehicles and then flown to different parts of the country, and no one had ever suspected a thing.

We code-named our case Operation Arctic Heat and set up meetings with our Los Angeles and Kansas City offices. On November 8, 2002, we took the traffickers down. When it was all over, sixteen subjects were named in federal complaints or indictments in Operations Heavy Hitter, Once Again, and So-Cal Snow, all based in Los Angeles. Forty-four subjects were indicted in Operation Arctic Heat, based in Anchorage, and thirty-eight subjects were charged in Operation Sword Blade, based in Kansas City, Kansas. The Los Angeles investigations were conducted by the DEA, the FBI, the IRS, the LA County Sheriff's Department, the LAPD, the Southern California Drug Task Force, and the San Bernardino West End Narcotics Task Force.

The LA cases focused on targets who imported cocaine from Mexico and delivered it to contacts in the Los Angeles area for further distribution nationwide. Operation Sword Blade was initiated in Kansas City after agents identified subjects there who were receiving cocaine from subjects identified in the Heavy Hitter and Once Again cases, which were based in Los Angeles. Operation Arctic Heat was initiated independently in Anchorage, but it later overlapped with the Los Angeles cases. I hoped that this initiative would improve Senator Frank Murkowski's attitude about Alaskan law enforcement's efforts to address the state's illegal drug problem.

While I was SAC in Anchorage, I received a few calls from FBI headquarters letting me know that one of our FBI jets would be landing at Elmendorf AFB for refueling; I was asked to arrange landing clearances for them and provide them on-the-ground security until they were "wheels-up." The jets would be coming from overseas after agents had conducted rendition operations there. I was more than happy to support the effort and glad to see we were still conducting these operations around the world.

Though I typically didn't know whom they had apprehended or why, I knew it had to be a major case if the FBI was using such significant resources to apprehend them. I usually found out their identity later, after the apprehension was made public.

Before I left Anchorage, President Bush wanted to personally thank the SACs who set up command centers around the country during the aftermath of 9/11, so we flew to the White House from all over the country. Unfortunately, my luggage got there too late for the meeting with the president, and I had to scrounge up some clothes for the occasion.

❧

Out of the blue I got a call from FBI headquarters asking me to put in for the SAC position at the San Francisco office. I had been in Alaska for four years: two as the ASAC, and two as the SAC. I knew it was time to start thinking about moving on to a larger office.

I flew to headquarters for an interview with Director Mueller and others. I was aware that I wasn't the only one interviewing for the position, and the man who ended up getting the post was the Denver SAC. When I was asked to replace him in Denver, I accepted with gratitude. I became the first black SAC in the Denver office; I had been the second black SAC in Anchorage.

This was a welcome change for me and my wife, and it was a great opportunity because I was three years away from the mandatory retirement age of fifty-seven. For the last couple of years I had been the highest-paid employee in the FBI, because in addition to my SES-4 salary, I received a 25 percent wage increase for living in Alaska, along with 25 percent Automatic Uncontrollable Overtime (AUO) pay—but most of that did not count toward retirement pay. Although taking over an office in the lower forty-eight would mean an overall income reduction, in the long run I was boosting my retirement earnings because that number was based on the highest-paying three years of my salary.

CHAPTER 16

▲

THE VAIL FIRES

The Final "Mississippi Burning" Case

We took a house-hunting trip to Denver in August 2002 and really liked the area. We made great money from the sale of our Anchorage home and bought a very large house in Aurora, in a golf course community. It was our dream home. If we looked out the corner of our living room window, we could see the Rocky Mountains.

I was surprised by the welcome I received from the federal, state, and local law enforcement agencies, and I was also surprised by the warm reception I received from the media. As a matter of fact, the *Denver Post* published a very thorough and heart-warming feature story on my background soon after I arrived. They not only interviewed me, but they interviewed one of my colleagues back in Alaska as well. The article was well-written and positive.

I'll have to admit that I was very concerned about getting altitude sickness in "the Mile-High City," especially after my very bad experiences in La Paz, Bolivia. But I certainly wasn't going to let that stop me from accepting the new position. After we got settled, I realized that as long as I stayed hydrated I was fine, but initially I did find myself lightheaded and susceptible to headaches.

When I officially reported to the office on September 25, I received an exceptional briefing from the assistant special agent-in-charge—who, by the way, was born in Cuba. (America is a great country!) He made it immediately clear that I had to make some quick organizational changes to support the FBI's investigative priorities, which had been changed subsequent to 9/11. At that time I was responsible for all FBI investigations in Colorado and Wyoming. I was in charge of more than 250 FBI agents and 150 support employees, including analysts. I was also responsible for various task forces (Domestic Terrorism, International Terrorism, Drug, Safe Streets, Regional Computer Forensics Lab, etc.), which included representatives from various federal, state, and local law enforcement agencies.

It soon became clear that some of the local law enforcement agencies were still smarting from the JonBenét Ramsey murder investigation and the Columbine High School shootings. The police departments responsible for those investigations were still answering questions from the media several years after the incidents occurred. While I was the SAC, there were requests for us to get involved in the JonBenét Ramsey murder investigation; I declined because I believed the matter had already been extensively and thoroughly investigated by the Boulder police, and I didn't see where our involvement would add value. Some of the employees in my office, both agents and professional support, had children at Columbine at the time of the attacks on April 20, 1999. They were still trying to recover almost six years later.

I established some aggressive and ambitious goals for the Denver division. In addition to our top priority, terrorism prevention, I wanted to build a regional computer forensics laboratory with the support of state and local law enforcement; a new, stand-alone Denver field office that included space for intelligence analysts; a sensitive compartmented information facility (SCIF); and an emergency operation center where I could establish a command center when needed. I wanted to forge the strongest possible working relationship with our federal, state, and local law enforcement agencies, as well as with the military departments located in Colorado and Wyoming. I made sure that we had an effective Safe Streets Task Force and worked very hard to build a facility for them to work out of.

Our investigative priorities needed to be made clear to office personnel, the public, the media, and other law enforcement officials. I also wanted to move agents assigned to the Colorado Springs RA into a newer, more secure facility.

I delivered quite a few speeches as an SAC, but not all of them went as planned. When I attended my first regional law enforcement conference in Colorado, I stayed up late preparing my presentation. The next morning, just as I was about to deliver it, some last-minute changes were made, leaving me no time to adjust. When I got up to the podium to speak, I totally blew my presentation in front of Colorado's law enforcement leadership, which included our US attorney and senator, Ben Nighthorse Campbell. It was one of my most embarrassing moments. I can't remember if I took gingko biloba that morning or not.

✑

During one of the early briefings in Denver, several agents and analysts told me about a 1998 arson that had caused more than $12 million in damage to a brand-new housing development in Vail. There were no identified persons of interest and no solid leads to follow, but it was rumored that an Earth Liberation Front (ELF) group was involved. I assured the agents and staff that I would make this investigation one of the division's priorities. In order to develop some substantial leads in the case, I suggested we take a "Mississippi Burning" approach: if we identified weak-link members of ELF that we could charge with federal, state, or local violations, they might tell us who was responsible for the arson or become our informants in order to save themselves. To that end, I suggested we contact all the field offices and other federal agencies that had ongoing investigations with the ELF and the Animal Liberation Front (an eco-terrorist group with similar goals and tactics) and assemble the case agents in Denver so we could compare notes, form a joint investigation, and identify any potential weak links.

That meeting produced solid results. It turned out that the ELF had been linked to fires set at SUV dealerships and construction sites in various states, while the ALF had been blamed for arsons and bombings targeting animal research labs and the pharmaceutical and cosmetics industries. We identified some weak links we could charge with lesser, unrelated violations, and we were able to convince them to save themselves by informing on the leadership responsible for the Vail arson fires.

In December 2005 and January 2006, with assistance from the Bureau of Alcohol, Tobacco, Firearms, and Explosives (ATF), the FBI indicted six women and seven men on a total of sixty-five charges, including arson, conspiracy, use of destructive devices, and destruction of an energy facility. Some of these charges were connected to the Vail fire.

On December 15, 2006, two subjects pleaded guilty to $20 million worth of arsons committed between 1996 and 2001 by the Oregon-based cell of the ELF known as "The Family." These arsons included the fire-bombing of the Vail housing development. "Mississippi Burning" worked once again!

∞

While assigned as SAC at the Denver office, I worked very closely with the commander of the United States Northern Command (NORTHCOM), which was created on October 1, 2002, in the aftermath of the 9/11 attacks. Its mission is to protect the homeland and support local, state, and federal authorities. Its area of responsibility includes air, land, and sea approaches, and encompasses the contiguous United States, Alaska, Canada,

Mexico, and the surrounding water up to approximately five hundred nautical miles.

Every six months the commander and I briefed each other, either at his facility on Peterson Air Force base or at my office. My briefings covered potential threats that we had identified in his immediate area and what was going on in our antiterrorism investigations. The commander's presentations to me included his views on potential threats on the state and national level.

The commander and I established a great working relationship that NORTHCOM hadn't been able to establish with FBI headquarters. Once I became aware of this disconnect, I worked very hard to repair the problem. Eventually I was able to set up a meeting between the commander and FBI officials back at FBI headquarters.

ぐ乃

While we lived in Denver, one of the agents assigned to our Colorado Springs RA convinced me and Bernadette to attend our first US Air Force Academy football game at the academy's stadium in Colorado Springs. While we were sitting in the stands enjoying the game, an air force officer came up to me and asked if we would join the air force commandant up in his glass booth. We were, of course, surprised, but we accepted the invitation. We spent the rest of the game in the commandant's booth, where he introduced us to other special guests and treated us to plenty of food and drinks.

The leadership of the academy eventually became embroiled in a controversy involving a series of rape reports by female cadets; the cadets further alleged that the academy had a culture of blaming the victim in sexual assaults. Ultimately four top officers at the US Air Force Academy were replaced, at least two of them by women.

One of my best and most memorable speeches was for the Air Force Office of Special Investigations (OSI) at an annual awards ceremony at Peterson Air Force Base. I had done a lot of homework and preparation before delivering that speech and found out that there was a strong historical relationship between the FBI and the Air Force OSI. I practiced that speech over and over because I was delivering the keynote. At the ceremony, the room was packed with air force officials and family members. I gave the speech, which was very emotional, and when it was over, I got a standing ovation.

ॐ

In the summer of 2003, the sheriff's office in Eagle, Colorado, arrested NBA superstar Kobe Bryant in connection with a sexual assault complaint filed by a nineteen-year-old hotel employee, Katelyn Faber. The news media reported that Bryant had checked into The Lodge and Spa at Cordillera in Cordillera, Colorado, on June 30—he was scheduled to have surgery near there on July 2. Faber accused Bryant of raping her in his hotel room on July 1, the night before the surgery. Bryant married and the father of a seven-month-old daughter acknowledged that he had had sex with her, but he insisted it was consensual. I offered the FBI's investigative and laboratory resources to the sheriff, should he need them. The case was dropped after Bryant publicly apologized to Faber, Faber declined to testify, and a civil suit was settled out of court.

The FBI got involved in the matter when a twenty-two-year-old Iowa man, John Roche, allegedly threatened to kill Faber for accusing Bryant of rape. He was arrested and taken into custody without incident by FBI agents and officers of the Iowa City Police Department. A federal grand jury in Denver indicted Roche for allegedly making a threatening phone call across state lines. According to the indictment, Roche allegedly left an obscenity-laced message on Faber's home answering machine, threatening to use a coat hanger in a vulgar fashion and saying, "I'll kill you."

ॐ

I thought I seen a lot of snow in Alaska, but on March 20, 2003, it started snowing in Denver and didn't stop until the snow was four feet high. This happened just as President Bush was initiating the war in Iraq, and I needed to get to my office to open the command center. I ended up calling my good friend, the Arapahoe County sheriff, who handled snow removal for the county. He had trucks come into my subdivision and remove just enough snow for me to get out of my garage and up to the main roads, where the streets were passable. Thanks to the sheriff, I was able to get into my office and open the command center to monitor potential threats in Colorado and Wyoming resulting from our invasion of Iraq.

❧

One day I received a call from Director Mueller asking me to come back to FBI headquarters as acting assistant director of the Office of Professional Responsibility from December 2003 to January 2004. Mueller was in the process of reorganizing the office and needed someone with OPR experience to run it in the interim, no longer than two months. I was to put one of my ASACs in charge of the Denver office in my absence. I had once been assigned to OPR as a supervisor; now I was being asked to run it. Even if it was only for a couple months, it was a great honor.

The timing was fortuitous, as well, because my mother was very sick at the time, and it gave me an opportunity to be with her. Though I had visited Baltimore many times, I had been living away from home for more than twenty-five years. I guess this was another instance where God intervened, because I was there with my mother when she died. I wrote and delivered the eulogy at her funeral and was glad to be with my brothers during this difficult period.

❧

In June 2004, to my pleasant surprise, one of the CIA regional directors presented me with a plaque from CIA headquarters in appreciation for my many years of working joint operations with them in the United States and abroad. I was truly honored have treasured the plaque ever since.

On December 7, 2004, I was asked to give a speech to the City Club of Denver on the state of terrorism and the FBI's efforts to combat it nationally and in Colorado. This was one of my best speeches, and it was certainly the longest—it lasted about forty minutes and was followed by some good questions. It was videotaped by C-SPAN and aired nationally for several months, titled "FBI Efforts against Terrorism." I was surprised to discover that C-SPAN was actually *selling* the DVD of my speech; I ended up buying three or four for myself. The speech was well-received and I was very proud of it, but I was also relieved when it was over. I had taken several gingko biloba to get through it. The ginkgo seemed to kick in when I needed it, particularly when I had to answer questions.

∝∫ρ

Some of my greatest experiences in the FBI involved working with community groups and their charitable activities. Organizations like the YMCA, Boys and Girls Clubs, the Kiwanis Club, the VFW, the Lions Club, the Elks Club, the Shriners, and the Rotary Club are an integral part of the national social safety net, and they do their work quietly, without fanfare. Over the years I had the opportunity to speak to these groups about the FBI, and it was a pure pleasure.

When I got to Denver I became aware of Dave Liniger and the incredible charity work that he and his wife, Gail, were doing in Colorado. The Linigers are the cofounders of RE/MAX International. In 1997, they established the Sanctuary Golf Course in Sedalia, Colorado, as a private enclave for charity golf tournaments. Since its opening, the private course has raised more than $50 million for hundreds of charitable organizations. Among the beneficiaries are the Big Brothers and Big Sisters of America; the Boy Scouts of America; Colorado Youth at Risk; Boys & Girls Club of America; the Colorado State Patrol, which provides educational and financial support to the children and families of fallen and seriously injured state troopers; the Douglas County Sheriff's Office, which uses the donations to benefit eight Douglas County youth and community services, including the Women's Crisis Center, the Violence Prevention Institute, DARE, the Senior Services Foundation, and the Victim Assistance Program; the National Benevolent Association of Colorado Christian Home; and Junior Achievement. On December 30, 2004, I presented Dave and Gail Liniger with the FBI Director's Community Leadership Award. Since 1990, the FBI has used this award to publicly recognize the achievements of individuals and organizations in the areas of drug and violence education and prevention.

ঙ৶৶

One morning my wife called me at the office from her new job at the headquarters of a group of health clubs; she sounded very upset about something that had happened to her at work. During her lunch break I met her at a restaurant, where she explained that a couple of her subordinates did not seem to like her and had been doing things to make her look bad in the eyes of her boss. The latest incident involved someone changing the call-back phone number on a letter she had written to the club's members. The number had been changed to a toll-free phone-sex line.

My wife talked about quitting and finding a new job. I told her that she shouldn't think about quitting—that instead she should go back to work, call her boss (who was out of town), and tell him what had happened. I also told her to prepare a new letter to the club members explaining the need for a corrected phone number, and to solicit her boss's help in identifying the person who had altered the number. I said to make sure she made it clear to her boss how upset she was that other employees would do such a foolish thing and put the reputation of the company in jeopardy.

When other employees realized that my wife was leading the company's investigation into the incident, a couple of them told her what had happened and who had changed the number. Once the culprits were identified, they were immediately fired. My wife found out afterwards that they had done the same thing to another supervisor they did not like. But this time they did not get away with it—they were dealing with an FBI family. The entire episode was a shame, because the fired employees had families depending on their income. They could not find other jobs and ended up on welfare.

❧

While I was an SAC in Denver, the Colorado attorney general was a very nice and intelligent gentleman named Ken Salazar. As head of the law enforcement community, he held monthly meetings with the leadership from federal law enforcement assigned to the state. I attended most of these meetings, and he and I got along really well. Later on, Salazar would join Barack Obama's presidential campaign and eventually become President Obama's secretary of the interior.

The state's attorney for Denver, meanwhile, was Bill Ritter. Little did I know when he served his last term that he would go on to become governor of Colorado. When he retired as the state's attorney he was well-respected across Colorado; a big retirement party was held in his honor and attended by the state's most prominent people. I'd hoped to give him a plaque that evening in appreciation of his support for the FBI over the years, but I didn't see an opportunity. I later invited him to one of our law enforcement meetings, where I presented him with our plaque.

❧

As SAC of the Denver division I got to work with the governors, senators, congressmen, and US attorneys from both Colorado and Wyoming. The governor and the US attorney of Wyoming asked our office to give top priority to the federal Wind River Indian Reservation, inhabited by Shoshoni and Arapahoe, because of crime related to illegal drugs and alcohol abuse. I spent a lot of time traveling to the reservation to speak with tribal council members and attend their meetings. I also worked with my agents on investigations to help stem the flow of drugs into the reservation. We set up programs for the children there to address the community's high suicide and school dropout rates, and we worked with the reservation's law enforcement on domestic violence, child abuse, and rape cases.

Wyoming US Attorney Matt Mead was very intelligent, savvy, active, and intense, and he made sure the FBI gave a lot of attention to his state. I once challenged him to participate in a traditional sweat lodge: if he did it, I said, I would join him. He took me up on the challenge, and it was a very sobering experience. The tribal council members really seemed to appreciate both of us taking part.

Mead came from a very prominent Wyoming family that was heavily into politics and owned one of the largest cattle ranches in the state. I had no doubt that he was destined to become a major political figure, and I was right: Matt Mead is currently the governor of Wyoming. He is also a good dancer, a fact that probably helped his political career. Whenever we visited our favorite bar in Jackson Hole—a saloon where they had saddles for barstools—he always found an opportunity to get out on the dance floor and show off his moves. (Every once in a while I would get out and do my humble moves, too.)

When I was in Denver, the Wyoming governor was David Freudenthal, who was very interested in the FBI protecting his state's critical infrastructure, including missile silos, from any terrorist acts. His director of homeland defense was a former FBI agent who had been assigned to Wyoming and developed a very close working relationship with the governor. After the agent retired, the two became good friends. I joined Governor Freudenthal for a couple of terrorism training scenarios and public forums dealing with issues related to the Wind River Indian Reservation. He was very personable.

I enjoyed working closely with Sen. Ben Nighthorse Campbell, who was a legend in Colorado. One day we were flying to Washington, DC, on the same plane, and it was struck by lightning. The aircraft went into free fall, and we both thought it was over for us. The pilots eventually regained control of the plane, and we made it safely to Washington. We have been counting our blessings ever since. By the way, I first met the senator and his wife when I arrived in Colorado and they invited me to a rodeo. I got to wear a ten-gallon hat and ride with the senator in a stagecoach through the crowded arena.

ᏯᏆᎦ

When I first visited our Colorado Springs RA, I was excited to see the Olympic Training Center again. The last time I had been there was in the mid-1980s, when I was the FIT advisor for the Washington field office; each year several advisors were sent to the Olympic Training Center for a conference. When I went, we were there for about a week and were allowed to use all the facilities and eat in the cafeteria. I was doing triathlons at the time, so I was able to use the center's swimming pool and gym, which included weights and stationary bikes.

ᏯᏆᎦ

The Administrative Maximum Facility (ADX), the supermax prison in Florence, Colorado, houses some of the world's most notorious criminals, those deemed the most dangerous and in need of the tightest control. The ADX houses around 430 male prisoners, each assigned to one of six security levels.

I'll have to admit that I was not aware of this prison's existence or who its inmates were until I was assigned to the Denver field office. Although I was familiar with the history of many of these criminals, I did not know they were being held in a Colorado federal prison. Because of many of the inmates' terrorist backgrounds, I was concerned that there might be an attempt to help them escape, so I reached out to meet the warden, who gave me a tour of the facility. When I saw it myself, I realized how difficult it would be for anyone to escape from the ADX.

After learning about the complex's design, I looked more closely at some of the prisoners there. They included Ramzi Yousef (the bomber in the first World Trade Center attack in 1993; Ted Kaczynski ("the Unabomber"); Robert Hanssen (FBI agent turned spy); Richard Reed (the "shoe bomber"); and the blind sheikh Omar Abdel-Rahman (serving a life sentence for the 1993 World Trade Center bombing, conspiracy to use explosives against New York landmarks, and plotting to assassinate US politicians). The prison population also included several major drug lords, gang leaders, and mob bosses. It was like a who's who of world terrorism and international crimes. The warden took the time to introduce me to Robert Hanssen, Ted Kaczynski, Ramzi Yousef, Sheikh Omar Abdel-Rahman, and Richard Reed. I can't say it was a pleasure to meet them.

Whenever FBI headquarters officials, including the director, came to my territory, I made sure that we included a tour of the ADX. Obviously, Robert Hanssen was always of special interest to bureau officials.

I started planning for a major training exercise with federal, state, and local law enforcement agencies around the scenario of an attempted breakout of inmates like Yousef, Abdel-Rahman, or Reed from ADX by members of an international terrorist group—possibly using a school takeover as either a diversion or a negotiating tool. I retired before I could ever get the training organized.

⋰⋱

Not too long before my retirement, I received an unexpected call from my former assistant special agent in charge in Alaska, who informed me that there had been some terrorist threats made against the Valdez terminal of the Alaskan pipeline. He said he just wanted to let me know that the training exercise I had initiated a couple of years before had helped prepare federal, state, and local law enforcement officials to address the threat. That was very gratifying.

✒

By then I was getting close to mandatory retirement, so I started looking for jobs in the private sector. I was very fortunate to be hired by Boeing's CFO to head the company's security team in Chicago.

On May 5, 2005, after twenty-eight years with the FBI, I finally retired as the Denver special agent in charge. I was given a great send-off by the federal, state, and local law enforcement officials in the area and representatives from various community groups. I was overwhelmed by the gifts, plaques, and citations, and the speeches and comments. It was truly a great way to end a career.

I remained with Boeing for almost two years and then moved to Florida where I took a position as director of security for Collier County Public Schools, in Naples.

CHAPTER 17

▲

CLOSING THOUGHTS

I n 1969, when the colonel from the draft board gave me the option of how I could serve my country, I chose a law enforcement career, and I never looked back. That decision allowed me not only to serve my hometown as a policeman, but also my country as an FBI agent.

I was fortunate to have had such a successful and interesting thirty-six-year law enforcement career. Pivotal to that success was the discovery of the power of Three Sisters Ponds to focus my attention on tangible goals, such as finishing college while working full-time and then expanding my administrative and investigative experiences in the police department and the FBI. When I look back, I shudder at the thought of *not* discovering Three Sisters Ponds when I did. Setting and pursuing personal goals, accomplishing them, and then setting new ones became a way of life for me. And it allowed me to achieve even more than I ever imagined.

I certainly took full advantage of the educational opportunities, career paths, and career advancement opportunities a law enforcement career offered. I remain indebted to LEEP for all that program did for me, and to the Community College of Baltimore, which designed its courses to accommodate law enforcement officers' irregular work hours. I am also grateful to the professor at Morgan State University who suggested that I consider a career with the FBI. The audacity!

Obviously, I had to be able and willing to adapt to the changes presented by new opportunities. Every opportunity came with its own challenges to overcome, but they all provided me with unforgettable experiences. I was very fortunate because I naturally welcomed and embraced change, and so did my wife. I was always ready to do something different, but I didn't always wait for change to happen—sometimes I did whatever it took to *make it happen*. I truly believed that if I wanted something, no matter how slim the odds of success seemed at the time, I had to get aggressive about it.

As I noted early on and throughout this book, there were many points in my career when I experienced great luck and fortune that I couldn't explain, other than to attribute it to God's intervention on my behalf. These were always pivotal points, times when I was offered a choice that at first was surprising and later turned out to be momentous.

When I retired from the FBI, I left with the feeling that the country was safer from terrorism and major organized criminal activity thanks to the development of law enforcement joint task forces that cover the entire United States. They are made up of representatives of federal, state, and local law enforcement agencies who share resources, expertise, and intelligence to address every major potential criminal threat. They even solicit help from private citizens, which creates a "force multiplier" effect and further enhances everyone's security. With today's technology, law enforcement across the country is more coordinated and united than ever. They can now connect the investigative dots. And we are all are safer as a result.

I am truly proud of the success I had as a black law enforcement officer. Every day I tried to represent my race in the most exemplary fashion, on the job and off. It is my belief that black citizens need to have a significant presence and hold important roles in law enforcement to ensure fair and equal justice in our communities. Although I encountered my fair share of what could be interpreted as racism or prejudice in the BPD and the FBI, I never let it stop me. I hope that in the pursuit and achievement of my personal goals, I have inspired, motivated, and blazed a few trails for other blacks to follow.

Because I am so grateful for the career that I had, I felt obligated to take some time during my retirement to revert back to my days as a police recruiter and use my own experiences to convince as many readers as possible to consider a career in law enforcement. If I haven't convinced you to do that, I hope that you found in my journey a route to your own life's dreams and goals. I also hope you find your own version of Three Sisters Ponds, and that the good people of Baltimore restore theirs.

Best of luck!

To Protect and Serve

I dedicate my life to honor and respect
the Constitution of the United States,
which we are sworn to protect.

My badge is a symbol of public faith bestowed,
and I accept it as a public trust that I reliably behold.

With God as my witness,
I will uphold the law of the land.
There will be no question as to my fitness
to enforce our laws with an even and unbiased hand.

The lives and property of the American people we serve
will be protected with unrelenting vigilance
that is nothing less than deserved.

I will never allow my personal beliefs to take control
and influence my actions or decisions, at any toll.

I will keep my public and private life an example to all.
Where honesty, integrity and courage are required,
I will stand tall.

I will uphold all secrets
that I've been entrusted to maintain.
That commitment has no limits,
or time of refrain.

I am a law enforcement officer,
given respect I hope to deserve.
It's a profession that I have chosen
So that I can Protect and Serve.

Phil Reid

APPENDIX

A

I n late 2002, not too long after I arrived in Colorado to take over as the special agent in charge of the Denver FBI field office, I was contacted by Jim Hughes, a staff writer from the *Denver Post*, who wanted to write an article that would introduce me to the paper's readers—the public whom I would be serving. I was and still am very proud of how well this article was written. Having received the *Post's* permission, I am honored to use Jim's article to introduce myself to the readers of this book.

Local FBI chief adapts to agency's new roles

Phillip Reid, the special agent in charge of Denver's FBI field office, finds himself working on familiar terrorism-related issues, but with many more people watching.

By Jim Hughes
Denver Post staff writer

December 16, 2002—When he arrived in La Paz, Bolivia, in 1988 to investigate the attempted bombing of then-Secretary of State George Shultz's motorcade, Phillip B. J. Reid was riding a new FBI wave that was just then carrying the bureau outside U.S. borders.

Soon, he was lugging around an oxygen tank he had found at the U.S. Embassy to combat the headaches and dizziness he found in La Paz, 11,916 feet above sea level. It was a strange experience for Reid, who has completed triathlons and marathons.

In that investigation and in subsequent assignments to places like Malta, Pakistan and India, the FBI agent found himself in more new situations—working in other foreign climes and cultures and, increasingly, with CIA agents, military intelligence officers and embassy staff.

"Going overseas, the reality is that the CIA is out there," said Reid, the new special agent in charge of the FBI's Denver field office. "They've developed sources. They've got contacts out there. They live out there, and we're just out there visiting. It was common sense for us to knock on their door and sit down with them and develop a relationship." Now, with a U.S. war on terrorism blurring the lines between domestic and international concerns and Congress demanding more than ever of the bureau, Reid finds himself working on the same terrorism-related issues, but with many more people watching.

He took charge in Denver in September after staffing FBI offices in Virginia, Washington, D.C., Honolulu, and, most recently, Anchorage, Alaska. From 1988 to 1991, Reid was assigned to the investigation of the Pan Am Flight 103 bombing that killed 270 people over Lockerbie, Scotland, on Dec. 21, 1988.

Reid, 54, is responsible for helping agents in Colorado and Wyoming adapt to an urgent, expanding mission for the FBI, said Reid, who replaced Mark Mershon. Mershon was transferred to the bureau's San Francisco office.

Reid said the FBI's top priority today is to prevent crimes, especially terrorist attacks like those of Sept. 11, 2001, from happening—not just to find and arrest the people responsible.

The bureau was told to focus on preventive investigations after those terrorist attacks, for which the FBI, along with the CIA, has been blamed.

Fair or not, that criticism does not overly discourage Reid, he said.

"The American people look to the FBI to provide a certain protection from these types of threats, and certainly, when something like a 9/11 goes down, it's natural for them to point the finger at the FBI," he said.

Complicating the FBI's post-Sept. 11 paradigm shift is that it now reports not only to the Justice Department in this regard, but also to the new Homeland Security Department, signed into existence by President Bush last month.

It also works with military leaders at Northern Command, the new military command post based in Colorado Springs. It assumed military responsibility for North America in October.

And if the congressional panel that last week ended its review of intelligence failures leading up to 9/11 gets its way, there could one day be a Cabinet-level director of national intelligence, too.

In short, the FBI's world is changing, even as Reid settles into Denver.

But he does not anticipate too much confusion among these overlapping chains of command, he said.

"We all know that ultimately, we all are here to protect and serve the American people," he said. "We are all on the same sheet of music in that regard."

The mounting interagency-communication challenge plays to the Baltimore native's strengths, said Robert Burnham, who worked as Reid's assistant special agent in charge in Anchorage and still holds that position.

"Phil's strongest attribute is his ability to interact with other law enforcement agencies," Burnham said. "He was very active in the community, and he forged very strong relationships with a number of agencies that elsewhere in the country people might not think the FBI worked quite so well with."

Reid created the Honolulu office's international investigations squad, which today investigates terrorism and other crimes along the Pacific Rim. That and his other terrorism work allowed him to hit the ground running in Alaska well before homeland security became a mainstream priority, Burnham said.

"He established some relationships in the intelligence community, and especially in the military, that really helped us take care of our counterterrorism responsibilities here in Alaska," he said. "It was his vision, really, that did that."

Reid began his law-enforcement career with the Baltimore Police Department in 1969. As an African-American and "child of the '60s," he wanted to improve the department's relationships with Baltimore's minority neighborhoods, he said.

His experiences during the 1960s may be why Reid does not dismiss liberal skepticism of the FBI, the lead agency in Attorney General John Ashcroft's domestic war on terrorism.

In the months after the 2001 attacks, Ashcroft won congressional approval for the Patriot Act, which gave federal agents far more leeway in investigating and incarcerating suspected terrorists.

Civil rights advocates say the new powers, some of which will expire in 2005, are too broad. They make it too easy for the FBI and other agencies to lock up and harass innocent people while pursuing terrorists, they say.

While those tools are helping them do their jobs, federal agents do not expect to be able to act with impunity, Reid said. They have no interest in eroding American freedom—they just want to avoid a repeat of what happened on Sept. 11, 2001, he said.

He welcomes the scrutiny, he said.

"Give us the tools, but watch us," he said. "But give us the tools."

ABOUT THE AUTHOR

▲

hillip B. J. Reid was born in Baltimore City, Maryland, on October 27, 1948, one of four sons of Wendell and Ernestine Reid. His early childhood began in Day Village, a small black enclave in the Turner Station section of Dundalk, Maryland. His family later moved to Baltimore City, where he graduated from Edmondson High School in 1966 and joined the Baltimore City Police Department (BPD) in 1969.

Mr. Reid was a member of the BPD for eight years. During that time he was assigned to street patrol duties for three years; the personnel division, where he recruited police officers, for two years; and finally the BPD training academy for three years as a certified Maryland Police Training Commission instructor. In 1972 he received an associate's degree in law enforcement from the Community College of Baltimore, and in 1975 a bachelor's degree in sociology from Morgan State University. He was later appointed adjunct lecturer in the Division of Continuing Education of the Community College of Baltimore.

Mr. Reid joined the FBI in 1977, and after graduating from the FBI Academy, he was assigned to the FBI's Norfolk, Virginia, field office. In addition, he was assigned to FBI field offices in New York; Alexandria, Virginia; Honolulu; Anchorage; Denver; and Washington, DC.

In November, 1991, he was promoted to supervisor at the FBI's Office of Professional Responsibility (OPR), located at FBI headquarters in Washington, DC, where for two years he conducted investigations involving employee misconduct, including that of former FBI Director William Sessions. He subsequently was promoted to field office supervisor and assigned to the Honolulu, Hawaii, field office. Five years later he was promoted to assistant special agent in charge and assigned to the Anchorage, Alaska, field office. During his assignment in Alaska he was promoted in place to special agent in charge. After two years in that position, he was reassigned to the Denver, Colorado, field office, again as the special agent in charge, overseeing the FBI's investigative responsibilities in Colorado and Wyoming for the next two and a half years. He remained there until he retired in May 2005.

During his twenty-eight years with the FBI, Mr. Reid was assigned to various types of federal investigations that included bank and armored truck robberies, fugitives, extortion, white-collar crime, civil rights violations, cyber-crime, organized crime/ drugs, kidnappings, foreign counterintelligence, counterterrorism, and extraterritorial terrorism. He spent extensive amounts of time overseas conducting FBI terrorism investigations, such the 1988 attempted bombing of Secretary of State George Shultz's motorcade in La Paz, Bolivia. For three years (December 1988-November 1991) he was one of the full-time case agents assigned to investigate the bombing of Pan Am Flight 103 over Lockerbie, Scotland, in which 270 people were murdered. During that time, while traveling extensively, he provided coordination among the FBI, the American embassy, Scotland Yard, Scottish law enforcement, the CIA, and the Maltese government regarding the investigation, which eventually resulted in the indictments of two Libyan suspects in 1991. In 2000 he testified in the trial in the Netherlands that resulted in the conviction of one of the two suspects.

While assigned to the Honolulu field office, Mr. Reid was asked to establish and supervise a counterterrorism extraterritorial squad to investigate all murders, kidnappings, or serious assaults of American citizens in Asia and the Pacific Rim countries. He worked personally with US embassy officials, including ambassadors and CIA station chiefs, and with host-country law enforcement and military officials in those parts of the world. He traveled extensively throughout Asia and the Pacific Rim, including India, Thailand, Pakistan, Japan, Hong Kong, and the Philippines. Some of his investigations there included the March 8, 1995, execution-style murders of a CIA and a Department of State employee in Karachi, Pakistan (both were assigned to the American consulate there at the time of their murders). Also in Karachi, Mr. Reid led the investigation into the November 12, 1997, murders of four US citizens, all oil company auditors from Union Texas Petroleum Corporation, and their Pakistani driver. He also led the investigation of the July 4, 1995, kidnapping and murders of an American and four Europeans in Srinagar (Jammu/Kashmir), India.

Mr. Reid graduated from the FBI's Special Weapons and Tactics (SWAT) School at Quantico and was assigned to counter-sniper and assault teams in the Norfolk, New York, Alexandria, and Washington, DC field offices.

Prior to his retirement, Mr. Reid was asked by FBI Director Robert Mueller to return to OPR for sixty days as acting assistant director, providing guidance for that office, which was going through transition and reorganization.

Mr. Reid retired from the Denver FBI field office on May 5, 2005, and immediately began working as the director of security for the Boeing Corporation's world headquarters in Chicago, and the company's Executive Flight Operations Center in Gary, Indiana. While there, he became a member of Who's Who in Black Chicago. After approximately two years with Boeing, Mr. Reid was hired as the director of security and environmental management for Collier County Public Schools in Naples, Florida, where he remained until his retirement in June, 2013.

Mr. Reid's role in the Pan Am Flight 103 bombing investigation is chronicled in Richard A. Marquise's book *Scotbom: Evidence and the Lockerbie Investigation*. In addition, Mr. Reid's December 2004 speech to the City Club of Denver, titled "FBI Efforts against Terrorism," can be found in C-SPAN's video library.

Mr. Reid received the following awards, commendations, citations, and plaques for his law enforcement and community service:

- The United States Coast Guard Public Service Commendation
- The Governor's Alaska Legion of Merit Award
- The proclamation of a "Phillip B. J. Reid Appreciation Day" by the mayor of Anchorage, Alaska
- A plaque from CIA Headquarters reading, "In appreciation for your professional dedication and longstanding cooperation in the pursuit of Joint Operations"
- The Distinguished Service Award from the Douglas County (CO) Sheriff's Office

Mr. Reid was a member of the International Association of Chiefs of Police (IACP) and the National Organization of Black Law Enforcement Executives (NOBLE) during his law enforcement career. In addition, he is a graduate of the FBI's Executive Development Institute I and II and the recipient of a certificate for Leading Strategic Change from Kellogg School of Management. He retired from the FBI in 2005 as a member of its Senior Executive Service and joined Boeing as security director for its world headquarters in Chicago, attending its Executive Leadership Center. While employed with Boeing, he attended the Defense Security Service Academy and received a Facility Security Officer (FSO) Program Management Certificate. Mr. Reid is currently a member of the Society of Former Special Agents of the Federal Bureau of Investigation Inc. and Leadership Collier, in Naples, Florida.

Mr. Reid is married and has three (3) grandchildren by his daughter.